D1125921

ROMAN MYTHOLOGY

DAVID STUTTARD

ROMAN MYTHOLOGY

A Traveler's Guide from Troy to Tivoli

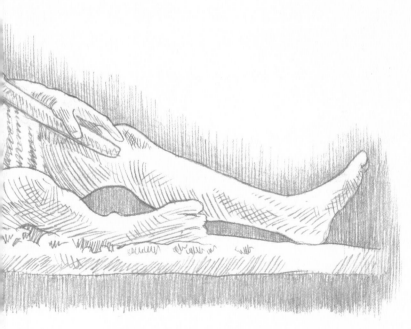

Thames & Hudson

To Sam, Fiona and Atticus Moorhead

Note: All translations are by the author unless
otherwise stated.

Pages 2–3 A cornucopia in his right hand and an oar
in his left, Tiber, the river god, reclines as the she-wolf
suckles Romulus and Remus beside him.

Roman Mythology: A Traveler's Guide from Troy to Tivoli
© 2019 Thames & Hudson Ltd, London

Drawings by David Bezzina

First published in 2019 in the United States of America by
Thames & Hudson Inc., 500 Fifth Avenue, New York, New York 10110

www.thamesandhudsonusa.com

Library of Congress Control Number 2019934321

ISBN 978-0-500-25229-1

Printed and bound in India by Replika Press Pvt. Ltd.

CONTENTS

Map of sites featured in the book.

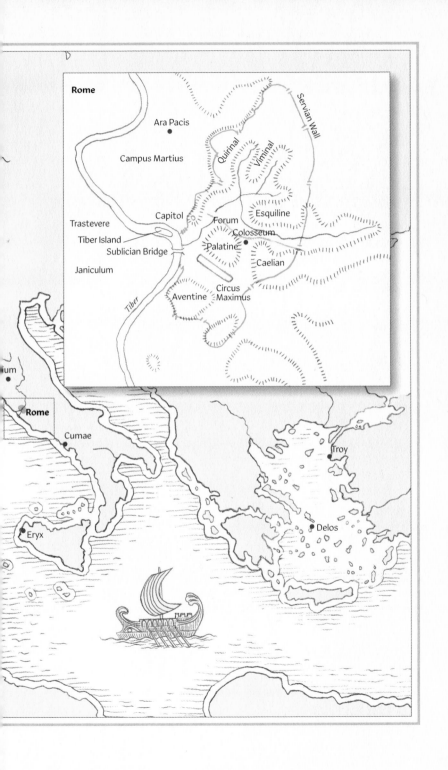

Rome

Ara Pacis

Campus Martius

Quirinal

Viminal

Servian Wall

Capitol

Trastevere

Tiber Island

Sublician Bridge

Janiculum

Forum

Esquiline

Colosseum

Palatine

Caelian

Tiber

Aventine

Circus Maximus

ium

Rome

Cumae

Troy

Eryx

Delos

INTRODUCTION
ALL ROADS LEAD TO ROME

A Brief History of Rome

In the first century BC the Roman world was convulsed by a succession of brutal civil wars. They were sparked, in part, by Rome's remarkable and relatively sudden rise to the status of world superpower, a process that climaxed in 146 BC when she crushed two rivals, Carthage and Corinth, annexed vast tracts of land and acquired almost unimaginable wealth. Just as lottery wins can ruin lives, so Rome's unforeseen success nearly destroyed her.

The traditional date for the city's foundation was six centuries earlier, in 753 BC. As a monarchy then a republic, for the first half of her life she behaved like any other contemporary city state, protecting her boundaries from attack, making alliances and finding ways to expand at others' expense. As she grew, however, she learned not only to subdue her neighbours but also to incorporate them into her political sphere, sometimes by force, sometimes by offering incentives they could not refuse, so that many inhabitants of these new territories thought it advantageous to consider themselves part of the wider family of Rome.

But families squabble. Even from the start there were tensions, and Rome was often plagued by internal strife: aristocrats overthrew kings; the city plebs (a non-pejorative term meaning 'commoners') fought ruling families for increased political rights; and among the senatorial elite, rampant egos strove for ever greater influence.

Expansion throughout Italy and into Sicily brought Rome into con-flict with that powerful controller of western Mediterranean trade routes, Carthage. From 264 BC three Carthaginian or 'Punic' Wars raged throughout Sicily, Spain, Italy and ultimately North Africa. Meanwhile, to the east, Carthage's Greek allies proved such dangerous neighbours that Rome was forced to open up a second front and engage in a series of 'Macedonian' Wars. At last in 146 BC Rome inflicted crushing defeats on both enemies, but checks and balances that had (sometimes only just) held old Republican Rome together proved insufficient for the new world order.

Within a generation, ambitious men backed by powerful legions, their loyalty inflamed by the lure of booty, were fighting for supreme power. In 44 BC the wily politician-turned-general Julius Caesar almost achieved it before being assassinated by a cabal of senators. Another civil war followed, this time between Caesar's heir, Octavian, and Caesar's trusted lieutenant, Mark Antony. The Battle of Actium in 31 BC, and the defeat the next year of Antony and his ally, Cleopatra, not only brought Rome's existing territories under the control of one man, but added wealthy Egypt, too. Subsequently known as the emperor Augustus, Octavian had emerged victorious, and – thanks to a combination of political genius and icy ruthlessness – he inaugurated an age of peace, stability and economic prosperity. Aided by his 'spin-doctor', the urbane Maecenas, he succeeded in part thanks to a clever propaganda campaign that tapped into long-held ideas of civic values and a sense of destiny contained in legends set in Rome's heroic past: one of the key foundations of Augustan peace was Roman mythology.

The Temple of Venus Genetrix ('Mother Venus') was dedicated by Julius Caesar in his new forum in 46 BC.

Rome and Mythology

Many educated Romans were suspicious of mythology. They believed that tales of roving, capricious gods and heroes undermined public morality and diminished the purity of religion. This, the philosopher-cum-politician Cicero maintained, consisted of three elements: ritual (the repetition of sacrifices and other rites, allowing humans to communicate their piety to gods); auspices (examining sacrificial entrails for divine signs); and prophecy (whereby gods communicated directly with humankind). A generation after Cicero, Dionysius of Halicarnassus, a Greek writing in Rome, praised (mythical) Romulus for rejecting myths that showed gods and heroes behaving badly.

Ironically it is chiefly these racy stories that we know today – for the most part thanks to authors writing in the immediate aftermath of Augustus's elevation to 'First Citizen'. Livy's history, *From the City's Foundation*, is steeped in legend; Virgil's *Aeneid*, tracing the Trojan hero Aeneas's adventures as he seeks a new home in Italy, blends mythology and Augustan propaganda; and Ovid's *Metamorphoses* weaves a heady tapestry of myths before culminating in fulsome praise of the now-deified Caesar and his heir, Augustus.

Yet what strikes Ovid's readers today is that many of these myths are not Roman but Greek. Only at the end of his sprawling epic does the scene switch from the Greek east to Italy, and his trove of native stories is surprisingly sparse. Indeed, many modern authors have suggested that Romans did not really possess a mythology of their own, but were so focused on preserving a relationship with gods through ritual and clean living that they had no time for the imaginative fiction that lies behind mythology, preferring instead legend – heightened accounts of dimly remembered historical events containing clear examples of good civic values.

The truth is more nuanced, and Rome and her Latin, Sabine and Etruscan neighbours (roughly to the south, northwest and northeast respectively) probably possessed a rich mythology. We shall encounter many examples: a king consorting with a local river nymph; a prophetic baby found in a field; divine voices booming from sacred groves; and phalluses emerging unexpectedly from hearths. At the same time there were other, non-Italian influences. From the eighth century BC Greeks colonized parts of Italy and traded with others, bringing not just stories but also artworks bearing scenes from their own (and other eastern Mediterranean) myths, which were both adopted and adapted by local Italians.

When Romans embraced literature in the third century BC, they turned to Greek models: the first work of Latin literature was a translation of Homer's *Odyssey* by a Greek slave, Livius Andronicus; Plautus and Terence based their comedies on plays by the Greek Menander; and poets such as Virgil, Horace and Ovid self-consciously drew inspiration from Greek masters. Meanwhile, Rome's citizens wholeheartedly embraced Greek myth, whether they were aristocrats dressing up to banquet as Greek gods, or bloodthirsty audiences in amphitheatres, thrilling at the sight of condemned criminals forced to play the roles of mythological characters in snuff dramas, torn apart by bolting horses or dropped from great heights like Icarus, when his wings melted.

Meanwhile, Romans invited conquered gods and goddesses to move to Rome. By Augustus's time, the city was a melting pot of not just people from across the Mediterranean and beyond but also myths and legends, heroes and heroines, gods and goddesses. With only a very few exceptions, most of the empire's expanding population was content to believe that seemingly foreign deities were simply their native gods by other names. Thus Greece's sky-god Zeus was Roman Jupiter; Hera, his wife, was Juno; Athene was Minerva; and so on, until religions and mythologies became inextricably intertwined in imperial Roman legend. It is this that forms the centrepiece of our book. Beginning in Troy and ending in the dream of an eternal Rome, it contains many strands – and, before embarking on our travels, it might be useful briefly to consider three that we shall encounter in a variety of places and contexts.

Foundation Myths

Most ancient cities had their own foundation myths. Rome boasted many. One told how, banished from Greece, the benign god, Saturn, ruled the land; another that Greek refugees from Arcadia first occupied the site; another maintained it was a son of Ulysses; another fugitive Trojans; another still twin boys, saved from their murderous uncle, the king of a nearby city. The sheer number of conflicting stories could have proved problematic – but, rather than dismiss any as false, the Romans reconciled them and embraced them all. For here was evidence, if evidence were needed, of the magnetic pull that from the very start had attracted the best of people from across the world to the city, as it continued to attract them in historical times.

In a modern age that has seen desperate waves of immigrants and refugees seeking Italy's shores it is, perhaps, salutary to recall that other Italian towns and cities, too, were proud to have benefited from foreign settlers. Many traced their origins to displaced Greek heroes such as Hercules, or fighters from the Trojan War such as Odysseus (called Ulysses by the Romans) and Diomedes. In part (as we have seen) this reflects historical truth: from the eighth century BC onwards Greeks did send settlers to found cities on foreign soil, so that much of Italy's coastline was studded with Greek-style city states, from which goods were traded and ideas exchanged. Today the extent of such cross-fertilization (not just with Greeks) can be seen in Italy's archaeological museums, where many high-end imported goods show signs of having been customized to suit a local market. Mythological heroes were believed to have founded more than simply cities. Many customs and religious rituals were attributed to them, too, and specific landmarks came to be associated with legendary exploits. Rome positively teemed with them.

Family Myth

In a city still dominated by powerful aristocrats, it was no wonder that many legends involved members of elite families such as the Horatii, the Fabii and the Julii. Romans placed great importance on revering ancestors. Upper-class funerals featured mourners dressed in death masks representing generations of deceased family members, and these masks took pride of place in houses, alongside effigies of household gods believed to watch over the living. For the Romans, time was not the linear phenomenon we know today. Instead, Romans believed that, just as a family might draw pride or shame from their ancestors' deeds, so the actions of present or future generations might colour the reputation of the dead. Indeed, some of the legends we shall encounter were preserved (if not invented) because they belonged to specific families. For example, the story of the Fabii, who died almost to a man in a scrap with the nearby city of Veii, was probably embroidered by surviving descendants to mirror the exploits of near-contemporary Spartans, who fell fighting at Thermopylae.

The Fabii traced their line back to Hercules, but others bragged an even greater lineage. The Julii claimed descent not only from the Trojan prince Aeneas, but from the goddess Venus herself. Since Augustus was a member of the Julian family, this was quite literally a godsend for poets and propagandists wishing to justify his role as emperor: just as Venus's spirit moved through Aeneas, so it moved too through Augustus; just as Aeneas led a confederacy of Italian states to victory over the barbaric rebel, Mezentius, so Augustus prevailed over Mark Antony; and just as Aeneas and his sons ruled prosperous Latium, so Augustus and his heirs would rule the world.

Others, too, could draw their own parallels with legend. Marcus Junius Brutus, one of the conspirators who assassinated Caesar, fearing he would crown himself king, was a direct descendant of Lucius Junius Brutus, who helped overthrow the monarchy in 509 BC. So deeply ingrained was this ancient act of patriotism that it inspired Caesar's assassins – but it also meant that not even Augustus's well-oiled propaganda machine could erase it from Rome's legendary history. Yet in one respect Augustus had reason to be grateful even to the disloyal Brutus: had Caesar not been killed, Augustus would never have been emperor; had Caesar not become a god, Augustus could not have styled himself *divi filius*, the son of god.

Destiny of Rome

Indeed, when viewed like this, the whole history of Rome appeared to have been building up to the inevitability of Augustus's reign. This theme runs through much Augustan literature. It is present in Livy's history. It is at the forefront of Virgil's *Aeneid*. Throughout the poem there are passages that proclaim not just Aeneas's destiny to reach Italy and prevail in war, but Rome and Augustus's destiny to rule the world.

Two set pieces stand out above all. In the first, Aeneas descends from Cumae to the underworld, where the spirit of his father, Anchises, shows him souls of those yet to be born and explains the fate of each, revealing among them 'Augustus Caesar, son of god, who heralds a new golden age for Latium'. In the second, Venus presents Aeneas with a shield on which the blacksmith god Vulcan has worked scenes from Rome's future history. At their heart is Augustus's victory over Antony and Cleopatra at Actium, and the triumph with which he celebrated their defeat. All this, Virgil proclaims, was destined before Rome was even born.

While some question Virgil's sincerity, after his death in 19 BC the *Aeneid* was co-opted as Rome's national poem, the ultimate validation of the new regime. And in 2 BC, when Augustus dedicated his new Temple of Mars Ultor (Mars the Avenger), he decorated niches on one side of the associated plaza with statues of Aeneas, his father, his son and other famous members of the Julii family, while in niches on the other side stood statues of great men from the Republic, thereby fusing the foundation myth, Augustus's family myth and the epic story of Rome's destiny into one.

Conclusion

The Temple of Mars Ultor was far from being the only sacred landmark in Rome's physical geography. The entire city was alive with memories of myths: the Capitoline Hill, where Saturn ruled; the Aventine Hill, where Remus watched for omens; the Palatine Hill, where Romulus first built his city; the Forum, where Marcus Curtius sacrificed himself to save Rome; the Tiber, across which Cloelia once led her fellow captives to safety... In the day-to-day geography of ancient Rome legend and history were inescapable.

Indeed, so sacred was the city that it was said to possess a secret name, known only to the goddess Angerona and a select few citizens, who were forbidden to reveal it lest their enemies find out and use it in curses. According to some, however, it was simply the common name turned backwards: instead of Roma, Amor. And, since Amor meant 'love', and this was the province of Rome's ancestral goddess, Venus, they may well have been right.

Today Rome is known as the Eternal City. As they wander its pavements, inspect exhibits in museums, drink espressos in piazzas, ride the Metro, shelter from the midday sun in churches in Trastevere, try to dodge traffic, view reconstructions of its ancient streets in Cinecittà's film lots, queue for the Vatican, or watch the Tiber's lazy waters drift green past reedy riverbanks, visitors can wonder at its palimpsest of history and at its rich mythology. Out in the country, too, they can step back in time: at Veii, Rome's ancient enemy; Alba Longa, where her kings were born; Lavinium, where Aeneas first set foot in Italy. And across the Mediterranean, in other lands – in Sicily and Tunisia, Greece and Turkey – the heartbeat of Rome's legends still resounds.

This book will take its readers on two journeys. The first is through time – from before Rome's foundation until the Gaulish invasion of 390 BC, after which (some argue) legend becomes history. The second is through space, following in the footsteps of Aeneas and his companions from Troy to Italy, travelling with his descendants into Rome, and finally enjoying a brief excursion into Tuscany and Latium to explore some later legends. While the closing chapter takes us to the idyllic setting of the emperor Hadrian's villa at Tivoli, most of the book views the myths through the eyes of authors of Augustus's time, since it is they who have left the most accessible material.

All the locations can be visited. Those exploring them may find this book a useful companion, while for armchair travellers the brief descriptions at the start of chapters evoke something of the atmosphere today. For, while the imagination may furnish landscapes of its own, location is important to mythology. As one author has recently observed:

> Movement through a landscape in the present enables us to unlock the mythical past and its narratives. As the traveller continues on his or her way, the past comes to life, and the landscape becomes not only the one being journeyed through, but simultaneously the one experienced by figures from the past, evoked by place names, artefacts, and stories.

Katherine Clarke, 'Walking Through History', in Greta Hawes (ed.), *Myths on the Map*, Oxford, 2017

CHAPTER 1
TROY:
ROME'S ANCESTRAL HOMELAND

'Almighty Jupiter, if you are moved by prayer, look on us now.
It's all I ask. And, Father, if we are at all deserving for our piety,
grant us a sign. Send us an omen.' No sooner had the old man
spoken than to our left we heard a sudden thunderclap, and from
the skies a star shot through the gloom, trailing fire in its wake –
a brilliance of light. We watched it glide above the rooftops before
burying itself deep in the woods of Ida, a sign for the road ahead,
a long scar in the earth that glowed with light, and all around it
sulphur, fuming. My father was convinced. Standing to his full
height he addressed the gods, honouring the holy star: 'No more
delay! No! I shall follow. Where you lead, there shall I be. Gods of
our homeland, save this family, save my grandson! This omen
comes from you. Troy is in your protection.'

Virgil, *Aeneid*, 2.689–703

The walls of Troy tower over you. Once-well-dressed limestone slabs slope gently as they rise, their smooth regularity rippling in a subtle curve to lead the traveller around towards the eastern gate. Now, on the right, another wall rears high, so that the roadway seems to tunnel, hairpinning back upon itself to mount the hummocky incline. Climb up. Stand on the grassy mound, and there – beyond the miles of flat fields, golden in the evening glow – the waters of the Dardanelles are sparkling, metallic blue. Container vessels glide like ghosts. And, spectral in the shimmering haze, the silhouette, stark and uncompromising, of the Martyrs' Monument, memorial to Ottomans who fought and died, where many thousand Allied soldiers fought, too, and died, too, in the hellfires of Gallipoli.

Yet it is not just for the view that we are standing on this knoll, its grasses dried and desiccated by the summer sun. It takes imagination and a leap of faith to comprehend, but here in a walled sanctuary once stood a Doric temple to Minerva, itself set on the site of a more ancient shrine that once housed a totemic statue. Said to have descended from the heavens, this effigy, the Palladium, possessed protective powers. Only when it was stolen could Troy be captured – though some said that the true Palladium was smuggled west by Trojan refugees and, many generations later, it safe-guarded their descendants and the city they had founded. For, at the heart of their fast-growing empire, in the elegant Temple of Vesta, as solicitously guarded as the eternal flame that signified the nation's soul, Troy's Palladium protected Rome.

The Palladium, Troy's Mysterious Protector

The Palladium was the product of bloodshed and remorse. When the goddess Minerva was first born, springing fully armed from the head of her father, Jupiter, she was fostered by the sea-god, Triton. He had a daughter, Pallas, Minerva's favourite playmate. One day, as the two were tussling in mock battle, Jupiter (who was watching) became fearful for Minerva's safety. So, shielding her with his aegis (a magical goat-skin fringed with hissing snakes), he intervened. Distracted, Pallas glanced away, but Minerva was already launching an attack. She tried to stay her hand. Too late! She struck her friend a mortal blow, and there was nothing she could do to save her.

Distraught, Minerva took her dead friend's name – she was known in Greek as Pallas Athene – and, already an accomplished sculptress, fashioned a statue of her, the Palladium, draping it with Jupiter's aegis, and investing it with awesome powers. At first, she housed it on the island of Samothrace, where it presided over ceremonies promising life after death. But when a local princess came to the shrine, Jupiter was scandalized: the princess was pregnant (with his child), and her presence threatened to pollute the Palladium's chaste sanctity. So he snatched the statue and hurled it in a great arc over the north Aegean sea, until it fell to earth at Troy. There the Trojans built a temple to Minerva, setting the Palladium in pride of place to honour it and keep it safe, knowing that it would guard them too – just as, years later, it guarded Rome.

Troy's Origins

According to the Greeks, the pregnant princess, who caused such havoc on Samothrace, gave birth to Dardanus, who later ruled Troy. Romans, however, knew another tale. For them, Dardanus was a native-born Italian, an Etruscan prince, who after many battles left Corythus (modern Cortona in Tuscany) and sailed east to Asia Minor. Here he was welcomed by King Teucer, himself a newcomer, having emigrated from Crete to escape a crippling famine. Impressed by the Etruscan refugee, Teucer gave him his daughter's hand in marriage – and (so this version goes) she brought with her the Palladium as part of her dowry. Dardanus fathered a dynasty of kings. Troas, his grandson, gave his name to Troy and the Troad (as the area around the city is called), while from Troas's son, Ilus, it gained its alternative name, Ilium. Some said that it was Ilus who first founded Troy and built the Temple of Minerva to house the Palladium.

Both now and in later generations, the beauty of Troy's princes fired gods' passion. Ilus's brother, Ganymede, attracted Jupiter. Transforming himself into an eagle, the god snatched the youth up to Mount Olympus, to serve as both cupbearer and catamite (as the Latin form of Ganymede's name, Catamitus, makes clear). When Aurora, goddess of the dawn, fell in love with another Trojan prince, Tithonus, she asked Jupiter to make him immortal – but she forgot to ask for his eternal youth. Incapable of dying, he withered, losing strength and looks until he could no longer move. So Aurora locked him away in a secluded cell, until Jupiter took pity and transformed him into the first cicada.

Yet another love affair between a goddess and a local prince would have significantly more profound, far-reaching consequences, and influence not only the mythology and literature but also the history of Rome.

Venus and Anchises: A Marriage Made in Heaven

As a young man, Ilus's grandson, Anchises, was looking after cattle on the slopes of Ida, the mountain southeast of Troy. A Homeric Hymn relates how Venus, goddess of love, saw him and immediately (at Jupiter's instigation) 'felt desire for him, and hungry lust consumed her'. Having dressed with care, and wearing her most stunning jewelry, Venus approached Anchises, pretending – somewhat implausibly – to be a mortal girl, and, although he suspected her true identity, Anchises was so bewitched that he ignored his fears that 'any man who sleeps with an immortal goddess is sapped of health and energy for ever afterwards'. Venus reassured him:

> Anchises, you are the best, the bravest of all mortal men. Don't be afraid. You will experience no harm from me, or any of the other gods, for they all love you dearly. You'll have a son, who'll have dominion over all the Trojans, and the generations still to come, a race that will last forever. And they shall call his name Aeneas, the Terrible One, because I felt such terrible distress to sleep with a mere mortal.

Others gave another meaning to the name Aeneas, deriving it not from the Greek *ainos* ('terrible' or 'dreadful'), but from *ainē* ('praise'). For Romans, who considered Aeneas their ancestor, both derivations might seem equally appropriate.

Stricken by post-coital shame, Venus made Anchises promise to tell no-one of their tryst on pain of being struck down by Jupiter's thunderbolt. Almost inevitably, however, Anchises broke his word. Jupiter did not. Some said he killed or blinded the boastful lover, though most artists and authors (including Virgil) imagined him surviving, injured, into old age, only to suffer the consequences of a misguided adventure in which his son Aeneas played a supporting role.

Judgment and Abduction

Aeneas was brought up by wood-nymphs on Mount Ida, but as a young man he accompanied his cousin, Paris, on a mission to Greece. Paris's fate and that of Troy were inextricably linked. His parents, Priam and Hecuba, were warned that he would be the cause of Troy's destruction, so they exposed baby Paris to die on Mount Ida; but a shepherd rescued him and brought him up as his own. Then, on the cusp of manhood, Paris experienced an epiphany: he was with his cattle on the mountainside when Mercury, the gods' messenger, approached him. With him Mercury brought a golden apple, inscribed 'for the most beautiful'. He also brought three goddesses: Venus, Minerva and Juno, wife of Jupiter. Paris, he said, must give the apple to whichever he saw fit.

Each offered Paris an incentive: Minerva that she would let him rule Greece; Juno that he should rule all Asia; and Venus that he could marry the most beautiful woman in the world. To Juno and Minerva's irritation, Venus won, and soon Paris was back in Troy to claim his birthright. Still wracked by guilt, believing they had killed their baby son, his parents were so overjoyed to find him unexpectedly alive that they happily granted Paris's request to let him undertake an expedition to seek Venus's reward. Aeneas was more than willing to accompany him – not knowing that the reward was Helen, queen of Sparta, wife of the possessive Menelaus. Soon, thanks to his good looks, Venus's assistance and her husband's absence in Crete, Paris not only seduced Helen but persuaded her to come back with him to Troy. When Menelaus found out, he was incandescent. When he married Helen, the other Greek kings had sworn to help him if she ever strayed. Reminding them of their oaths, he assembled an army (commanded by his brother, Agamemnon), and together they set sail for Troy.

Aeneas and the Trojan War

At Troy the Greeks made one last offer: return Helen and they would call off their attack. Paris refused, and both sides settled in for a long siege. Occasionally Trojans, led by their supreme fighter, Hector, attacked the Greek encampment, while the Greeks waged a war of attrition, laying waste to increasingly large areas of surrounding countryside. For much of this time, Aeneas was absent, since an oracle caused Priam to resent him and suspect his loyalty, as Neptune reminds the gods in Homer's *Iliad*:

> Already the son of Cronus (Jupiter) hates Priam's family. From now the Trojans will be ruled by Aeneas's authority, and that of his children's children, and of all the generations that will follow.

So, with bad blood between them, Aeneas prowled off into the wilderness of Ida to tend his cattle and to brood. Even here, however, he was not immune from the effects of war. The Greek hero Achilles led a raid into the mountains, where, surrounded and outnumbered, Aeneas was saved only when Jupiter gave him strength to run away. It was now that he returned to Troy, slipping into the besieged city, where (partly in an attempt at reconciliation, partly to turn the oracle to his own advantage) Priam married his daughter Creusa to Aeneas. In time they had a son, Ascanius, also known as Ilus, or Julus – a name that would echo loudly through the history of Rome.

As fighting swirled around the walls of Troy, Aeneas was often in the front line. Time and again he faced the bravest of the Greeks. Often his courage would have lost him his life, had not gods, mindful of his destiny, intervened. Once, the Greek Diomedes hurled a boulder at Aeneas with such force that it shattered his hip bone. He lost consciousness and might have died, but Venus, overcoming her innate dislike of warfare, ran onto the battlefield and carried him to safety. Even then she almost dropped him when Diomedes drove his spear through her hand, but fortunately Apollo was nearby. He rescued Aeneas, took him to his temple on Troy's citadel, and, assisted by his mother, Latona, and his sister, Diana, restored him.

Another time Aeneas faced Achilles, 'two men, better than all others'. His head helmeted in bronze, and clutching his shield and spear, Aeneas strode through the Trojan lines and into no man's land. Like a hungry lion, Achilles came to meet him, trying to rile Aeneas by reminding him of how he had been forced to run away on Ida. Aeneas refused to trade insults 'like children...or women quarrelling in streets', but drove his spear into Achilles' shield. His enemy, however, was unharmed. Now Aeneas heaved up a massive boulder, as Achilles, sword drawn, bore down on him. Once more a god intervened. Conscious of Aeneas's destiny, Neptune removed him from the fighting, warning him not to engage the enemy while Achilles lived. Thereafter no Greek would harm him. Soon, with Minerva's help Achilles slew Hector, said by the Greeks to be Troy's strength, while Aeneas was its soul. Then Achilles died, felled by the archer, Paris, an arrow through his heel. Still Troy proved impossible to take – even when Ulysses and Diomedes stole into the city in the dead of night and through the broad streets to Minerva's temple, where they removed the famed Palladium from its sanctuary and smuggled it back out to their encampment. Now only guile, it seemed, could end the war.

The Wooden Horse and Laocoön

One morning Troy awoke to a miracle. The bay, for years black with ships and teeming with Greek soldiers, was empty; and on the beach stood a massive horse, artfully constructed from well-planed wood. Virgil describes how, tentatively, the Trojans went out to investigate. Some were suspicious, among them Neptune's priest Laocoön. Suspecting a trap, he speared the horse's side, exclaiming: 'Whatever this is, I fear the Greeks – especially when they offer gifts.'

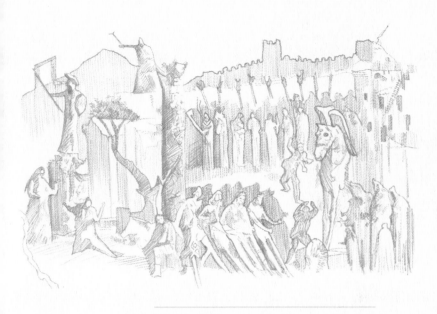

'I fear the Greeks – especially when they offer gifts':
a fresco from the Villa Ariadne, Stabiae, depicts
the Trojan horse.

At that moment, however, a young prisoner was dragged in. His name was Sinon, and he claimed to have escaped being sacrificed by the Greeks to ensure a safe homeward voyage. The horse, he said, was an offering to Minerva to placate her for their theft of the Palladium, which had no sooner been set up in the Greek camp, than it began to sweat profusely, fire blazing from its eyes, as it lunged three times from its base. Like the statue, the horse possessed protective powers. So, fearing that the Trojans would drag it inside their walls, the Greeks made it so huge that it could not fit through the gates.

All who heard Sinon believed him. Then from the island of Tenedos two monstrous sea serpents glided through the waves and up onto the shore, making straight for Laocoön and his two sons. Each wound round one of the young boys, tearing and consuming him, and, when Laocoön ran to help:

> They seized him, too, and wound around him with their massive
> coils. Already they had looped twice round his waist, twice with
> their scaly bodies round his neck, towering over him with heads and

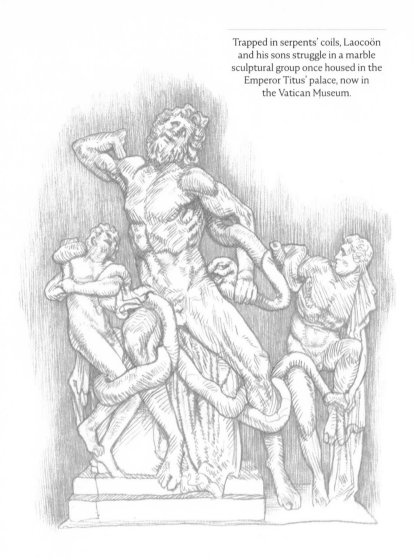

Trapped in serpents' coils, Laocoön and his sons struggle in a marble sculptural group once housed in the Emperor Titus' palace, now in the Vatican Museum.

necks raised high. And all the while, he strained against the knots, his priestly ribbons stained with blood and black bile, bellowing horrendously, like a bull that blunders, wounded, from the altar, shaking the ill-aimed axe out of its neck. And then the twin snakes slid away, slithering towards the towering sanctuaries, seeking out Minerva's citadel, where they nestled beneath the goddess's round shield, beneath her feet.

This gruesome omen further convinced the Trojans. At once they dismantled one of the city gates and dragged the horse on rollers up to the Temple of Minerva. Then the celebrations started. Long into the night they lasted, and Helen led them, dancing through the streets, brandishing a torch, whose firelight could be seen far out to sea. At last the city slept. So no-one saw the Greek ships slipping back across the black waves, or the trapdoor in the belly of the wooden horse swinging open, or the hand-picked killers sliding down the ropes. By the time the Trojans knew what was going on it was too late. The Greeks had poured into their city; the slaughter had begun.

Escape from Troy

Aeneas awoke from a dream. In it, dead Hector had appeared to him, warning him of danger and urging him to flee, taking with him the city's icons, her Penates (protecting gods), sacred vestments and the statue and fire of Vesta, goddess of the hearth. But Aeneas's instinct was to fight, not fly, so with a small band of companions he ran into the street – and mayhem. As flames rolled through Troy, lines of armed Greeks blocked escape routes, while others smashed down doors in an orgy of killing and looting. Hacking their way through the enemy, they reached Priam's palace, but they were already too late. Achilles' son, the bloodthirsty Neoptolemus, had broken in and butchered the old king on the altar steps, while his widow Hecuba and her surviving daughters 'huddled like doves before a lashing, driving storm'.

As Aeneas looked on, fearful for his family's fate, he caught sight of Helen, the cause of all this suffering. He was about to kill her in revenge, when his mother Venus appeared before him in a radiance of light, 'as she appears to gods', urging him to save himself and those he loved. Troy's fall, she said, was fated: divine anger had decreed it; the gods – Neptune, Juno and Minerva – were fighting for the Greeks. Only Aeneas had a future, and he must escape.

Convinced, Aeneas made for Anchises' house, where Creusa and Julus had taken refuge, but at first his father refused to leave – until two portents convinced him. A halo of fire shone round Julus's head, and moments later a fireball shot through the sky and across the rooftops until it crashed far off into the slopes of Mount Ida: the gods would protect his family, but they must leave Troy now. Carrying Anchises on his shoulders, and leading young Julus by the hand, Aeneas and his household followed back roads through the burning city, until they reached the safety of the countryside. But Creusa was nowhere to be seen. Frantic with worry, Aeneas dashed back inside the blazing walls trying desperately to find her.

It was then that he met the third of that night's apparitions: Creusa's ghost. Jupiter had forbidden her to accompany her husband. Instead (according to Virgil, who follows a tradition that the Etruscans came from Lydia), she told Aeneas:

> For you there is long exile, vast voyaging across the sea; and you will come to Hesperia, the Western Land, where Lydian Tiber flows between rich pasturelands, the home of sturdy men. There you will find happiness, empire and a royal wife.

Aeneas tried to embrace her, but she evaporated from his touch. As dawn broke he rejoined his household, swollen now by other Trojan refugees, and (taking the rescued Penates with them) they headed for the hills. The journey to Italy had begun.

Other Versions

So writes the Roman Virgil in his *Aeneid*, but Greeks knew other reasons for Aeneas's escape. Some said that he left before the city fell, sent on a mission to Phrygia, or forewarned by Venus; others that, on the night that Troy was taken, he fought valiantly, rallying his troops, saving the royal treasures and beating a retreat only when it was clear that to resist was pointless. He then held out courageously on Ida until at last, after lengthy negotiations, the Greeks let him and his followers go free, in recognition of Aeneas's efforts throughout the war to persuade the Trojans to return Helen to Menelaus. Still others (less well-disposed to Rome's founder) claimed that Aeneas colluded with the Greeks, betraying Troy because of his long-lasting feud with Priam, and his irritation that Paris received greater honours than he did. As Dionysius of Halicarnassus concludes, 'you may believe whichever tale you wish'.

The fate of the Palladium was equally contested. Julius Caesar minted coins that clearly show his ancestor, Aeneas, clutching the Palladium in his right hand, while escaping Troy with Anchises on his back. Other artworks show the same scene. From where, though, did Aeneas get the Palladium, if it had been stolen by Ulysses and Diomedes? Again, there were variations to the traditional myth: according to one the Greeks stole a fake Palladium, set up in Minerva's temple as a decoy. Another said that there were two Palladia: the Greeks took one; Aeneas took the other. An ancient commentator on the *Aeneid* knew a third version: Diomedes had the Palladium with him, when he returned home only to discover that his wife was being unfaithful.

On a silver denarius struck by Julius Caesar in 47 BC Aeneas flees Troy carrying his father Anchises on one shoulder and the Palladium in his right hand.

Pragmatically he sailed to Italy, where he founded many cities including Brindisi, before meeting Aeneas in Calabria. Setting their hostility aside, he tried to give Aeneas the Palladium. Since Aeneas was sacrificing at the time his head was covered, so he did not see Diomedes. Instead another Trojan, Nautes, took the statue – 'which is why today', the commentator writes, 'it is the family of the Nautii and not the Julii who conduct Minerva's rites'.

Troy in History and Today

For the Romans, and especially the Julii (who traced their lineage back to Julus, Aeneas and Venus), Troy held a special significance. In this city that was at once legendary and real they discovered much to inspire them, not least the story of Aeneas's protection by gods determined that he should fulfil his destiny to found Rome. In more modern times this mix of the mythical and material again made for a heady cocktail, so it is sobering to recall the real-life history of the settlement we now call Troy.

The city was inhabited for almost 4,000 years. From the start (around 3000 BC) it was strongly walled, a maritime settlement in the fold of a great bay at the western mouth of the Hellespont (modern Dardanelles), exchanging ideas, trade and technologies with partners throughout the Aegean, and boasting a wealthy elite. However, around 2300 BC both citadel and lower town, an area embracing some 9 ha (22 acres), were destroyed by fire, perhaps as a result of war – certainly its inhabitants never salvaged their hastily buried treasures, including items made from gold, silver, bronze, electrum, carnelian and lapis lazuli. When Heinrich Schliemann discovered exquisite jewelry from this period, he identified it as belonging to the mythical Helen. In fact, it was a thousand years too early.

Thanks to both Schliemann's over-enthusiastic excavations and the flattening of much of the earlier citadel during the building of a new Temple of Minerva in Hellenistic times, evidence for Troy's next phases is scant, but by 1750 BC the city was enjoying renewed prosperity. Large two-storeyed buildings, many with defensive ground-floor walls, include one (the 'Pillar Hall') apparently dedicated to textile manufacture and another which was perhaps a temple. Tall towers and limestone walls, 5 m (16 ft) wide, angling gently inward as they rose, their line softened by subtle vertical offsets, protected the citadel. Outside, a thriving town covering 30 ha (75 acres), surrounded by a ditch and palisade, was served by a sophisticated water-course of artificial shafts and tunnels. However, around 1300 BC both town and citadel were partially destroyed, probably by earthquake.

Almost immediately the citadel was rebuilt. Now, smaller houses crowded once-open spaces, and new towers were added, perhaps suggesting a city under siege. Correspondence from Hittite archives provides tantalizing evidence that Wilusa (another name for Ilium or Troy) was fought over on more than one occasion. A thick layer of ash up to a metre (3 ft) thick, along with unburied human remains, arrowheads and slingshot, suggests that around 1180 BC this Troy fell in an attack that involved a fierce conflagration. The date chimes with classical calculations for the Homeric siege, but not with archaeological discoveries in mainland Greece, where the cities of Troy's mythical enemies had already fallen by this time. This was a period of unrest across the eastern Mediterranean, and the true identity of Troy's attackers is unknown. The city was quickly rebuilt, albeit less grandly, and our impression of an ensuing dark age may reflect lack of evidence rather than historical reality.

By now the shoreline was receding, the bay was shrinking, and consequently Troy was no longer the commercial hub it had once been. Intriguingly, however, by the eighth century there are signs of cult activities and ritual feasting apparently connected with the city's heroic past. Troy was turning into a heritage site, while the Trojan War became a paradigm for East/West tensions and aggression. In 480 BC, Persia's King Xerxes is said to have sacrificed a thousand cattle at Troy's Temple of Minerva before launching his unsuccessful invasion of Greece (partly to avenge Troy's sack). In 334 BC, before invading Persia, Alexander the Great, who kept a copy of the *Iliad* under his pillow, ran naked to Achilles' grave mound and sacrificed, vowing to build the world's largest temple to Minerva at Troy. He died before it was begun, but his successors enhanced and enlarged the city. Under Rome's

Julio-Claudian emperors, Troy prospered, assuming renewed significance as Rome's spiritual homeland. Later, Constantine considered making Troy his capital before settling instead for Constantinople (modern Istanbul). Under the Byzantines Troy's importance diminished, and in AD 1452 their nemesis, Mehmet the Conqueror, visited the site to mark his victory over the crusading infidels, now couched as successors to Homer's Greeks.

For 400 years the site lay almost forgotten, but in 1865 the British Frank Calvert, believing reports that Hisarlık ('The Place of the Fortress') was Homer's Troy, bought the land and began digging. Six years later a chance conversation in nearby Çanakkale so enthused a romantic German, Heinrich Schliemann, that he took over, ploughing much of his wealth into unwittingly destroying valuable archaeology. Excavations have continued ever since, and the site is no longer the 'vast, untill'd and mountain-skirted plain' that greeted Byron on a visit that inspired the lines: 'where I sought for Ilion's walls, / The quiet sheep feeds, and the tortoise crawls.'

· ·

TROY Some Important Dates and Remains

3000 BC	Troy I: first settlements.
2550–2300 BC	Troy II's Citadel and Lower Town show signs of wealth. Destroyed by fire.
2300–1750 BC	Troy III–V: an upturn in fortunes follows a period of relative poverty.
1750–1300 BC	Troy VI: fine houses on the Citadel and a Lower Town covering 30 ha (75 acres). Partially destroyed by earthquake and fire.
1300–1180 BC	Troy VIIa: further houses on the Citadel and an expanded Lower Town are eventually destroyed in conflict.
1180–950 BC	Troy VIIb: resettlement (perhaps by immigrant population?).
950–85 BC	Troy VIII: rise of Troy as heritage site.
480 BC	Xerxes sacrifices at Temple of Minerva.
334 BC	Alexander the Great sacrifices at Troy.
85 BC	Roman general Fimbria sacks Troy, but Sulla restores the city.
85 BC–AD 500	Troy IX: under Rome, Troy assumes a renewed spiritual importance.
48 BC	Julius Caesar visits Troy and inaugurates building works.

20 BC	Augustus visits Troy and rebuilds Temple of Minerva and theatre.
c. AD 318	Constantine considers making Troy his eastern capital.
AD 1452	Mehmet II (the Conqueror) visits Troy.
AD 1865	Frank Calvert buys site and begins excavations.
AD 1871	Heinrich Schliemann takes over excavations.

Troy is situated off the E87 southwest of Çanakkale in a gated compound amid flat wheat fields. From the car park (dominated by the replica wooden horse) the path leads past the old dig house (now a museum containing models and photographs) before forking (right) to a vantage point.

Steps (left) lead down to the fine **city walls** and **eastern gate** (from Troy VI). From here the designated walkway climbs to the **Temple of Minerva** (**Athene**) with its Roman altar and good views towards the Dardanelles. After traces of **early walls** (Troy I) and **houses** (Troy II), the path skirts Schliemann's trench before reaching the magnificent **ramp** into the citadel of Troy II and a stretch of city walls from **Troy VI**. Beyond is a sanctuary. The track now curves back past the **Roman Odeon** and **Bouleuterion** (Council Chamber), between which is a narrow **towered gateway fronted by altars**, identified as Homer's Scaean Gates. The Lower City lies beneath wooded terrain, from which can be seen the tumulus known as the **Grave Mound of Achilles**.

Turkey's President, Recep Tayyip Erdoğan, proclaimed 2018 'The Year of Troy', with a new museum opening at the site under the auspices of its chief archaeologist, Rüstem Aslan. Meanwhile, some finds from the site are housed in **Istanbul's Archaeological Museum**. Others, including the 'Jewels of Helen', enjoyed a peculiar and very modern adventure. Taken by Schliemann to Germany, they were kept in the Royal Museums in Berlin until the Second World War, when they were hidden for safekeeping in vaults beneath Berlin's zoo. Liberated by Russia's Red Army at the end of the war, they were taken to Moscow, where they are now displayed in the Pushkin Museum.

. . . .

CHAPTER 2
DELOS AND
APOLLO'S PATRONAGE

Mid-ocean lies an island, the favourite of both Doris, mother of
the sea-nymphs, and of Aegean Neptune. It used to float around
the coasts and shorelines, but the dutiful Apollo, archer-god,
anchored it fast to towering Myconus and Gyarus, and let it lie
there motionless, untroubled by the winds. My journey brought
me here, and tranquil Delos welcomed my tired crew to her safe
harbour. So we disembarked and paid respects to Apollo's city.
And Anius, who was both the island's king and Apollo's priest,
came rushing down to meet us, his head garlanded with ribbons
and the sacred leaves of laurel.

Virgil, *Aeneid*, 3.73–82

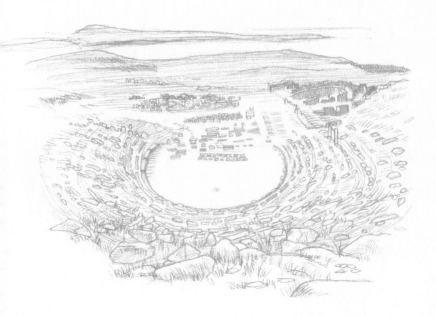

Away from the jetty, where gentle ripples lap sun-baked rocks – away, too, from the dust-dry hollow, once a sacred lake, still flanked by ruined temples and (on the seaward rise) an avenue of proud stone lions – the theatre is deserted. The only sounds: the breeze rustling among arid grasses, the scuttle of a lizard, the clucking of a family of quails as they skitter up the hill behind us. Sit here in the auditorium, its stone seats skewed and overgrown, and you can watch the boats arriving – private yachts; day trips from nearby Myconus (Mykonos); smart tenders frothing in from towering cruise ships anchored out to sea. You can watch their passengers debouch, many apparently bewildered by this seemingly so unimpressive isle, while others, hot and listless, wait wanly to be ferried back, some curiously enervated not just by the beating sun but by the barrenness, the sense of wistful loneliness that can assail you here.

Few come to the theatre. Few scale the slopes behind it: the extravagantly named Mount Cynthus, a mere 112 m (367 ft) high, with panoramic views of the surrounding Cyclades. Few even climb up to the Roman houses on the rise above the theatre, so they do not see the breathtaking mosaics which now lend them their names: the House of the Dolphins; the House of the Masks, on whose floor young Bacchus sits side-saddle on a prancing panther, a work of superb artistry. It is not to the anarchic wine-god Bacchus, though, that Delos is devoted, but to one in some respects his opposite: Apollo, god of the sun, of music and of reason, the god whom Augustus, first emperor of Rome, claimed as his special patron.

Aeneas on Delos and Beyond

Virgil relates how, once the victorious Greeks had set sail from Troy for home, Aeneas and his followers built a fleet and (with Creusa's prophecy still ringing in their ears) put out to sea. Soon fair winds carried them to Delos, an island sacred to Apollo, god of prophecy. Here they were warmly welcomed by King Anius, an old friend of Aeneas's father, Anchises. Without delay, god-fearing Aeneas entered Apollo's venerable temple and made prayer, asking for a sign to set them on their way. At once an earthquake shook the island, and a voice came from the sacred tripod deep within the temple (the first of many disembodied voices that would steer the destiny of Rome):

> Hardy sons of Dardanus, your ancestral land will welcome you to her rich bosom when you return to her. Look for your ancestral mother! It is there that Aeneas's family, his children's children and all who will be born from them will rule every shore.

This fragment of a fresco showing Apollo holding
his lyre was found close to the site of the House
of Augustus on Rome's Palatine Hill.

Where was their 'ancestral land'? There were so many different stories
about Troy's foundation, and where her founder came from, that it was
unclear where Apollo meant them to go. Anchises, however, thought he
knew. Troy's first king, Teucer, he recalled, had come from Crete – and so
had the nature goddess Cybele, the so-called Great Mother, whose devotees
worshipped her in ecstatic rituals.

So without delay the Trojans sailed to Crete, and at Pergamea (perhaps
modern Platanias, a few miles west of Chania) they began to build a city.
Soon, though, a plague struck not just them but the land itself, and Anchises
urged that they return to Delos to consult Apollo, whose remit embraced
both health and sickness. Before they could sail, however, the Penates
(Troy's protecting deities, whose statues had been rescued from the flames)
appeared to Aeneas in a dream. Anchises, they said, had misinterpreted
Apollo's words. The land he meant was not Crete but Italy, from where
Dardanus once sailed to Troy. In Italy, they prophesied, 'we shall raise your

descendants to the stars and make your city the heart of empire'. This was the message, the Penates told Aeneas, that Apollo himself would have conveyed had they returned to Delos, so, fired by this renewed promise of their destiny, the Trojans embarked once more.

It was not the last time that Apollo intervened to bolster their resolve. Having sailed past the western coast of Greece – where they held athletic games on the shore at Actium (the site of Augustus's defeat of Antony and Cleopatra in 31 BC) – Aeneas and his followers reached Buthrotum (Butrint in present-day Albania). Here they were astounded to find not only what appeared to be a miniature Troy but also two Trojan survivors, both of whom had been enslaved by Greeks but subsequently freed. One was Hector's wife Andromache, the other Helenus, Priam's one surviving son, a priest and prophet of Apollo. Through him the god revealed many of the dangers that awaited Aeneas, before urging him once more: 'Get up and go now! Through your deeds raise great Troy to the stars!'

It suited a poet such as Virgil, writing a national epic, to be able to put such words into the mouth of a trusted prophet or (better still) the god of prophecy, and he chose the sites of his revelations carefully. Buthrotum (whose landmarks had for centuries been named after those of Troy) enjoyed close links with Augustus's friend, the general Agrippa, while nowhere boasted a closer connection to Apollo than Delos.

Delos, Apollo's Island

Delos was Apollo's birthplace. His mother, Latona, like so many both before and later, aroused Jupiter's lust, and soon she was expecting twins. But Juno was determined to punish her husband's lover by making her pregnancy problematic, and her delivery as late and painful as possible. Moreover, she commanded Iris, her messenger, and Mars, god of war, to proclaim that nowhere on earth should give Latona sanctuary. In mounting distress, Latona wandered incessantly until she came to Delos, which was at that time floating in the sea, and therefore not covered by Juno's decree. So it was here that, gripping tightly to a palm tree by the shores of its circular lake, Latona was eventually delivered of her divine children, the radiant Apollo and Diana, goddess of the hunt. It was here, too, on the island's tiny mountain that Roman poets such as Virgil often imagined the two gods:

> Diana...on the crags of Cynthus leading her dancers, a thousand mountain nymphs who crowd around her on both sides, following in her wake. On her shoulder is her quiver, and, as she runs on, head

and shoulders taller than all other goddesses, Latona's heart is filled with an unutterable joy.

Similarly:

Apollo, visiting Latona's island, Delos, sets up his dancing choruses, as round his altars throngs of Cretans, and Dryopians [early inhabitants of mainland Greece], and tattooed Agathyrsians [Dacian Scythians] raise their voices loud. Apollo himself stalks the crags of Cynthus, binding his flowing hair with soft leaves encircled in a band of gold, and his arrows clatter at his shoulder.

'Taller than all other goddesses', Diana contemplates her weapons on a fresco from Stabiae on the Bay of Naples.

As both descriptions reveal, the twins were accomplished archers, raining their deadly shafts on those who slighted them – or their mother. When Niobe boasted that she had more children than Latona, Apollo and Diana did not hesitate to turn their bows on Niobe's seven sons and seven daughters, killing them all.

Apollo, God of Plague and Medicine

Whereas Diana generally used her bow for hunting wild beasts on the mountainside, Apollo's arrows could inflict plague. The Romans were not alone in imagining this. In the first set-piece scene in Western literature, the beginning of Homer's *Iliad*, Apollo punishes the Greeks at Troy for kidnapping his priest's daughter by assailing both men and livestock with disease-bearing darts, 'and well-packed pyres burned constantly'.

In Italy, Etruscans suffered similarly from Apollo's wrath. Following their victory over Phocaean émigrés at the Battle of Alalia in 540 BC, they massacred their prisoners near Caere (modern Cerveteri). However, as Herodotus tells us in his *Histories*:

> Soon anything from Caere – sheep, draught animals or men – that went past where the Phocaeans were buried became crippled, dis-figured and disabled. So, wanting to make amends for their crime, the Caereans sent to Delphi, and the priestess of Apollo ordered them to do what in fact the Caereans still do: offer sacrifices to the dead Phocaeans along with athletic games and equestrian events.

At the same time, the Caereans built a treasury at Delphi, while shortly afterwards a statue of Apollo (called Aplu or Apulu in the Etruscan language) was created by the sculptor Vulca to grace his new temple at Veii.

Italians enthusiastically embraced the healer-god Apollo, happily introducing him into their own legends. At Lake Nemi, east of Rome, they wove an elaborate tale to associate him and his sister Diana with local ritual. A Greek myth told how Theseus, king of Athens, killed his own son Hippolytus (Diana's devotee), wrongly believing that he had raped his queen. But Apollo's son Asclepius (like his father a skilled doctor) restored Hippolytus to life, sending him to live at Nemi (called in some sources Aricia). Here, where in former times the nature goddess Egeria had ruled supreme, Virbius (as Hippolytus was now known) inaugurated the worship of Diana.

Even under Rome's emperors, Nemi's cult was notorious. According to Strabo: 'its priest is always a runaway slave, who has managed to kill the previous office-bearer. For this reason the incumbent priest always carries a sword and watches out for attack, always ready to defend himself.' As for Asclepius, who restored Hippolytus-Virbius to life, Jupiter, angered that he had upset the laws of nature, blasted him with his thunderbolt, but thanks to Apollo's intercession, he was subsequently deified. In the wake of plague, his rites were introduced to Rome around 291 BC, and a temple dedicated to him on Tiber Island.

Apollo and Daphne

Romans appropriated other Greek myths associated with Apollo, too, not least his pursuit of the beautiful young water-nymph, Daphne, who had sworn an oath of chastity. Like Apollo, Venus's son Cupid wielded a bow and arrows, and when Apollo boasted that, while his own weapons killed or caused disease, Cupid's could do nothing but enflame desire, the love-god resolved to teach him a lesson. So he caused him to fall desperately in love with Daphne.

The nymph would have nothing of it. Instead, she fled, 'her limbs bare in the wind, her tunic billowing behind her'. Apollo ran after her, but, when it seemed he might catch her, Daphne prayed fervently that she might escape by being somehow transformed. Immediately, as Ovid writes in *Metamorphoses*:

> A heavy tiredness crept across her limbs, her smooth stomach was embraced by a thin layer of bark, leaves grew from her hair and branches from her arms, while her feet – just now so swift – were held tight by restraining roots. Her face became a leafy canopy. Only her glow remained.

Daphne had turned into a laurel tree, which from that time on was sacred to Apollo. In recognition of the god, victorious Roman generals were crowned with laurel when they celebrated triumphs, riding in a chariot through the cheering streets of Rome and up onto the Capitol – and laurel trees grew beside Augustus's palace on the Palatine, 'the most faithful guards of all'.

Apollo, the Laurel and Augustus

Augustus identified himself closely with Apollo. Suetonius records that his mother, Atia, claimed to have been impregnated by Apollo disguised as a serpent, while the same god sent the emperor's wife, Livia, an unlikely gift:

She was visiting her villa at Veii, when an eagle flew past and dropped a snow-white hen into her lap. In its beak it still held the sprig of laurel that it had pecked at. Livia gave orders for the hen to be looked after, and for the laurel to be planted in soil. The hen had so many chicks that today the villa is called 'The Villa of the Hens'. As for the laurel-grove, it grew so vigorously that the emperors took from it the leaves and branches that they carry in triumphs. It was their tradition, too, to plant a new tree in the same location immediately after their triumph, and it was noticed that, a little before each of them died, the tree he had planted withered away.

At one particularly infamous dinner party, known as The Banquet of the Twelve Gods, where aristocratic Romans dressed as deities, Augustus appeared as Apollo. His choice was not accidental. With the Roman world on the verge of civil war, Augustus's enemy, Mark Antony, was already being hailed as a second Bacchus. The two gods were polar opposites. Bacchus's purview was populist licentiousness: wine and drama, liberation from social constraints, freedom to abandon mind and body to excess. Apollo, on the other hand, was the aristocratic god of civilization – not just of medicine and prophecy but of music and the arts, sobriety and order. Occasionally, too, he was envisaged as a wolf, a particularly talismanic creature for the Romans since a she-wolf was believed to have suckled the city's founders Romulus and Remus. If this were not enough, in his guise as Phoebus, Apollo drove his sun-bearing chariot across the skies, bringing light to the whole world, a task that only someone with his consummate skills could possibly achieve.

Phoebus Apollo and Phaethon

Phoebus Apollo had a son, Phaethon ('Fiery'), but the boy's friends refused to believe him when he boasted of his parentage. So Phaethon made the long journey east until he came to Apollo's palace. Here the god acknowledged that he was indeed his father, and swore to grant the boy whatever he might wish. However, when Phaethon asked to drive the chariot of the sun for one day across the skies, Phoebus was distraught. Even he needed all his strength and experience to control the horses; a callow youth such as Phaethon would be doomed. But he could not go back on his word. Phaethon was unable to rein in the team – which galloped wildly, swooping down to the earth, scorching much of Africa until it became desert, turning the Ethiopians' skin black and threatening to evaporate the seas – until Jupiter struck the chariot with his thunderbolt. Dislodged, Phaethon crashed down into the River Po, where in sorrow his sisters, transformed into black poplars, wept tears of amber.

Ovid's description of Phaethon's visit to Phoebus Apollo's palace is undoubtedly intended to remind his readers of a Roman temple, with its high columns inlaid with gold and bronze, its ivory roof and its polished silver doors. He may have had in mind one of the temples built or rebuilt by the victorious Augustus in Rome on the Capitol or at key sites such as Actium. Curiously Augustus did not build at Delos, which was by now a backwater. However, the god's birthplace still held sufficient significance in Roman minds for Virgil and his contemporaries to make the island a key stopover on Aeneas's journey from Troy, and its priest, Anius, a crucial character for him to visit.

Anius and His Daughters

Like Daphne, Anius experienced shape-shifting, albeit at second hand. Apollo's son and Bacchus's great-grandson, he and his family were renowned for piety. His three sons – Andros (himself a prophet), Myconus and Thasos (who was later eaten by a dog) – gave their names to islands where they ruled, while thanks to a gift from Bacchus, one of Anius's daughters could change anything she liked to wine, a second could make wheat, and a third could produce oil. When the Greek army docked at Delos on its way to Troy, keen to consult Anius about its future, the girls showed off their skills to Agamemnon, and this was their undoing. Realizing their worth, he abducted them and forced them to feed his troops, but the girls escaped. The Greeks pursued them, and even as they were fastening chains around the girls' waists, the three raised up their arms in prayer to Bacchus, begging him to help them escape captivity. At once they changed into snow-white doves and soared far away, the birds of Venus, the divine ancestress of Augustus.

Delos in History and Today

The Greeks considered Delos, site of Apollo's birth (Diana's birthplace was sometimes debated) to be a place of tremendous sanctity, as many of their offerings proclaimed. In the late seventh century BC, islanders of Naxos dedicated between nine and twelve marble lions (perhaps inspired by Egyptian avenues of sphinxes, such as those linking the temples of Luxor and Karnak) on a terrace overlooking the sacred lake. In the sixth century BC, the Athenian tyrant Pisistratus purified the area around the sacred lake and began building a temple to Apollo with a massive statue of the god.

Following the Persian Wars, in 478 BC Delos became the site of the Greek (Delian) League's assembly and treasury. Facing a 9 m (30 ft) statue of the god dedicated by Naxians in the seventh century BC, a colonnaded temple to Apollo was begun, though it was not completed until the end of the fourth century BC. When the League's headquarters were transferred to Athens in 454 BC, Athens continued to lay claim to Delos. In 426/425 BC she removed all its graves to nearby Rhenea, proclaiming that henceforth

DELOS Some Important Dates and Remains

pre-1200 BC	Centre of worship.
C7th BC	Ionian cult centre; Naxians dedicate lion terrace and colossal statue of Apollo.
546–527 BC	Pisistratus purifies Delos and builds Temple of Apollo.
490 BC	Persians spare Delos during invasions of Greek mainland.
478 BC	Delian League formed; Athenians begin Temple of Apollo.
426/425 BC	Athenians again purify Delos and begin third Temple of Apollo.
166 BC	Becomes a Roman 'free port'.
late C2nd BC	Major commercial and slave-trading centre.
88 BC	Attacked by Mithridates of Pontus and 20,000 inhabitants killed.
69 BC	Further piratical attacks.
late C1st BC	Delos, depopulated, experiences severe and irreversible decline.

Delos is a popular cruise destination, but independent travellers must take one of the frequent ferries (30 minutes) from nearby Mykonos. All must be prepared for the merciless sun and a lack of any real shade.

Facing the **Sacred Harbour** (separated by a narrow spit from the ancient **Commercial Harbour**, where most now disembark) is the site occupied no one might give birth, die or (in recognition of Thasos's fate) keep a dog on Delos. She also built a third temple to Apollo between the existing two.

In the early Roman era, Delos, a bustling free port and sizeable community with over 20,000 inhabitants, hosted a thriving slave market with room for 10,000 slaves. Temples were built to Isis and Ba'al, as well as the oldest surviving Jewish synagogue. Delos's isolation, however, left it vulnerable to attack. By the end of Rome's civil wars of the first century BC the island's fortunes were already in decline. In time, thanks to its lack of agricultural land, and despite its sanctity, it was abandoned.

· ·

by three sixth- and fifth-century BC **temples to Apollo**, their unusual west-facing entrances aligned to an earlier Bronze Age shrine. A path (left) leads towards the **Temple of Latona**, the **Avenue of Lions** and the (now drained) **Sacred Lake**. Enthusiastic walkers can proceed to the **Stadium** and **Synagogue** on the far side of the island. Other paths lead off (right) towards the fine **theatre**, above which remains of large houses contain well-preserved mosaics and wall-paintings. In this area, too, are the **sanctuaries of Syrian and Egyptian gods**. A paved pathway leads to the top of **Mount Cynthus** with panoramic views of the Cyclades.

The small Museum (which also sells refreshments) contains finds from Delos, including the originals of the Naxian lions, a Mycenaean ivory plaque showing a warrior with boar-tusk helmet, an archaic statue of a young woman, an impressive bronze mask of Dionysus and a second-century BC **statue of Apollo**. There is also a good collection of **pottery** and a stunning (if hastily drawn) **fresco** showing Hercules, two boxers and a musician.

In 2017 a major reconstruction programme was announced for Delos, aided by a €550,000 donation from the Paul and Alexandra Canellopoulos Foundation. Dimitris Athanasoulis, head of the Cyclades Antiquities Ephorate, spearheading the project, proclaimed that his vision entailed 'making Delos an archaeological hub just like Pompeii, which in turn could attract millions of euros in funding restorative actions'.

· ·

CHAPTER 3
CARTHAGE AND DIDO'S CURSE

There was an ancient city, home to colonists from Tyre.
Its name was Carthage, and it lay far off facing Italy and Tiber's
mouth, a city of enormous wealth, well-drilled in bitter arts
of war. They say that Juno loved this city more than any other
in the world, more even than her precious Samos. It was in
Carthage that she kept her weapons and her chariot, and it was
Carthage that, if Fate allowed, she meant to make the capital of
empire. Already she was lavishing her care on it, and grooming
it for greatness.

Virgil, *Aeneid*, 1.12–18

The air is loud with an exuberance of birds that chatter from lush shrubs and palm trees, and from sun-baked walls and columns rising tall into a perfect, cloudless sky. From the turquoise sea, where sunlight dances on the swell, a warm breeze bathes our cheeks as we gaze down across the Bay of Tunis, bustling with shipping, out towards the jagged mountains far beyond, which shimmer in the haze. The courtyard, where we stand, is rich with fine mosaics, a kaleidoscope of tesserae, a profusion of exotic birds, the stony cousins of the sparrows whose song so fills the air, pheasants and peacocks strutting, proudly preening, forever frozen in a blaze of colour.

It is always to the view that our eyes and thoughts are drawn: the great sweep of the shoreline from the palace (recently the presidential palace, now the Palace of the Tunisian Republic), south, where a maze of Roman baths squats in a leafy park, and further still to where a fleet of little fishing boats, their hulls painted jauntily in vibrant blues and reds, bobs in an ancient harbour. Its circular construction still remains (though the buildings that adorned it are long gone) and broken columns strew the baking earth. Such peacefulness belies its history. For this was once a tightly guarded naval installation, the military port of the most powerful trading nation of its age, and from this harbour, where now whitewashed houses flank the shore and trees sigh in the gentle breeze, the mighty Carthaginian war fleet, feared from Spain to Sicily, once put out to sea.

Dido-Elissa in Tyre

Like the Trojans, the founders of Carthage were refugees, and, like Aeneas, their leader had suffered her own share of personal tragedy. Today we know her as Dido, though Romans also called her Elissa, a name which, in Semitic languages, suggests a close relationship with the divine. Beautiful, resourceful and intelligent, she was Phoenician, from the wealthy island port of Tyre, where generations of her ancestors had ruled as kings.

As he approached death, Dido's father, Belus, decreed that the throne must pass not just to his young son, Pygmalion, but to Dido, too, as joint ruler. Pygmalion was outraged. His courtiers whipped up the people's anger, and Dido was forced to flee to her uncle on the mainland for protection. Called Sychaeus by Virgil, but by others Acerbas, he was the powerful priest of Melqart, 'Lord of Tyre', founder of the royal line, a god in whom Greeks and Romans found close parallels with Hercules. Soon passion played its part. Uncle and niece became husband and wife. But they could not escape Pygmalion.

The young king resented Sychaeus for his marriage to Dido, for his priestly power and (still more) for his wealth. So he despatched assassins and slew Sychaeus. Dido was heartbroken, but she had little time for mourning. Swearing to be forever faithful to her beloved Sychaeus's memory, she planned her escape, for she had no doubt that she would be Pygmalion's next victim.

Dido's Escape

Dido knew that there were some in Tyre who shared her hatred for Pygmalion, and secretly she took these men into her confidence. Meanwhile, to allay Pygmalion's suspicions, Dido sent him a letter. She was, she said, so haunted by her husband's memory that she wanted to turn her back on her marital home and return to live with Pygmalion. With her she would bring her husband's wealth.

Ecstatic, Pygmalion sent trusted servants to help Dido load her belongings onto a ship and that evening, with all aboard, they put to sea. As the vessel lumbered, laden, into open water, Dido ordered Pygmalion's men to heave overboard some sacks of sand that served as ballast. Then, knowing that from the shore Pygmalion could hear her words, Dido raised her arms towards the skies and theatrically prayed to Sychaeus's ghost, asking that he accept as offerings the riches that had caused his death. Pygmalion's men were terrified. They knew the sacks held only sand, but the king would never believe them – he would think that they had willingly consigned the treasures to the deep and surely execute them. So, they turned their coats, swore loyalty to Dido and, making sacrifice to Melqart, set sail with her for exile.

Pygmalion was incandescent with fury, and would have launched his fleet, but his mother held him back, and, when his priests had read the omens, they delivered baneful news. The king must not interfere with Dido's plans. If he did he would not escape unpunished, for it was his sister's destiny to found the richest city in the world.

Dido Sails West

The fugitives made landfall first on Cyprus, where they were met by Jupiter's priest, who not only welcomed them but offered to accompany the refugees, and bring his wife and children with him. Inspired with a new confidence, the Phoenicians began to think more seriously about their future, and some of Dido's shipmates felt the time was ripe to find a wife. It so happened that the Cypriots were celebrating a festival of Venus (or Astarte, as the Phoenicians knew her). Its rites dictated that unmarried girls were sent down to the beach to prostitute themselves. Part of the money they thus earned they offered to the goddess (in the hope that she might keep them faithful to their future husbands), while part they kept to swell their dowries. Now, with Dido's blessing, the refugees chose the eighty who most took their fancy, and escorted them on board their ship; then, with their newly press-ganged wives, the Tyrians continued on their voyage.

Founding Carthage

As they sailed on, keeping North Africa on their port side, they at last rounded a long, low promontory and, crossing the azure bay, they dragged their ship ashore. At once the local Berbers, who had been watching the ship's progress, rushed down to meet them, eager to trade and barter – and among them was their king, Iarbas. Dido enchanted him, and, when she asked him for a little piece of land where she and her companions could rest awhile, he asked, 'How much?' 'Oh, not much really,' she replied, 'only as much as an ox-hide will stretch over.' Delighted by what he took to be a charming joke, Iarbas readily agreed.

When the ox-hide was brought to her, Dido became deadly serious. She ordered her most skilful crew-members to cut the skin into the narrowest of strips, a mere thread's width, and with them she encircled not just the beach but the hill that rose behind it, which has ever since been known as Byrsa ('Ox-Hide'). Iarbas gallantly admitted he had been outplayed, and soon the enclosure became a thriving trading post, as Berbers and other Phoenicians from nearby Utica converged there to do business.

In truth, neither Dido nor her fellow refugees felt any inclination to sail further, and Iarbas was content to let them settle in exchange for yearly rent. So they set about digging foundations for strong walls. Almost immediately their spades unearthed an ox's skull. Priests crowded round. It was, they judged, both a good omen and a bad one: the city would enjoy great wealth, but (like an ox) it would be lumbering and enslaved. That would not do at all! So the diggers moved on to another spot. And here they found another skull – this time of a horse. 'Much better!' the delighted priests pronounced, for this foretold not only rapid power but victory in war. So it was founded: *Kart-hadasht*, 'The New City'. Today we know it as Carthage, the capital of the Carthaginian (or Punic) Empire.

Aeneas Arrives in North Africa

Like many other elements of his life, Aeneas's arrival in Carthage was closely choreographed by gods. Sailing west, the Trojans eventually made landfall on Sicily, but now – so tantalizingly near Italy – they suffered two major setbacks. Anchises (Aeneas's father), whose wisdom and experience had guided them throughout their voyage, died; and, as they set sail once more, their mortal enemy Juno, queen of the gods, persuaded Aeolus to unleash a storm. Aeolus had power over the winds, which he caged like wild beasts in a rocky cave. Now with a blow from his trident, he smashed the cavern's walls and the winds rushed out. Thunder cracked. Seas boiled. Aeneas's ship was pummelled. Virgil's account is vivid:

> Oars broke. The prow sheared off. Waves battered the ship's hull. Next came a massive roller, a towering mountain of sea water, soaring tall above them. At one moment they were hanging high on the wave's crest, then at the next they saw, so far below, the water sucked back and the ocean's bed exposed. And the sand seethed and boiled.

Now housed in Copenhagen's Ny Carlsberg Glyptotek, this second-century AD head of Juno encapsulates the goddess's unbending personality.

As the Trojans' ships splintered and wallowed, their crews clutching desperately to wreckage, Neptune intervened. Angered at Juno's meddling, he calmed the waves and cleared the storm winds. By now the Trojan fleet was scattered, and believing many of his comrades to be dead Aeneas mustered the seven ships that he could see and headed for land. They had been driven far off course, and made landfall not in Italy but in the territory of Carthage.

Welcoming Aeneas

Venus was indignant. What of Jupiter's promise that her son's descendants 'would hold sway over every land and sea'? The king of the gods was quick to reassure her, and Virgil imagines him outlining glorious Rome's future from Aeneas to Romulus to Julius Caesar and the civilizing reign of Augustus. 'I set them no limits of either time or space', his Jupiter declares. 'To them I have granted empire without end.' With which words, the god sent Mercury to Carthage to make its people and Queen Dido amenable to their new visitors, while Venus herself (poorly disguised as a huntress) confronted Aeneas as he was reconnoitring the land.

Having briefed him on Dido's history, Venus swept aside Aeneas's worries about his missing comrades, furnished a reassuring omen, and wrapped her son in a mist of invisibility to let him enter Carthage unseen. Aeneas looked in awe at the new city, whose buildings were already nearing completion. Especially miraculous was the Temple of Juno (or, more properly, her Punic equivalent, Tanit) with sculptures showing the Trojan War. As he was admiring them (even recognizing himself among the fighters), Dido arrived with her retinue, soon followed by a crowd of unexpected guests – Aeneas's lost companions. They had survived the storm, and, no sooner had they told the queen their story, than Dido welcomed them, even offering them homes as citizens in Carthage. Now the mist around Aeneas melted, his handsome looks enhanced by Venus. Reunited with his friends, he, too, was welcomed by Queen Dido and invited to dine with her. Eagerly, Aeneas sent for his son Ascanius to join them. Once again Venus intervened. Still fearing Juno's treachery, she disguised Cupid as the boy, with instructions to weave his magic and make Dido fall hopelessly in love with her Trojan guest.

Dido and Aeneas

Dido could not resist, and, when she confided her passion for Aeneas to her sister Anna (who had fled from Tyre with her), Anna urged her to forget her promise to stay faithful to Sychaeus's memory. A Trojan alliance would be good for everyone. So, 'like a doe that wanders through thick forests or high mountain passes, a Cretan shepherd's arrow lodged deep inside its flank' (in Virgil's memorable simile), Dido swooned over Aeneas. Nothing else mattered. Even work on building Carthage ground to a halt.

For Juno it was a godsend. If Aeneas stayed at Carthage, it would thwart Jupiter's plans for Rome. So, pulling rank on Venus, she cajoled her into colluding in her plans. The next day, the Carthaginians and Trojans went out hunting, but far from the city they were caught in a sudden storm. As hail and thunder lashed the countryside, and all fled for cover, Dido and Aeneas found themselves alone in the same cave. It all seemed so propitious – as if Nature herself were conspiring to bring them together. But, as Virgil caustically remarks:

> On that day was first born death and suffering. From now on, Dido had no more concern for reputation or appearance; her passion was concealed no longer. She called it marriage, and with this word disguised her sin.

However, if Dido was delirious with happiness, Iarbas, her Berber neighbour, considered the Trojans to be a threat. So he prayed to Jupiter, whose son he was (one of many that the god had fathered by a hapless nymph), and he demanded reparation.

Aeneas's Betrayal

Jupiter, too, was unhappy. For Aeneas to lose his head over an African queen was never part of his grand plan. So he sent Mercury to Carthage to reprimand the Trojan, reminding him of his destiny and that of Rome. Aeneas was terrified, and ordered his lieutenants to make the fleet ready for departure; but how could he break the news to Dido? As he kept putting it off, he discovered that he had no need. Dido had observed his preparations. She was no fool. Seeking Aeneas, she poured out her heart, accusing him of betrayal, begging him to stay, imagining her bleak future with him gone.

Aeneas was resolute – so resolute, in fact, that he seemed callous, peevish. He must honour his obligations to his Trojans! He had his destiny; he must fulfil it! 'Stop unsettling yourself – and me – with your complaining. It's not my choice to go to Italy.' His words further inflamed Dido. Promising that her memory would haunt Aeneas while she lived, while in death her ghost would plague him, she left him standing paralysed and speechless, before, contemplating his great future, he strode down to his ships.

Dido's Curse

From her window Dido watched the Trojans make their preparations. Repeatedly she sent Anna with messages for her faithless lover, begging him to stay a little longer. Still 'Fate constrained him, and the gods checked his compassion', and Dido, plagued increasingly by nightmares and bad omens, and haunted by Sychaeus's ghost, resolved to die. Pretending to know rituals to cure her passion, she had a massive pyre built in the palace courtyard. At its summit she placed the bed that she and Aeneas had shared, together with his sword, his portrait and the gifts he had once showered upon her, before, with Carthaginian priestesses, she made offerings and prayers to the gods of the underworld. That night Mercury again appeared to Aeneas, reminded him that 'women are forever fickle', and commanded him to leave at once.

Next morning, when she saw the harbour empty, Dido, distraught, called down a terrifying curse upon Aeneas, praying that, even if he was fated to reach Italy, he should be afflicted by war and suffering, and ordering her fellow Carthaginians:

> From this day harrow his descendants, hate every member of his family! Make this his payment to my ashes. Let there be no love lost between our peoples, and no treaty made. And from my bones one day will rise up an avenger to plague these Trojan settlers with sword and fire, now and tomorrow and whenever strength is yours. Shore against shore, sea against sea, weapon against weapon, this is my curse: from generation unto generation total war!

Then, ordering Sychaeus's old nurse, Barce, to bring Anna to the sacrifice, Dido climbed onto the pyre, and, seizing Aeneas's sword, she plunged it deep into her chest. As the shocked household raised ritual laments, Juno ordered Iris to swoop down from heaven, a rainbow trailing in her wake, to ease Dido's death, 'and warmth left her body, as her life evaporated into the surrounding breeze'.

Dido and Iarbas

Aeneas was not always part of Dido's story. The Roman historian Justin (citing the first-century BC Trogus) tells how in a meeting with ten Carthaginian ambassadors the Berber king, Iarbas, demanded Dido's hand in marriage, adding that her refusal would mean war. The ambassadors were unwilling to convey the message in these terms. Instead, they told Dido that Iarbas had requested that the Carthaginians send someone to 'civilize' him and his people. But who would be prepared to endure the Berbers' way of life? When Dido replied that, since this would benefit Carthage greatly, no-one must refuse, the ambassadors informed her that Iarbas had insisted that she herself should join him as his wife. Outmanoeuvred, Dido delayed for three months. Her oath of fidelity to Sychaeus, and the memory of their love, haunted her. So, announcing that she would make a final offering to him before 'joining in the marriage to which her city forced her', she made lavish sacrifice and raised an ornate pyre – before climbing onto it and stabbing herself.

Justin relates that the Carthaginians then worshipped Dido as a goddess, and for a time all turned out well. Later, though, when plague and discord gripped the city, 'they embraced cruel rites and hideous abominations: they offered human sacrifice, dragging children to the altars, asking for the gods' goodwill by killing those for whom gods more usually are asked to care'.

Dido, Hannibal and Cleopatra

In Augustan Rome, Dido assumed a fresh political significance, which comes to the fore in Virgil's *Aeneid*. Here, Dido personifies historical hatreds between Rome and Carthage. Her prayer for an avenger and her curse unleashing total war are presented as the cause of the three Punic Wars, and especially the destruction of much of Italy and the slaughter of many of its legions by Hannibal Barca (whose family name echoes that of the old nurse, Barce).

At the same time, however, Virgil cleverly compares Dido with another, more contemporary, enemy of Rome. In 32 BC, rather than declare civil war on the Roman Mark Antony, Augustus (then Octavian) declared war instead on his consort, the Egyptian Queen Cleopatra, and at the same time did all he could to blacken her name. Propaganda presented her as a schemer who had seduced the noble Antony, diverting his attention from his duty to Rome. Like Dido, the powerful Cleopatra was accused of witchcraft, while her marital status with Antony seemed as ambiguous as that of Dido and Aeneas. There were other similarities, too. Both queens were famed for their beauty, both fought with younger brothers, and both (it was said) committed suicide. Yet, despite Virgil's parallels between Dido and not only Cleopatra but also notoriously cruel women from mythology such as Medea, he presents a surprisingly rounded and sympathetic portrait of the Carthaginian queen, and many readers cannot condone Aeneas's apparently cold treatment of her.

Carthage in History and Today

Chronology suggests that, even if Dido and Aeneas existed, they could never have met. For, while some ancient historians placed Carthage's foundation in the twelfth century BC, archaeology confirms the views of others such as Justin who set it in the late ninth century. Indeed, it is possible that Roman myth preserves names of real characters: Belus (Dido's father) may be a Latin corruption of Ba'al-Eser (II), who ruled Tyre (now in Lebanon) in 841 BC, while epigraphic evidence calls his successor 'PMY', perhaps an abbreviation of Pygmalion. While it is possible that Dido, too, was a real person, it is more likely that in her we have a memory of a protecting deity (whose name meant 'The Beloved') maybe connected to Tanit/Juno, believed to have nurtured Carthage's first settlers.

Flanked by two Muses, the poet Virgil clutches a scroll on a third-century AD mosaic now in the Bardo Museum, Tunis, near Carthage.

As Tyre's empire grew and trading networks expanded across the western Mediterranean, its Phoenicians established an increasing number of safe anchorages, settlements and entrepôts along the North African coast, as well as in eastern Spain and Sicily. One was Utica (in modern Tunisia), and it was probably from here that colonists first recognized the potential of Carthage's natural harbours and the acropolis of Byrsa Hill. In the century after its foundation (perhaps in 814 BC, or more likely a century later), Carthage continued to maintain close relations with the Phoenician metropolis of Tyre, while cultivating diplomatic ties with African neighbours. However, in the sixth century BC Tyre lost its autonomy following wars with Assyrians, Babylonians and Persians. Cut adrift, their numbers perhaps swollen by Tyrian refugees, western Phoenicians looked for leadership, and soon, thanks to Carthage's acumen for commerce and warfare, the city was confidently facing down her trading rivals (Etruscans in western Italy; Greek colonists expanding into Sicily and south Italy) in a successful bid to control the sea-lanes.

With an insatiable appetite for raw materials, Carthage pushed into mineral-rich Spain and despatched intrepid voyagers to explore the coasts of Africa and southwest Europe. Meanwhile, her generals annexed huge swathes of North Africa and tried doggedly to conquer Sicily. Here, however, despite a treaty made in 510 BC, their ambitions brought them into direct conflict with Rome. The first of three Punic Wars (264–241 BC) saw Carthage driven out of Sicily; in the second (218–201 BC), Carthage's brilliant general Hannibal famously crossed the Alps with a squadron of war-elephants to launch a blistering sixteen-year-long attack on Italy, which almost conquered Rome but ended in defeat back on African soil; in the third (149–146 BC), after a prolonged siege, the Romans, heeding the advice of their politician, Cato the Elder, that 'Carthage must be destroyed', burned the city to the ground and enslaved its few survivors.

In 49 BC Julius Caesar began resettling Carthage as a Roman city, and the site began to prosper once again. Within a century it was North Africa's provincial capital, the fourth largest city in the empire, responsible for shipping much of the grain on which Rome depended for survival, and an increasingly important hub of Christianity. For ambitious warlords its wealth was irresistible, and with Rome's decline the Vandal king Genseric succeeded in capturing Carthage, overrunning North Africa in AD 439 (a prelude to his sack of Rome sixteen years later). A century later, it was back in the hands of Rome (or, rather, its western incarnation, Byzantium), but Carthage's glory came to an abrupt end in 698, when it fell to Hassan Ibn al-Numan and his Muslim army. Al-Numan relocated the defeated population to his new settlement of Tunis, a few kilometres to the south, for which the ruins of Carthage provided a useful quarry. Today, with Carthage both a UNESCO World Heritage Site and one of Tunis's more wealthy suburbs, the relationship between archaeologists and developers is not always the most harmonious.

CARTHAGE Some Important Dates and Remains

c. 1000 BC	Phoenicians establish safe anchorages along North African coast.
? 814 BC	Foundation of Carthage as Tyrian colony.
586–539 BC	Decline of Tyre enables Carthage to acquire autonomy and empire.
530s BC	Conflict with Etruscans and Greeks. Carthage annexes Sardinia.
510 BC	Treaty between Carthage and Rome.
c. 500 BC	Voyages of exploration, including by Hanno the Navigator (perhaps to Gabon).
C5th–4th BC	Three wars fail to establish Carthaginian control over Sicily.
264–241 BC	First Punic War ends in Carthaginian defeat and loss of Sicily.
218–201 BC	Second Punic War: Hannibal invades and terrorizes much of Italy but baulks at besieging Rome. Outflanked, he is lured back to North Africa and defeated at Zama. Carthage loses Spain to Rome and is forced to cede many North African territories to Rome's Berber allies.
149–146 BC	Defending itself from Berber attack, Carthage becomes embroiled in Third Punic War, ending in its sack.
122 BC	Rome founds a small colony at Carthage.
49–27 BC	Refounded as Colonia Junonia ('Juno's Colony'), Carthage becomes the capital of the Roman province of Africa, heralding centuries of relative stability and wealth.
AD 416	A major Christian city, Carthage hosts a synod to discuss (and condemn) the Pelagian heresy.
AD 439	Vandals under Genseric take Carthage.
AD 534	Belisarius recaptures Carthage for Byzantium.
AD 698	After three years of fighting, a Muslim army under Hassan Ibn al-Numan takes and destroys Carthage.

Note: A state of emergency was declared in Tunisia in November 2015 and was still in place at the time of writing. Travellers should confirm the current security situation before visiting (in the UK, consult the Foreign and Commonwealth Office website).

Carthage's remains are widespread, and an attempt to visit all in one day may prove frustrating. At their southern bounds, near the traditional site of Dido's landing, is the haunting **Salambo Tophet**, the cemetery for young children (30 per cent newborn, 68 per cent aged between one and three) said to be victims of sacrifice to Ba'al. Close by to the east is Carthage's rectangular **Commercial Harbour**, with the round **Military Harbour** to the north. Although it is now silted and ruined, it is still possible to appreciate the scale of this once stunning installation. Originally 325 m (1,066 ft) in diameter, it held a circular island, 106 m (347 ft) in diameter, site of the admiralty headquarters; facing inwards towards the harbour was a complex of two-storey buildings with shipsheds for up to 220 ships and warehouses for storing equipment.

North past the **Magon Quarter** with Punic and Roman houses lie the sprawling second-century AD **Antonine Baths**, while scarcely a kilometre (half a mile) northeast and inland are a heavily overgrown **odeon**, a much-restored **theatre** and spectacular **Roman villas**. The **Maison la Volière** has fine mosaics and panoramic views. Further south is steep **Byrsa Hill**, now home to the **National Museum of Carthage**, whose galleries contain material from the Punic and Roman periods, including stelae, masks, mosaics and objects from the siege of 146 BC.

Even more impressive is Tunis's **Bardo National Museum** with its wonderful collection of Roman mosaics, one of the largest and most comprehensive in the world, taken from Carthage and the equally important Tunisian sites of **Utica**, **Dougga** and **Hadrumetum**, the subject of one of which should appeal to anyone interested in the myth of Dido and Aeneas. It shows Virgil flanked by the Muses of poetry and drama. Visitors should note that, following a terrorist attack on the museum in 2015, security here has been heightened.

· ·

CHAPTER 4
ERYX, SICILY AND
THE CULT OF VENUS

Fortune controls us, so let us follow where she guides.
Let's change course now! Nearby, I think, is Eryx, your brother's
land, a true and trusted place, and the safe harbours of Sicily!

Virgil, *Aeneid*, 5.22–24

The air is limpid, the sky a perfect blue. And from our vantage point atop the limestone spur, where cobbled streets squeeze steeply up between well-weathered medieval walls, the view is breathtaking. Here, on the castle's belvedere, it seems that we are hovering. All Sicily luxuriates beneath us – its patchwork fields, its corrugated hills, even Mount Etna far off to the east – while, far below us, the sea's face is so glassy that the jagged pyramid of Mount Cofano appears mirrored in its stillness. The coastline curves, and there, southwest beyond the sprawl of Trapani and its glistening salt-flats, the low humpbacks of the Egadian Islands bask in the sun like porpoises. Look hard to the horizon and you might just make out Cape Bon. And Africa.

Today we have been lucky. Erice is not always so pellucid. Mists often swathe the sudden up-thrust of the mountain, rolling – spectacular and obscuring – from the plain below, swirling around castle walls, coiling about churches and obliterating bell towers. The locals have a name for this phenomenon, a name whose origins stretch back through time until they blur with romance and mythology. They call it '*il velo di Venere*', the veil of Venus, a homage to the goddess who once ruled this rock.

The Sons of Venus

Some said that Eryx, the town's founder, was the son of Neptune, but most commonly it was believed that his father was a mortal, Boutes, one of the Argonauts. When he leapt overboard in his longing to listen to the Sirens, those mythical half-bird, half-maidens whose songs lured many sailors to their deaths, Venus fell in love with him and safely brought him ashore in Sicily. Here, she bore him a child, Eryx, who grew up to found a mountain city, on whose highest peak (as the Sicilian historian Diodorus writes), 'he consecrated a sanctuary to his mother, adorning it with a graceful temple and many gifts and dedications'.

Eryx was not fated to enjoy a long and happy life. Hercules came to Sicily and killed him in a wrestling match. Quite why was open to debate, but it involved cattle stolen from Geryon as Hercules' tenth labour. Some said that Hercules was simply indulging in a spot of tourism, herding the creatures around Sicily so he could see the sights. Others connected his arrival with one specific bull: either hero and beast swam from Italy together (with Hercules clutching the bull's horn), or the creature broke free from the herd and crossed the Strait of Messina on its own. According to this version, it wandered west, and when Eryx saw it he was so impressed that he introduced it into his own herds. When Hercules discovered this, he demanded the bull back, but Eryx would relinquish it only if Hercules defeated him at wrestling. Hercules agreed, adding that if Eryx lost he must surrender his kingdom. Since Eryx did not survive the encounter, this is indeed what happened – and Hercules gave the land to the local people, with the proviso that they were merely its custodians, should he or his descendants ever wish to claim it back. (Another version absolves Eryx of the bull's theft, suggesting that it was Hercules who insisted on wrestling him for the kingdom, but the outcome is the same.)

It was a gruesome little tale, but a useful one, for Sparta's kings claimed descent from Hercules, and when Dorieus (brother of Leonidas, the hero of Thermopylae) tried unsuccessfully to found a colony (called Heracleia) in Sicily in 510 BC, he cited the story as evidence of his right to do so. In fact, the myth may be intended to explain why at Eryx there were major Carthaginian and Greco-Roman shrines to both Melqart/Hercules and Tanit/Aphrodite/Venus.

When Venus's more famous son, Aeneas, came to Eryx, he found both safe haven and sorrow. For here (or at nearby Drepanum/Trapani) his beloved father Anchises died. It was as Aeneas sailed, grieving, from Eryx that the storm blew his ships to Carthage, and when, a year later (having abandoned Dido), he was again sailing past Sicily and winds once more carried him ashore, he took the opportunity to organize athletic games in Anchises' memory.

Games for Anchises

These mythological games at Eryx enabled Virgil to draw parallels between pious Aeneas's devotion to Anchises and the allegiance of another of Venus's descendants, Augustus, to the memory of his adoptive father, Julius Caesar – and he based his description squarely on Patroclus's funeral games in Homer's *Iliad*.

Almost immediately the decision to hold games has been made, the gods signal their approval. Aeneas has made sacrifice, and, as he addresses Anchises' spirit, a huge serpent encircles the tomb seven times before tasting each of the offerings and disappearing. As snakes were often believed to embody dead heroes, this is a splendid omen, the first of several that mark the Trojans' stay at Eryx.

The first three contests are a race between ships (whose captains, Virgil writes, are all founders of distinguished Roman families), a foot race and a boxing match in which one of the contenders owns the very boxing 'gloves' – strips of ox-hide wrapped round the fighter's hands – that once belonged to Eryx (for in Virgil's version of the tale Eryx and Hercules have boxed, not wrestled). The fourth and final contest, however, is the most notable: an archery competition, in which the target is a dove tied by a cord to a ship's mast. One bowman misses the bird but cuts the cord; another shoots the dove. But the arrow of Aeneas's friend, Acestes, catches fire, soaring high to vanish in the air 'like comets which often plunge, detached from heaven, and trail their burning hair behind them'. Roman readers needed no reminding of the comet that blazed shortly after Caesar's death.

Even more resonant is the final event of the games, a cavalry display by Trojan youths led by Aeneas's son, Julus (aka Ascanius). Three regiments of young riders swathed in golden garlands, their hair wreathed in laurel and carrying two spears apiece, perform intricate manoeuvres 'as if in a dance', sometimes charging one another with levelled spears, sometimes galloping abreast, sometimes crossing and twining in labyrinthine patterns. Again, the spectacle was familiar to Virgil's contemporaries. As he writes:

> Later Ascanius revived this intricate tattoo and when he built the walls of Alba Longa, taught the Latin people to perform it just as he and Troy's young men had done. The Albans taught their people. At last Rome, greatest city in the world, inherited and honoured the tradition, and today we call the young men who perform it 'Trojans'.

In Augustan Rome 'Trojan Games' were performed by young noblemen at games celebrating victories, temple dedications or imperial funerals. They were introduced by Caesar and espoused enthusiastically by Augustus in a bid to cement their family's connection with Troy and Venus, but if they were really a revival of an ancient spectacle it is more probable that they originated with the Etruscans. A sixth-century BC wine jug from near Caere (Cerveteri) shows riders beside a labyrinth next to which appears the word 'TRUIA'.

Aeneas and the Temple of Venus

Aeneas's games are rudely interrupted. A messenger brings dire news: the fleet is burning! As part of her vendetta, Juno has sowed discontent among the Trojan women, who, unwilling to go further, have set fire to the ships. In horror, Aeneas prays to Jupiter for help – and is rewarded by a sudden deluge that douses the flames. Although four vessels are destroyed the rest remain seaworthy. That night, Anchises' ghost appears, advising Aeneas to leave the old and weary in Sicily under the command of his comrade, Acestes.

Obedient to the last, Aeneas ploughs the boundaries of a city (Segesta, named after Acestes), delineates its forum and establishes its laws. Before he sets sail, he performs one last action. 'As high almost as the stars, on Eryx's peak, he founds a sanctuary to Venus of Mount Ida, while at Anchises' tomb and sacred grove he consecrates a priesthood.'

Like cities, temples sometimes boasted multiple founders. Diodorus tried to solve the problem of who founded this shrine by relating that, while Venus's son Eryx first established it, his half-brother Aeneas embellished it with many offerings. He adds a further intriguing detail: the temple was enhanced by the great inventor, Daedalus, who fled Crete to escape the wrath of Minos after Theseus breached the labyrinth and slew the Minotaur. At Eryx, writes Diodorus:

> Where the rock towers vertiginously high, and (because of its confined space) the temple was built next to the cliff edge, he extended the overhanging spur. In addition, so they say, he made a ram from gold with such skill that it seemed the perfect likeness of a real animal.

Typhon, Enceladus and Etna

Wider Sicily, too, was rich in myths, not least thanks to Mount Etna, for whose volcanic fires both Romans and Greeks suggested a number of intriguing causes. According to one, they were red-hot exhalations from the monstrous Typhon, the earth-born god of storm winds, who once tried to usurp Jupiter's throne. Typhon was the stuff of nightmares. Some said he was winged, others that he possessed a hundred snaky heads, whose mouths bellowed like bulls, barked like dogs or emitted high-pitched whistles; others believed his eyes shot flames, while his lower body was a writhing mass of serpents. Vengeful because the gods of Olympus had killed his Titan siblings, Typhon launched a whirlwind attack on Jupiter. It was a battle on a cosmic scale. As they grappled with each other, thunder roared and lightning cracked, and many lands became so scorched that they turned to desert. At last Jupiter blasted Typhon with his thunderbolt, and shackled the dazed giant deep inside the earth, his body stretching south from Vesuvius and Cumae's Phlegrian Fields as far as Etna. From here (in Pindar's words) 'shoot forth pure, sacred flames, which no man might come near. Rivers of burning vapour billow out by day, while in the dark of night, with clattering thunder, searing fire hurls rocks down to the glassy sea...a miracle to watch, a miracle to hear of'.

Others said it was another giant, Enceladus, who was imprisoned beneath Etna, maintaining that, in the battle between gods and giants, Minerva hurled a massive rock, which crushed Enceladus before settling in the sea as Sicily. Virgil, however, writes that Jupiter himself destroyed Enceladus, whose body now lies 'charred by the lightning bolt, imprisoned, while over him vast Etna exhales fire from fissured furnaces. Whenever he turns his sleepless body all Sicily groans and thunders, and fumes blot out the skies.'

Vulcan and Mount Etna

Still others believed that Etna's fires were the flares from Vulcan's forge (the god who gave his name to all volcanoes) situated deep beneath the mountain. Here, they said, in a network of subterranean galleries stretching to the nearby Aeolian islands of Lipari, Stromboli and Vulcano, where 'booming anvil-blows are heard reverberating as the din resounds', Vulcan forged weapons for the gods and armour for those heroes of the Trojan War, Achilles and Aeneas.

Venus asked Vulcan to make weapons for her son shortly after Aeneas reached Rome. Virgil imagines the god hard at work with his team of one-eyed Cyclopes, whose brothers had once built many a Greek city's walls. Now Vulcan put all other work on hold – twisting thunderbolts for Jupiter from threads of fire, rain, cloud and storm winds, building a chariot for Mars, forging an aegis breastplate for Minerva – while the smithy focused solely on Aeneas's shield, a breathtaking creation showing Rome's fate as it unfolded to its glorious destiny: Antony and Cleopatra's defeat at Actium; Augustus riding through the cheering streets of Rome in triumph before sitting enthroned outside Apollo's temple, as prisoners from the conquered nations of the world shuffled in line before him.

Cyclopes

Besides Vulcan's subterranean assistants, more Cyclopes lived above ground in Sicily, a lawless, antisocial race of shepherds, who, writes Homer, 'neither plant nor plough.... They have no assemblies or laws, but live on towering mountain peaks in caves, each governing his own wives and his children.' Most famous was Polyphemus, who, appropriately for one whose name means 'much-sung', was the subject of a slew of myths. Many described his love for Galatea, most beautiful of all sea-nymphs, whom he wooed with singing or by playing his shepherd's pipes. While some imagined the unlikely couple – beauty and the beast – swooning in each other's arms,

On a fresco from Pompeii (now in
Naples' Archaeological Museum),
a ram watches unperturbed as
Polyphemus embraces Galatea.

most maintained that Polyphemus's love was unrequited. Ovid includes
a grisly detail: when jealous Polyphemus catches sight of Acis, son of Pan,
embracing his beloved Galatea, he hurls a rock and kills him. But Venus
will not allow the lovers to be separated. From beneath the rock, where
Acis's blood once flowed, spring water bubbles up to flow into the sea and
mingle with Galatea's waters. The river (near Catania) is still called after
him: Fiume di Jaci.

Ulysses and Aeneas both met this violent Polyphemus on their voyages.
Leaving his fleet beached on a nearby island, Ulysses and twelve companions explored the Cyclops's cave, while Polyphemus was out pasturing his

flocks. In it they found pens full of lambs and kids, and shelves laden with cheeses – on all of which they feasted. When Polyphemus returned, he was unimpressed by Ulysses' presumption, so he dashed two Greeks against the wall and ate them. Then he positioned a huge boulder in the cave mouth, too heavy for mere mortals to shift. Ulysses and his men were trapped. At daybreak Polyphemus breakfasted on two more Greeks before returning to the mountainside, leaving the survivors once more penned inside the cave.

The Cyclops, however, was no match for Ulysses' cunning. He had brought wine with him, and that night, after another two men had been consumed, he offered it to Polyphemus, proclaiming that his name was 'No-man'. Unused to alcohol, the giant quickly became drunk and soon he was asleep. At once the Greeks dragged from its hiding place a huge tree trunk, whose tip they had already sharpened, and now heated in the fire. Then they skewered it deep into the Cyclops's eye. Polyphemus bellowed in agony. The other Cyclopes hurried to his cave, but when he shouted, 'No-man is attacking me!', they thought him mad and went away.

Next morning, good shepherd that he was, Polyphemus let his flocks out to pasture, but he was determined that the Greeks should not go free. So, as each creature passed him, he felt its back in case his prisoners were riding it. Again Ulysses thwarted him: clinging beneath the sheep, he and his comrades escaped. Once out at sea, Ulysses mocked Polyphemus, but he went too far. When he boastfully revealed his true identity, the Cyclops cursed Ulysses, praying to his father Neptune that the Greek would endure a painful homecoming, the cause of his long wandering.

A year later (Virgil writes), Aeneas had anchored in the Cyclops's bay beneath Mount Etna, when a piteous figure burst from the undergrowth and begged his mercy. He was Achaemenides, one of Ulysses' crew who had been forgotten in the hurry to be off. As the Greek told his adventures (so earning Aeneas's protection), Polyphemus lumbered down the mountain and strode into the bay to wash his suppurating eye. At once the Trojans put to sea, but the Cyclops heard the splashing of their oars and roared in anger. Within moments other Cyclopes:

> rushed from the woods and high mountains and stood thronging
> the seashore. We saw them, the grim brotherhood of Etna, eyes
> blazing, heads towering to the sky, a terrifying gathering.

It was one of the last sightings of the Cyclopes. When Jupiter killed Asclepius for restoring Hippolytus to life as Virbius, Apollo, god of Delos, massacred the Cyclopes in retaliation.

Ceres and Proserpina

Another story told that Etna's flames first flared in sympathy for Ceres, goddess of crops and harvests. As beautiful Proserpina, Ceres' daughter by Jupiter, gathered violets and lilies by the shores of Lake Pergusa near Enna in the heart of Sicily, Pluto, king of the underworld, erupted from Mount Etna on a chariot drawn by four black horses. Swooping down, he snatched Proserpina and thundered off. He arrived at Syracuse, where the water-nymph, Cyane, refused to let him pass. In fury Pluto flung his sceptre into Cyane's pool, causing a portal to gape open to the underworld. Both chariot and riders vanished, and Cyane, traumatized, dissolved in tears.

Ceres was distraught. Lighting pine torches from Etna's fires, she searched throughout Sicily for Proserpina – including, Ovid tells us, at Eryx 'exposed forever to the western breeze'. Nearby she dropped a sickle (in Greek, *drepanon*), which, when found, gave its name to the curving bay today called Trapani. Only at Syracuse did she find evidence: the belt Proserpina had dropped into Cyane's pool. Finally, frustrated, Ceres unleashed her wrath on Sicily, causing 'the soil which had been famed throughout the world for

Proserpina (or perhaps Flora) plucks flowers for her basket in this exquisite fresco from the Villa Ariadne, Stabiae.

its fertility' to grow barren and its crops to fail. At last Arethusa, another Syracusan water-nymph, whose stream flowed underground from Greece, revealed that Proserpina had married Pluto in the underworld.

Armed with this information, Ceres begged Jupiter to help her, reminding him that Proserpina was his daughter, too, and Pluto was his brother. Reluctantly Jupiter agreed: Proserpina must return to Ceres on condition that while staying with Pluto she had eaten nothing. But a spirit of the underworld, Ascalaphus, screamed out that he had seen Proserpina eat seven pomegranate seeds. Distraught, Proserpina turned the informant into a screech owl. Too late! For eating the seven seeds she was condemned to spend half the year beneath the earth (when the land lies barren), and half above it (when all things grow to fruitfulness).

Proserpina had much in common with her Greek equivalent Persephone, venerated with her mother Demeter at Eleusis and elsewhere. Worship of Proserpina was introduced to Rome only at the end of the third century BC, but Ceres had long been important to Italian farmers. Even in urban Rome a spring festival of many days' duration was celebrated in her honour, including sacrifices, theatrical events and a horse race in the Circus Maximus, after which in a bizarre ritual foxes with lighted torches tied to their tails were let loose to scatter terrified across the race track. This was a punishment (writes Ovid) for a vixen setting fire to a field of ripened wheat. Not that it was the creature's fault. A boy had caught her killing birds, wrapped her in straw and hay, and set her alight. The fox escaped, the crops were burnt and the annual ritual was established to protect them in the future.

Scylla and Charybdis

Before Aeneas reached the Cyclopes' land, his ships almost came to grief in the strait that boils and eddies between northeast Sicily and the Italian mainland. For close to the island's coast, where 'spray shot up, and sand churned in the heaving surge', lurked monstrous Charybdis. Once Charybdis, daughter of Earth and Neptune, had been a nymph, normal except for a voracious appetite that caused her downfall: as Hercules passed by driving Geryon's cattle, Charybdis's stomach growled ravenously; she rustled some cows and wolfed them down. Jupiter saw her, and in fury hurled his thunderbolt; Charybdis fell into the sea, where she remained beneath a rock, her hunger unabated. Three times a day she sucked down all she could, causing tremendous whirlpools and consuming any sailor unlucky enough to get caught. Although today the current is not nearly so lethal, in Augustus's time the geographer Strabo expressed his wonder, writing of Charybdis's great depth, into which vessels can be so easily sucked thanks to its back-flowing currents, plunging prow-first into its fast-flowing whirlpool. When these ships are swallowed and shattered, the wreckage is carried down to the shore at Taormina, which for this reason is called 'Excrementia'.

Opposite Charybdis on a cliff by the Italian mainland crouched another terrifying creature: Scylla. She had once been a water-nymph of such exquisite beauty that Neptune was consumed by love for her. But Amphitrite, the sea-god's jealous wife, found out and dissolved potions in the pool where Scylla bathed. As the nymph sank down into its waters, she felt her body change. While her upper body still preserved its loveliness, from her hips six dogs' heads coiled out on snaky necks, their jaws, with three rows of teeth, salivating, while beneath them twelve dogs' legs dangled down beneath a fishy tail. Shunned now by Neptune, Scylla perched in a cave, her only distraction the ships that entered the strait beneath her. Then her dog-head legs concertinaed out, snatching sailors from decks and rowing benches, whipping them back into her lair, where she would eat them. (Curiously, while still imagining her barking, Virgil describes Scylla's lower half formed like a mighty whale from which numerous wolves' bellies grew, each tipped with a dolphin's tail.)

Another version of poor Scylla's myth said it was the witch Medea who transformed her, while yet another (which appears in Ovid's *Metamorphoses*) claimed that it was Circe, jealous of the lesser sea-god Glaucus's love. For when Glaucus asked Circe for a love charm to help him seduce scornful Scylla, Circe suggested he forget the water-nymph and make love to her instead. Glaucus was outraged. 'While she still lives as she does now, leaves will grow deep in the sea, and seaweed on high mountain peaks before my love for Scylla fades!' Humiliated, Circe wrapped herself in a dark cloak and stalked off down to Rhegium (Reggio di Calabria), where Scylla lived. There she poured into her pool the bitter potions that transformed the luckless nymph. Yet another myth relates that Hercules killed Scylla, who then became a guardian of the underworld.

Eryx in History and Today

Dominating the surrounding landscape, Eryx's imposing Monte San Giuliano, after Etna the second highest peak in Sicily, has long been an important site. While its slopes were occupied from the Neolithic and Bronze Age, the first temple (sacred to Astarte) was built on its summit by Elymians, according to Thucydides refugees from Asia Minor, whose capital was at nearby Segesta. For centuries these Elymians maintained close relations with Carthage, thwarting the Spartan Dorieus's attempt to found a colony near Drepanum (Trapani) in 510 BC, but in 415 BC, in a dispute with their neighbour, Selinus, they enlisted help from Athens, dazzling that city's envoys by displaying treasures kept in Eryx's temple (whose goddess they identified with Aphrodite, the Greek equivalent of Astarte). Six years later, after the Athenian expedition was defeated at Syracuse, Segesta again sought help, this time from Carthage, sparking a war that raged throughout Sicily.

Carthage was but one superpower that coveted Sicily. In 278 BC Pyrrhus of Epirus (the disaster-prone cousin of Alexander the Great) briefly captured Eryx, and during the First Punic War it twice changed hands before falling to Rome in 241 BC. Although the town was abandoned, its temple (now sacred to Venus, Rome's equivalent of Astarte/Aphrodite) thrived. After their disastrous defeat by Hannibal's Carthaginians at Lake Trasimene in 217 BC, the Romans, prompted by the Sibylline oracle, successfully turned the tide by building a temple to Venus Erycina (Venus of Eryx) on the Capitol in Rome, bringing the goddess (embodied in her statue) to reside there, and honouring her with an annual festival on 23 April. Her connection with Rome's founding father, Aeneas, caused her to be known as Venus Genetrix ('Mother Venus'). In this guise she was especially honoured by the Julii, whose members included Caesar and Augustus. In 181 BC, following war with north Italian Ligurians, a second temple to the goddess – Erycina Ridens ('The Laughing Lady of Eryx') – was built outside Rome's Porta Collatina. Here, amid fine colonnades, roses were offered to her.

After the collapse of the Roman Empire, Sicily passed through the hands of Vandals, Byzantines and Arabs before finally being conquered by the Normans in AD 1091. While besieging Eryx, their leader, Comte Roger de Hauteville, saw a vision of St Julian, prompting him to rename the mountain 'Monte San Giuliano'. Despite being subsequently occupied by Swabians, Angevins, Aragonese and Bourbons, it continued to be so called until 1934, when (under Mussolini) it reverted to a form of its Roman name: Erice.

Eryx's temple, one of the most important dedicated to Venus-Aphrodite in the Greco-Roman world, was undoubtedly breathtaking. The second-century BC Polybius observed that it 'without doubt surpasses all Sicily's sanctuaries in wealth and splendour', but, despite its connection with Aeneas, Strabo reports that by the Augustan period it was relatively deserted, although 'previously it was thronged with female temple-slaves [sacred prostitutes], dedicated to the goddess in fulfilment of promises by Sicilians and foreigners

VIRTVS · HONOR · IMPERIVM

Dating from the fourth century AD, a fresco now in Rome's
National Museum shows Venus enthroned as the
personification of the Roman Empire above the
caption 'Virtue · Honour · Imperial Power'.

alike'. A generation later, Claudius responded to ongoing appeals to rebuild
it, but today, since the Norman Castello di Venere occupies its site, we
can gauge its importance only from images, mythology and descriptions
of rites performed there. Perhaps the most romantic involved the doves of
Venus. In mid-August every year (when Erice's patron saint, Our Lady of
Custonaci, is now honoured) hundreds of doves were released outside the
temple. All were pure white, except one, whose red plumage identified it
with Venus. From Eryx the birds flew southwest on a journey of nine days,
until they arrived at the Temple of Sicca Veneria (El-Kef in modern Tunisia),
where on another high peak Venus was similarly worshipped with rites of
ritual prostitution.

3000–2000 BC	Early habitation in Trapani and around Monte San Giuliano.
c. 1200 BC	Elymians settle Eryx.
c. 750 BC	Phoenician sanctuaries of Astarte (Venus) and Melqart (Hercules) built on Mount Erice.
510 BC	Dorieus fails to establish Spartan colony.
415 BC	Athenian envoys shown temple treasury.
278 BC	Captured by Pyrrhus of Epirus.
260 BC	Destroyed by Hamilcar Barca but subsequently rebuilt.
249 BC	Captured by Romans and besieged by Carthaginians.
244 BC	Retaken by Hamilcar.
241 BC	Abandoned after Roman victory at Battle of the Egadi Islands, though temple remains important.
217 BC	Temple of Venus Erycina established on Rome's Capitol.
181 BC	Temple of Erycina Ridens built outside Rome's Porta Collina.
c. AD 54	Claudius rebuilds temple.
AD 831	Conquered by Aghlebid Arabs.
AD 1091	Normans take Eryx, before renaming it Monte San Giuliano. Castello di Venere built over temple ruins.
AD 1934	Town renamed Erice.

Erice, with its sixty churches, cobbled streets and houses dating mainly from the fourteenth to seventeenth centuries, is charming, and views from the Castello di Venere are some of the best in Sicily. However, apart from remains of limestone city walls begun by Elymians and Phoenicians and reinforced chiefly by Romans and Normans, it contains virtually no classical remains. Visitors in search of Punic and Greco-Roman archaeology should not be put off, though. Nearby are **Segesta** with its theatre and unfinished Greek-style temple and (beyond **Palermo** with its fine museum) the Punic settlement of **Solunto** perched high above the sea.

Wider Sicily vaunts an embarrassment of riches, of which only highlights can be included here. On the south coast, **Selinunte** (classical Selinus) and **Agrigento** (Acragas) boast some of the finest Greek temples in existence; to the west, **Syracuse** with its Arethusa Spring has a fine theatre and museum, while views of Etna from **Taormina**'s theatre are superlative. Meanwhile, the fourth-century AD Roman villa at **Piazza Armerina** contains magnificent mosaics (showing scenes of hunting and so-called 'bikini girls' playing ball), while at Cozzo Matrice near Enna by the shores of **Lake Pergusa** (where Proserpina was once abducted) are remains of the Temple of Ceres. Once a quiet haven, the haunt of migrating birds, the lake is now encircled by the Autodroma di Pergusa, a Formula One racetrack.

CHAPTER 5
CUMAE:
WHERE PAST MEETS FUTURE

For I myself – with my very eyes – have seen the Cumaean Sibyl hanging in a jar. And when the boys asked her, 'Sibyl, what do you want?', she replied 'I want to die'.

Petronius, *Satyricon*, 48

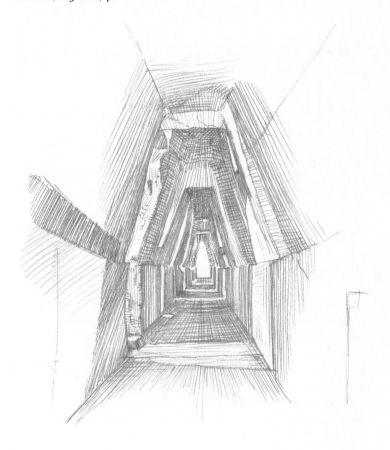

This should be an infernal place, a place of death and terror. Dire warnings of impending doom lie all around. Close by across the bay broods the hunch-backed giant, Vesuvius, whose explosion in a terrifying surge of ash and magma grows more likely by the year, and whose destruction of property and lives seems inescapable. Nearer, on the Phlegrian Plain, mud boils and scalding steam shoots forth from cracks and fissures in the earth, beneath which (though not far beneath) a lake of molten rock is bubbling and shifting, building pressure that cannot be contained much longer – a supervolcano, some scientists say, a ticking time bomb with potential to kill millions.

Yet on a day like this Cumae is quite heavenly. Below us, as we stand here by Apollo's temple, the pale blue sea is sparkling. Long waves wash lazily ashore to whisper in a hiss of foam along the beach, where trotters train to race at Naples's hippodrome, their one-horse modern chariots cavorting modishly across the sand like their ancestors two millennia ago. There, too, separated from the sea by the narrowest of spits, Lake Fusaro, famed for oyster beds and mussels, glints in the sun; there Cape Miseno shimmers in the heat; and on the faint horizon Ischia's Mount Epomeo basks as hazy as a dream. At Cumae beauty – fragile and sublime – cohabits with the threat of an apocalyptic hell, which made this liminal location not just a portal to the underworld but a place where past and future met, where hidden cosmic secrets might be revealed by Italy's most famous oracle: the Sibyl.

The Sibyl

A beautiful young girl, who lived near Cumae's wooded hill, Deiphobe, daughter of the lesser sea-god Glaucus, caught Phoebus Apollo's roving eye. So he attempted to seduce her, promising whatever she might ask in return for favouring him. Coyly she pointed to a pile of dust that she had swept into a corner, and said: 'Count those dust particles! I want to live as many years as that!' Phoebus agreed, though he knew she had forgotten to request one crucial thing: eternal youth. No matter! 'If you sleep with me, I'll grant you this as well.' But Deiphobe did not want to sleep with him. She spurned him, and was condemned to live to great old age, becoming ever more infirm, a fate made harder thanks to another of Apollo's gifts, an ability to see into the future that earned her the title Sibyl ('Prophetess'). By the time Aeneas met her on his voyage up the coast of Italy, she had survived seven generations, and knew that she must still live for another 300 years. In the end, shrivelled and tiny, she crouched, suspended in a jar, and even when her body crumbled her voice remained to tell the future to all generations yet to come.

Another story brought the Sibyl right into the heart of historical Rome. It told how, during Tarquin the Proud's reign, she came, old and wizened, to his court, offering to sell nine scrolls of prophecies, the so-called Sibylline Books, written in Greek hexameters and said to have originated on Mount Ida before reaching Cumae by a circuitous route. When Tarquin discovered the asking price, he laughed dismissively. No books were worth that much! Calmly the Sibyl picked out three and flung them into the fire. As flames consumed the dusty parchment, she repeated her offer: the remaining scrolls were still for sale, but at the same price as before. Again Tarquin rebuffed her, and again the Sibyl burned three manuscripts before again making her offer. Three scrolls survived. The price remained the same. By now the king was growing uneasy, so he consulted his priests. They were unanimous: pay whatever she asked, but buy the prophecies! He did so, and immediately the Sibyl disappeared.

Stored on the Capitol in the Temple of Jupiter Optimus Maximus ('Jupiter, the Best and Greatest'), the sacred texts were venerated and consulted in times of national emergency, but in 83 BC the temple and its books were destroyed by fire. As many of the prophecies as could be found (copied and circulated throughout the Roman world) were rewritten. When Augustus assumed power he realized the books' importance to his authority, carefully removed such prophecies as seemed unhelpful to him, and had new manuscripts placed in the Temple of Apollo next to his palace on the Palatine.

Aeneas and the Golden Bough

It was at Cumae that, guided by prophecies and dreams, Aeneas and his Trojans first set foot in Italy. Virgil describes how at Buthrotum (Butrint in present-day Albania) the Trojan seer Helenus advised Aeneas to come ashore at Cumae's 'sacred lakes and Avernus's murmuring forests' in order to consult the Sibyl, 'the manic prophetess, who from her cliff-cave sings men's destiny, and writes her prophecies on leaves'. He added that, although she tried to catalogue these writings, a sudden breeze would send them flying, so that their order and meaning were largely incomprehensible. Nonetheless, she would reveal Aeneas's destiny and that of Rome. At Eryx, when Anchises appeared in a dream, Aeneas learned a further, terrifying truth: from Cumae he must descend into the underworld to see Rome's future at first hand.

Aeneas's first encounter with the Sibyl led to dire predictions. Inspired by Apollo, she foretold 'wars, horrendous wars, and the River Tiber foaming with much blood' (a phrase that would haunt late twentieth-century AD

British politics). Nonetheless, Aeneas remained resolute and proclaimed his determination to journey to the underworld. Pithily observing that 'the descent is easy; what's hard is to return and re-emerge into the upper air', the Sibyl declared that in Juno's sacred grove he must first pluck a self-regenerating golden bough from a dark oak tree. This was to be his passport to the underworld, a sign that his journey was divinely sanctioned, and a gift demanded by Proserpina, queen of the dead. As Aeneas trudged through the forest a pair of doves, birds of his mother Venus, flew before him until, near the shores of Lake Avernus, they settled high in trees. There he saw the golden bough jangling and shimmering 'like mistletoe, which even in coldest winter remains verdant with young growth, and, although unseeded, wraps its golden berries around tree trunks'. And, reaching up, he tore it down.

Entering the Underworld

Much of our knowledge of Roman views of the afterlife comes from the first century BC and later, and shows significant influence from Greek philosophy and popular beliefs. Some embraced the Epicurean standpoint that death with its dissolution of the body's atoms is the end of everything; others followed Stoic teachings of an eternal world soul of which all are a part; still others adhered to Pythagorean notions of reincarnation. Most, though, believed souls descended to the underworld, where, preserving a ghostly body, the deceased were punished or rewarded according to their behaviour when alive. Virgil combines many of these beliefs in the *Aeneid*, making him, his hero and the Sibyl ideal guides.

Lake Avernus near Cumae was long considered to be a portal to the underworld. It gained its Greek name, Aornos ('Birdless'), from a belief that its sulphurous gases killed birds flying above it. So it was here, as ghostly hounds bayed around the shores, that Aeneas and the Sibyl began their journey to the underworld. Almost at once, the horrors crowded in. Grim figures lurked in shadows of dark passageways, embodiments of torment – Sickness and Old Age, Famine, Poverty and Terror – while Furies, who track down criminals, squatted in iron cages. Next came hybrid creatures of mythology and nightmare: the part-lion, part-goat, part-snake Chimera; the many-headed Hydra; Harpies, half-bird, half-woman; and Gorgons, whose bulging eyes, fang-like teeth and lolling tongues were petrifying.

At last they reached murky River Acheron, its banks crowded with innumerable ghosts, 'as many as the forest leaves that fall and flutter to the earth at the first chill of autumn or the flocks of birds flying in from stormy waves to crowd the earth when icy weather chases them across the sea to make for warmer lands'. All yearned for the farther side, but only those who were properly buried could cross – in a ferryboat, propelled by Charon, a squalid character 'with straggling grey beard...and a filthy, coarse blanket hanging knotted at his shoulder'. Only when he saw the golden bough did Charon admit Aeneas and the Sibyl aboard, and after an uncomfortable voyage – the living bodies' weight caused the boat to rest low in the fetid water – they reached the sludgy sedge of the far shore.

Romans imported their concept of Charon largely from the Greeks, but the Etruscans, too, knew of a guardian of the underworld called Charun. Occasionally shown in art in association with the winged goddess Vanth, who led souls to the underworld, he is a terrifying figure armed with a hammer, with which he strikes the heads of the deceased, either to ensure that they are properly dead or to release their spirits. Following fights in Roman amphitheatres an attendant dressed as Charun delivered the *coup de grâce* to losing gladiators by smashing in their skulls.

On a painted gravestone now in Paestum's
Archaeological Museum, a winged spirit –
possibly Etruscan Vanth – waits to ferry
the dead to the Underworld.

Cerberus, Fields of Sorrow, Fields of War

Watching the entrance to the underworld was Cerberus, a terrifying three-headed hound with snaky hair (the infernal equivalent of the chained dogs that guarded homes across the Roman world; images of them appear on several mosaics, while a plaster cast of a real one, killed in the eruption of Vesuvius, is displayed at Pompeii). The Sibyl was prepared. Like an accomplished house-breaker she threw it a drugged honey-cake (or maybe three?) and the creature sank sleeping to the ground.

It was now that the underworld's efficiency became apparent. Three judges, Minos, Rhadymanthus and Aeacus, were responsible for assigning each soul its place, and the first zone that Aeneas came to were the Fields of Sorrow. Here languished not just souls of newborn infants and people executed on false charges, but those who had died for love. Among them was Dido, whose shade Aeneas saw 'as at the month's beginning a man sees or thinks he sees the new moon rising in the clouds'. Ardently Aeneas tried to reassure her that he had never wanted to leave her, but destiny controlled him. Dido remained unconvinced, 'as hard as flint, as obdurate as marble', her one consolation her beloved Sychaeus, her husband again in death, into whose incorporeal arms she fled.

Progressing further, Aeneas came to another region, where he was delighted to discover many of his Trojan comrades among the souls of heroes killed in battle. Even in death they preserved their partisanship: each side in the war stayed separate, and, far off, dead Greek fighters huddled round their leader, Agamemnon, eyeing Aeneas with hatred and suspicion, trying to bellow out their war cry, though all they could produce was a faint ghostly whisper.

Tartarus

It might be thought that for a fighter to lose his strength was dreadful punishment, but this was nothing compared to what faced those consigned to Tartarus. Already for the Greeks this was a place of terror, as far beneath the earth as heaven is above it, the distance an anvil falls in nine days. For Romans it became a sadist's torture chamber, the inescapable home of those who committed offences against not just gods but family and state, and where the Cretan king Rhadymanthus ruled with a rod of iron. Virgil's description is gothic:

> On the left beneath a cliff Aeneas saw walls stretching out on either side – three sets of walls surrounding the whole cliff – while,

round it raged Phlegethon, a racing river of molten fire that bears down massive rocks that roil and thunder in its current. There is a massive gateway, whose posts are hewn from adamant, so solid that no mortal's strength or even warring gods could dent them. And, on an iron watchtower looming high, Tisiphone the Fury squats, her blood-soaked tunic belted, as, awake, both night and day she guards the gateway. Screams fill the air, the whip's harsh thump, the grate of iron, the rasp of chains.

Here exquisite and eternal punishment is meted out on those who (like the Titans) tried to challenge Jupiter's authority or defy the bounds of human decency: Tityus, pegged spread-eagled to the ground, his entrails gnawed by vultures, for attempting to rape Latona; Ixion, tied to a fiery wheel for trying to seduce Juno; Tantalus, condemned to perpetual thirst and hunger for serving his son Pelops to the gods at a banquet; and countless others – not least those who accepted bribes to undermine the state, who ruled as despots, who arbitrarily made laws, then rescinded them.... As the Sibyl (who has seen the horrors) describes them to Aeneas (who, pious as he is, will not) she is forced to admit: 'even if I had a hundred tongues, a hundred mouths, and an iron voice, I could not tell you all their crimes or name their punishments'. The fate of one other so-called criminal, however, the epitome of vice, was later embossed onto Aeneas's shield, where Catiline (whose bid to overthrow the Roman Senate in 63 BC was interpreted by them as an attempt on the Republic) was shown 'hanging from a rock, shuddering as he looked upon the Furies' faces'.

Elysium

What a relief to escape Tartarus unscathed and emerge in the Elysian Fields. Here, on a well-watered plain dotted with shady copses, and wearing pure white ribbons in their hair, the virtuous danced and sported. These were men (and they *were* mostly men) who had died for their fatherlands, been god-fearing priests, prophets and inventors, and had generally benefited humankind.

The Elysian Fields, too, were walled off, and before Aeneas could tread their dewy swards, he was obliged not just to show his credentials, leaving the golden bough at the gateway in offering to Proserpina, but also to purify himself with sacred water. Almost immediately he was rewarded by meeting the souls of Troy's dead heroes. They were taking their rest, surrounded by grazing horses and unyoked chariots, as they listened to the unworldly voice of the great Thracian singer, Orpheus, one of the few who, while still living, had succeeded in entering and leaving the underworld, when he tried to rescue his beloved wife Eurydice from the dead. Although he persuaded Hades (Pluto) to release her, he failed to observe one key condition: that, as he walked ahead towards the upper world, he should not glance backwards. Orpheus had almost completed the journey when fear overtook him that Eurydice was there no longer. One look back, and he saw her – already turning to withdraw for ever into the shadowy underworld. In classical times, Orpheus was regarded as a mystic, collections of his purported prophecies were held in great esteem, and mystery cults allegedly devised by him promised a blessed life after death.

A third-century AD fresco from the Octavian family hypogeum (underground tomb) in Rome shows Mercury with the deceased child Octavia Paolina in Elysium.

Anchises' Prophecies

It was with life *before* death that Aeneas's visit to the underworld ended. Some Romans maintained that after a thousand years (occasionally endured in a form of purgatory) certain people's souls were reincarnated, their memories erased by drinking from Lethe, the river of forgetfulness. Making brilliant use of this belief, Virgil imagines Aeneas in a remote valley of Elysium meeting the soul of his father Anchises. Frustration at not being able properly to hug (Anchises' spirit body slips through his son's arms) is forgotten when Aeneas sees a crowd of souls thronging the riverbank, 'like bees in balmy summertime that alight on flowers of every kind when pure white lilies stud the fields and the air is loud with insects' humming'.

These, Anchises explains, are the Romans who will shape history, and in a *tour de force* of propagandist writing suggesting the inevitability of his city's rise to greatness, Virgil takes readers through a turbulent millennium ending in his own age. Among the souls is 'Augustus Caesar, whom you have heard so often promised, son of god, who will re-establish a golden age for Italy'. In this scene of future generations jostling eagerly to forge destiny, Virgil encapsulates the essence of Rome's world mission, brilliantly melding mythology and political expediency:

> Others will hammer bronze with greater art to make it seem to breathe – I know this well – and magic the look of life from marble; others will plead lawsuits more convincingly, measure with instruments the movements of the skies, predict the rising of the stars; but you, Roman, must remember always that your destiny is to rule the nations with authority. These will be your special skills: to make peace a way of life; to spare the defeated; and to defeat the domineering.

Enthused by this vision, Aeneas and the Sibyl leave the underworld; but as they head back to Cumae, Virgil introduces a moment of doubt. For there are, he says, two Gates of Sleep, one made of horn, through which true dreams reach the upper world, the other of ivory, for false mirages. It is through the latter that the mortals depart – but whether because they are not themselves dreams or because the vision of the future they have seen is flawed remains ambiguous.

Monkeys of Pithecusae

In antiquity Ischia, glinting blue across the sea from Cumae, was known as Pithecusae, Monkey Island. These monkeys were originally two brothers, the Cercopes ('Tail Faces'), from the Greek island of Euboea, tricksters and trouble-makers, who left their native forests to play mischievous pranks. When they stole the armour of Hercules (at the time enslaved to Omphale, an eastern queen), the hero sought them out and tied them by their feet onto a pole, which he hoisted over his shoulders. As he walked on, the Cercopes burst into howls of laughter. What, he asked them, was so funny? 'Your bottom!' they replied. 'It looks so dark and hairy!' Even Hercules could not resist the humour, so he untied the brothers and let them go.

However, Jupiter was not so forgiving. Angered by their lies and japes, he turned them into what Ovid calls 'deformed humans, similar to men yet at the same time unlike them', monkeys with bent limbs, flattened noses and wrinkled faces. 'Then he covered their whole bodies with wiry tawny hair, robbed them of speech (that had so often led them into perjury), and sent them to this island, where he left them to complain forever with their raucous gibbering.' Like so many others, the myth contained a grain of truth, for, although not monkeys, the Greek first settlers on Ischia-Pithecusae did indeed come from Euboea.

Cumae in History and Today

In the Bronze Age, when Cumae was first inhabited, the shoreline was further inland than today, and Monte di Cuma was effectively a promontory. A village of huts until the mid-eighth century BC, it became Italy's northernmost Greek colony when it was settled around 730 BC by Euboeans, fellows of those on nearby Ischia, guided (it was said) by a dove or the sound of clashing cymbals. Soon afterwards, another Greek city, Parthenope, later resettled as Neapolis (Naples, 'Newtown'), was built on the bay to the south.

In the sixth and fifth centuries BC, surviving both volcanic activity and attacks by Carthaginians, Cumaeans fortified their acropolis, giving pride of place to sanctuaries of Jupiter and Apollo, a god who was central to their civic life. During this time Cumae's tyrant, the misleadingly named Aristodemus the Effeminate, not only twice defeated Etruscans in battle and consolidated his powerbase by enslaving aristocrats and freeing slaves, but also in 496 BC granted asylum to Rome's fugitive King Tarquin the Proud, inheriting his property the next year. Six years later, Cumaean aristocrats overthrew Aristodemus, torturing him and his family to death.

At the end of the fifth century BC, Cumae passed under Samnite control and later became a faithful ally of Rome, remaining loyal during the depredations of Pyrrhus and Hannibal. The first century BC saw a frenzy of building work – further fortifications, a new amphitheatre, and (during the future Augustus's war with the piratical Sextus Pompey) a broad tunnel linking the town to Lake Avernus. Under Augustus's principate the sanctuary of Apollo was considerably restored and enhanced, and a sacred way constructed, but although the town continued to prosper well into the second century AD, the harbour's silting led to trade being diverted to nearby Pozzuoli (founded in 531 BC with Cumae's permission by refugees from Samos).

By the sixth century AD, Cumae was mostly deserted, its temples converted into Christian basilicas. Nonetheless in his war with the Byzantine Empire, the Ostrogoth king Totila saw Cumae's strategic importance, making it a regional capital, but his death in 553 saw it 'liberated' by the Byzantine Narses. It continued to be enthusiastically fought over by Lombards, Neapolitans and Saracens, until in 1207, now a pirates' lair, the citadel was destroyed by the Neapolitan Godfrey of Montefusco and the town abandoned.

The Sibyl enjoyed a kinder fate. In his fourth *Eclogue*, Virgil wrote:

Now the final age predicted by the Cumaean Sibyl has arrived. The great progression of ages begins anew. Now the Virgin returns, and with her the Golden Age [literally Age of Saturn]. Now a new generation descends from heaven above. Lucina [goddess of childbirth], welcome the boy's birth! Thanks to him conflict will end and a golden age will blossom across all the world!

Since this can be interpreted as a prophecy of the coming of Christ, the Sibyl was enthusiastically embraced by the emperor Constantine and the early Church Fathers, playing such an important part in the burgeoning religion that she appears not only in the thirteenth-century poem 'Dies Irae' ('Day of Anger, that day will dissolve secular time into ash – as foreseen by David and the Sibyl'), but also in Michelangelo's early sixteenth-century paintings in the Sistine Chapel.

Virgil, too, was believed to be prophetic. While Dante chose him as his guide through Hell and Purgatory in the *Divine Comedy*, the superstitious used his collected works to tell the future, framing a question, opening the book at random, and interpreting whatever line the finger happened to fall on as the answer for which they were searching.

1200–730 BC	Bronze Age and Iron Age settlements on Monte di Cuma.
730 BC	Cumae settled by Euboeans.
late C7th BC	Evidence for Sibylline oracle (sacred originally to Juno, later to Apollo).
565 BC	Foundation of Parthenope (site of later Neapolis).
531 BC	Foundation of Pozzuoli.
524 BC	Cumaeans defeat Etruscans at Battle of Cumae.
505 BC	Allied with Romans and Latins, Cumaeans defeat Etruscans at Battle of Aricia.
474 BC	Cumaeans and Syracusans defeat Etruscan navy off the coast of Cumae.
470 BC	Foundation of Neapolis.
421 BC	Samnites occupy Cumae. Walls and sanctuaries reconstructed and reorganized.
338 BC	After Roman–Samnite war, Cumae becomes a Roman ally.
215 BC	Hannibal beaten back from Cumae and Phlegrian Fields.
38 BC	Agrippa carries out defensive work against Sextus Pompey, reinforcing port at Cumae, using Lake Avernus to build and train a fleet, and building a tunnel between the two.
27 BC	Under Augustus, sanctuary of Apollo enhanced.
C2nd AD	Forum Baths built; Temple of Jupiter enhanced; colossal statues installed.
C5th/6th AD	Temples converted into Christian basilicas. Cave of Sibyl and Roman Crypt used as catacombs.
AD 535	Belisarius occupies Cumae for Byzantium.
AD 542	Totila takes Cumae.
AD 553	Narses takes Cumae.
AD 717	Cumae passes first to Lombards, then to Neapolitans.
AD 915	Saracens pillage Cumae.
AD 1207	Godfrey of Montefusco annihilates pirate stronghold on Monte di Cuma. Now malarial, the site falls into disrepair.

Though slightly difficult to find, **Cumae** more than repays the search. A spur from the Strada Provinciale Cuma Licola cuts through fields in which lie remains of the Roman forum, including a bath complex and the Temple of the Giants, named from the size of statues discovered there. From the car park a path leads through a remarkable **tunnel** beyond which lies (left) the **Sibyl's cave**, a trapezoidal passageway 4.5 m (15 ft) high, 2.5 m (8 ft) wide and over 42.5 m (140 ft) long running on a north–south axis, pierced by three galleries to the east and six to the west, and culminating in a chamber with three niches. Nearby is the entrance to the **Roman Crypt** (usually closed), a straight tunnel 182 m (600 ft) long, originally a continuation of the 1-km (3,200-ft) **Grotta della Pace**, which emerges by Lake Avernus, wide enough for wagons to pass with ease, probably constructed for military purposes on Augustus's orders by Agrippa. The steep **Sacred Way** ascends to a terrace off which sits (right) the **Temple of Apollo**, a Greek foundation remodelled by Augustus, now extremely ruinous but with fine views. Further on the path climbs through lush woodland to the summit of Monte di Cuma and the equally ruined **Temple of Jupiter**, converted into a Christian basilica in the fifth to sixth centuries AD.

Artefacts from Cumae, including a marble statue of Diomedes stealing Troy's Palladium discovered in the Roman Crypt, are displayed in the stunning **Archaeological Museum** of Naples along with finds from the bay cities of **Pompeii**, **Herculaneum** and **Pozzuoli** and villas at **Stabiae** and **Oplontis**. All these sites are a must for any traveller with an interest in Roman history, while closer to Cumae the remains of **Baiae**'s notorious pleasure resort (some of which now lies underwater) should not be missed, especially as some claim that a tunnel complex leading to a geothermally heated stream is the true site of the Sibyl's cave.

J. M. W. Turner's nineteenth-century painting *The Golden Bough*, which transfers the location of this arboreal phenomenon to Lake Nemi, provided both inspiration and title for Sir James Frazer's seminal, if profoundly controversial, study of comparative religion, mythology and anthropology. The painting now hangs in London's Tate Britain.

CHAPTER 6
LAVINIUM:
PIGS, PIZZAS AND PENATES

Looking from out at sea, Aeneas saw a sprawling forest, through
which Tiber with his lovely river raced down to the shore,
his eddying currents rich with golden sand. The riverbanks
and waters were the haunt of birds of every colour, hopping,
circling, filling the sky with song and flitting through the trees.
Aeneas ordered his companions to change course and turn their
ships to land, and happily he sailed into the shaded river.

Virgil, *Aeneid*, 7.29–36

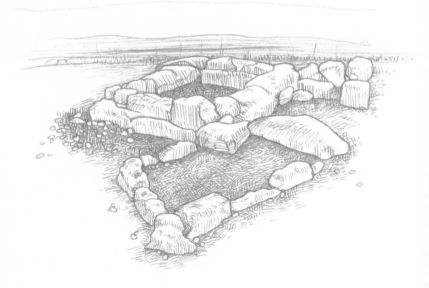

Turn off the narrow country road, pass through the factory checkpoint, and you will find yourself on a well-rutted track. Far to your left, beyond the stubbled fields, where flights of swallows swoop and dive around the tiny ruined Church of Santa Maria delle Vigne, the sea glints lazily, the only blot on the horizon an array of brutal high-rise flats that sprawl along the coastline. To the right, a lane leads up towards a low hill on the skyline ringed with trees that rises gently from the vibrant fields. Don't be distracted! That hill is not your goal. No, follow the track that you are on – it's only a few hundred metres – towards where sheep are bleating in the field beyond, and you will reach an open-sided, roofed construction that protects ancient foundations.

Examine them carefully. Although at first they may seem difficult to understand, they are of profound significance. Here, closest to the trackway, aligned towards the distant mouth of the river called in ancient times Numicus, is a hero's stone-lined grave, and next to it, one corner intersecting, well-cut foundations of a later shrine, whose massive false doors carved from tufa once faced Lavinium and Rome. That intersecting corner is not accidental. It was meant deliberately to link the shrine with the protecting magic of the buried warrior and serve as a symbolic hinge. For it was on this spot that a nation's fortunes turned: from sea to city; from an exile's wanderings to a conqueror's triumphs; from Troy's past defeat to the future victory and power of Rome. The hero in the grave was thought to be Aeneas. The shrine was consecrated in his honour. And to the huge mound heaped above them, and encircled by tall trees, Rome's great and good came every year to make their sacrifices. Lavinium is one of Italy's most sacred sites.

Saturn and the Age of Gold

When Aeneas arrived in Italy, the land around Lavinium was ruled by King Latinus (who gave it the name Latium). There were several versions of Latinus's ancestry. According to one, he was the son of Hercules by a hostage from the frozen lands of the Hyperboreans (identified by some as Britain); when she fell pregnant, Hercules gave her as bride to Latium's King Faunus, and the couple brought the child up as their own. Another version claimed Latinus as Ulysses' son, conceived during that hero's wanderings. A third version (that Virgil follows) said that, while Latinus was indeed of immigrant stock, his great-grandfather was Saturn. In Greek legend Saturn's equivalent, Cronus, was castrated by Zeus, and imprisoned forever in Tartarus. But Romans believed that Saturn, exiled by his son Jupiter from the Greek east, came to Italy, setting up court on Rome's Capitoline Hill, where he ruled so wisely that his reign became known subsequently as the Age of Gold.

Picus the Woodpecker

Saturn's son, Picus, was Latium's first ruler, and his was a curious tale. Smoulderingly handsome, he was so skilled in training warhorses that some thought Mars was his father. Although every nymph and dryad longed to wed him, he married Canens, daughter of two-faced Janus and Venilia, goddess of winds and sea. Canens sang with a sweet voice, and, like Picus, she was skilled in prophecy, but still she could not know her own fate.

When Picus was hunting in fields around Lavinium, Circe, daughter of the sun-god, saw him. She was a sorceress, a woman of beguiling beauty and extraordinary powers, whose home was a headland to the southwest (now known as Monte Circeo), where in later years she turned Ulysses' shipmates into beasts. One glimpse of Picus, and Circe burned with lust, but he was far away on horseback, and surrounded by his retinue, and she could not reach him. So, undeterred, she magicked up a bristling boar that led the king in hot pursuit into deep undergrowth. Then she caused mist to swirl between the trees, so thick that Picus's companions, bewildered, lost him. Once he was alone, she set about seducing him.

Picus, however, had eyes only for his Canens. The more Circe entreated him the more he swore that he would never be unfaithful, until at last, rebuffed and furious, the sorceress touched him three times with her magic wand and uttered three prayers. As Picus, terrified, took flight, feathers sprouted, his mouth became a beak, and he was transformed into a woodpecker; and when his retinue found out, and threatened to attack her, Circe turned them, too, into animals. When Picus failed to come home, Canens was disconsolate. For six days and nights she wandered Latium, neither eating nor sleeping, until exhausted she lay down on Tiber's banks, where she wasted away, still singing her lament, until only her song remained.

Faunus the Nature God

Picus and Canens had one son, Faunus. Like his forefathers he loved outdoor pursuits, and he was worshipped as a god of not just agriculture, cattle-rearing and domesticating nature, but (being an ardent hunter) also of untamed wilderness. Even as a god of prophecy he embraced the wild – any wishing to consult him had to visit sacred groves where, sleeping on fleeces of freshly slaughtered sheep, they heard his terrifying, otherworldly voice resounding through the trees. Perhaps because his voice appeared to echo, he was imagined as one of many – a multiplicity of fauns, half-man, half-goat, with shaggy legs and hooves and horns, lecherous and mischievous, cousins of the Greek Pan, delighting (like him) in causing panic among men and beasts.

Nor was Fauna, his female counterpart, safe from his advances. His wife or sister (no-one really knew), she stayed at home, indulging in secret drinking, never going outside, forever honouring her vow of chastity – which caused Faunus such frustration that he beat her to death with branches of Venus's sacred myrtle. As if this were not bad enough, another myth said Fauna was his daughter. Lusting after her, he made her drunk and tried to rape her. When she resisted he transformed himself into a snake and overcame her.

For august, patriotic poets – for Virgil – what made Faunus especially important was that he welcomed to Italy Evander and his Arcadian refugees (characters who, as we shall see in Chapter 9, would play an important part in the story of Aeneas), enabling them to settle on the future site of Rome. A few years later, Latinus, Faunus's son by the local nymph Marica, in like manner welcomed Aeneas and the Trojans. Two portents encouraged Latinus's hospitality. The first was a swarm of bees that settled in a tree within his palace, foretelling that foreigners would soon arrive and make Latium the centre of a mighty empire. The second involved Lavinia, Latinus's daughter. When she was sacrificing, her hair and coronet caught fire – a sure sign she was marked out for great things, but that war, too, was inevitable.

Pizza Proclaims Journey's End

When Aeneas's ships touched land, he and his thirsty comrades disembarked, and flopped beneath the trees. At once, up bubbled two freshwater springs, beside which Aeneas set two altars and made grateful sacrifice. Then, ravenous from rowing, and too hungry to unload plates or tables, the Trojans spread spelt pancakes on the grass, heaping on top whatever vegetables or herbs or fruit that they could find. Even these could not satisfy their appetites, however, so each picked up his spelt cake and ate it too. At which Ascanius merrily observed: 'Look! We're eating our tables!'

While his comrades laughed politely at his son's mordant wit, Aeneas was awestruck. He remembered the curse of the harpy Celaeno, half-bird, half-woman, whose goats and cattle they had killed on their voyage across the Ionian Sea. As they tried to eat the meat, the savage harpies had swooped down, attacking them, driving them away with fiercely beating wings, voiding themselves and making everything they touched inedible. At the height of the attack, Celaeno squawked out her prophecy: 'You will reach Italy, but you will never have a city of your own or build protective walls until, in punishment for your wrongdoing in attacking us, dire hunger makes you eat your very tables!'

Thanks to the gods' kindness, the curse had been fulfilled in an unexpected way. The promised land had been attained, the prospect of a settled home seemed so much closer, and (according to some more imaginative modern commentators) the concept for one of Italy's most well-loved dishes had been discovered.

Suckling Pig

Another good omen delighted Aeneas. A second prophecy commanded that, having eaten their tables, they must follow a four-footed beast, building their future city wherever it lay down to rest. Excitedly the Trojans set up altars and – as women sang and danced – unwrapped statues of the Penates, gods of Troy, so that they might preside over the ritual. But before the sacrifice could start, one of the intended victims, a pure white pregnant sow, broke free of her handler and, squealing, raced inland. Surely this was the beast which had been prophesied!

Hotfoot – but carefully – Aeneas pursued it, determined not to scare it from its fated path. Three miles they went, until on a low hill the sow lay down exhausted. Aeneas was disheartened. The site was too hard to protect, and too far from the sea. Surely there must be some mistake. Even as he hesitated, a disembodied voice boomed from a nearby thicket: this would not be the Trojans' home for long. Rather, in as many years as the sow had piglets, they would build a new city that would rule the world. So next day, when the beast gave birth to a remarkable (and biologically impossible) litter of thirty young, Aeneas sacrificed them all to the Penates on the site (Dionysius records) 'of the present temple, which the people of Lavinium consider sacred, and from which they bar all foreigners'. In historical times the sow's corpse was still kept in the temple, pickled in salt brine, but the tale of her pursuit would not sit easily in Virgil's storyline. In his somewhat mundane version (just five lines long), Aeneas sees the suckling sow on Tiber's banks, and sacrifices it at once to Juno.

Penates

The location of Aeneas's sacrifice at Lavinium was significant, for throughout history the town jealously guarded Troy's ancient Penates. According to one Sicilian historian, the artefacts associated with their worship included bronze and iron *caducei* or heralds' wands and a Trojan earthenware pot – which is oddly appropriate, since *penus*, from which 'Penates' is derived, means provisions or storage space.

A scene from the Ara Pacis
Augustae (Altar of Augustan Peace)
shows Aeneas sacrificing a sow in
front of a shrine to the Penates.

Once housed, the Penates would not leave. A few years later, the Trojans migrated to the hills, where they founded Alba Longa. Naturally they wanted their Penates near them, so they built a splendid temple, to which they conveyed the statues with all care and ceremony. They placed them in the inner sanctum and closed it for the night. But next morning the Penates were nowhere to be seen. What could have happened? The doors had been locked tight; there was no sign of forced entry; it was impossible that anyone had stolen them. Then a messenger came breathless from Lavinium. The statues had returned! They were back on their old bases. Again they were removed to Alba Longa; again rites were performed and sacrifices offered; and that night again the statues vanished. To try a third time would be sacrilegious; but although the Trojans had no wish to leave idyllic Alba Longa and return to Lavinium, they longed for their Penates. At last they reached a compromise. Choosing 600 men, they sent them with their families back to Lavinium to attend the Penates, which was why the town became the spiritual heart of Latium and, later, Rome.

One of the most important of all Penates was Vesta, whose specific care was for the hearth. Later, she would merit sanctuaries of her own, including one by Rome's Forum, where her round temple also housed Rome's own Penates and Troy's Palladium. There was no statue of Vesta, but instead an eternal flame, considered so sacred that any deviancy on the part of the Vestal Virgins, the six priestesses who tended it, was punishable by death. However, even more sacred was Vesta's first shrine on Italian soil – at Lavinium.

Aeneas and King Latinus

As soon as Aeneas declared Lavinium to be the promised land, the Trojans began constructing ramparts around its low mound, while sending young men out to forage. But since the food, clothing and iron implements that they brought back in triumph were stolen from the local population, they soon found themselves preparing for war. Immediately, Latinus broke off his existing conflict with the neighbouring Rutulians, and marched with all haste to Lavinium. Quickly the Trojans strapped on armour, seized their weapons and poured through half-completed gateways to line up outside the uncompleted walls – so warlike and experienced that Latinus hesitated to engage with them. Instead, he pitched camp and spent the night in fitful sleep, ready to do battle at dawn.

In his dreams a figure came, a local god, perhaps his father Faunus, warning Latinus not to fight the Trojans, but to make them friends and allies, since this would benefit them both. Meanwhile, in the watchful city, the Penates visited Aeneas in his sleep and gave him the same message. So as the sun rose gold across the farmland and low-lying marshes near the sea, Aeneas and Latinus met in no man's land, sorting out their differences, swearing oaths of lasting friendship, and agreeing to share customs, laws and rituals, and to call their united peoples Latins after the old king.

Lavinium and Lavinia

Honouring their treaty, Latinus gave Aeneas all the land within 8 km (5 miles) of Lavinium, including a good stretch of beach. But as the Trojans hurried to complete their walls, fire broke out in a nearby copse. Almost immediately – how strange! – a wolf loped up, a bundle of dry branches in its mouth, and flung the kindling on the flames, while at the same time an eagle swooped from the clear sky, beating its wings, encouraging the conflagration. Meanwhile a determined fox appeared, and tried to extinguish the blaze with its wet tail, which it dipped into a nearby stream. Now the wolf and eagle, now the fox seemed to be winning, but at last the flames caught hold. The spinney was consumed. For Aeneas it was a sign: like the inferno, his city would grow and prosper, devouring everything it touched – but others would envy it and attempt to curb it. So well-loved was this local myth, that bronze statues of all three creatures – as well as of the suckling sow – were set up in Lavinium's main square, in pride of place amid its shrines and temples.

In addition Latinus gave Aeneas his daughter, Lavinia, in marriage, and it was from her that the city took its name. Yet Juno's anger was not yet assuaged. Powerless to reverse Aeneas's achievements, she could

On a much-damaged fresco from the tomb of Statilius Taurus (now in Rome's National Museum) the Trojans hurry to complete Lavinium's walls.

still obstruct them. Virgil imagines her predicting conflict and bloodshed, a wedding gift from the war goddess Bellona. And in case his readers fail to pick up the parallel, he reminds them of another, equally incendiary marriage: Helen's. 'Venus has borne a second Paris and more funerary flambeaux to engulf this newly rising Troy.' For, like Helen, Lavinia was not entirely free to wed. She was betrothed to Turnus, the local Rutulian prince, whose capital was Ardea, and whose jealous anger Juno now provoked against the Trojans.

Latium at War

Presenting the conflict in Latium as a second Trojan War, Virgil draws parallels with Homer's *Iliad*. Early myths, while agreeing with his account in their essentials, were probably much sketchier. They told how, encouraged by Latinus's scheming wife, Amata ('Beloved'), Turnus joined forces with local Volsci, as well as the Etruscan King Mezentius. Virgil (wishing to win favour with powerful Etruscans of his day) claimed that, like Evander, who ruled the future site of Rome, all the Etruscans (led by their wise king, Tarchon) supported Aeneas, making Mezentius a wicked renegade and exile, whom Aeneas killed in combat. But Livy (mentioning the war in just one paragraph to illustrate Rome's ancestral pluck) writes that Mezentius was Caere's reigning king, who, fearing for the safety of his Etruscan confederacy ('which stretched the length and breadth of Italy from the Alps to Sicily'), brought an army south to Lavinium, where 'rather than skulk behind his walls, as he might easily have done, Aeneas led his men to battle'.

In essence the war was a struggle between an old world order (embodied by Turnus) and a new one (embodied by Aeneas) for control of Italy (embodied by Lavinia). While many leaders fell in battle – including both Latinus and Evander's son, Pallas – the conflict culminated in a duel between the warring commanders. Drawing on Homer's description of the encounter between Hector and Achilles, Virgil imagines his heroes slugging it out manfully before Turnus's sword shatters and, defenceless, he turns and flees. At last, hurling a spear that sinks into his rival's thigh, Aeneas overtakes him, looming over Turnus, who concedes defeat and begs for mercy. For a moment, Aeneas vacillates, but, when he sees, slung over Turnus's shoulders, a sword-belt stolen from dead Pallas, he explodes with rage and plunges his sword deep into Turnus's chest. So ends the *Aeneid* and the first phase of the war.

The Fleet Transformed

Turnus should have known the gods were on Aeneas's side, for they had already sent many portents. One came when, unable to subjugate Lavinium, Turnus had tried to burn the Trojan fleet. Even as flames caught and smoke billowed, otherworldly music filled the air – clashing cymbals, shrilly sounding flutes. The goddess Cybele had come hotfoot from Mount Ida, where the pines providing the ships' timbers had once grown. She could not bear to see them ruined, so, accompanied by terrifying claps of thunder, she sent an icy flight of hailstones to extinguish the flames, while lashing winds and swelling seas tore the vessels from their moorings. Then (as Ovid writes in his *Metamorphoses*):

> The hard wood softened and turned into flesh, the curving sterns changed into heads and faces, oars became hands and legs that swam through water, keels became spines, rigging became hair, and masts' spars became arms. [The ships had turned into sea-nymphs.] Their colour (as before) was azure blue; but whereas before they had been frightened of water, now they splashed and dived through waves like playful girls. Born on a harsh mountain, they now luxuriated in the liquid swell, forgetful of their homeland.

At Lavinium the Trojans, too, experienced a transformation, for here they ceased longing for their abandoned fatherland, and started to look forward to the future destiny of Rome.

Aeneas's Death and Hero Cult

Turnus's death did not end hostilities. The Rutulians and Mezentius (and maybe the entire Etruscan army) kept up the attack, and four years later, Aeneas, now king of Latium, led his troops through pouring rain to one last battle. As thunder crashed and lightning flashed around them, Aeneas was cut down by the banks of the River Numicus. Mysteriously, his corpse was nowhere to be found. Ovid tells us why: Jupiter had empowered Venus to bestow upon her son 'a portion of divinity'.

> Venus was glad. She thanked her father and, borne through the wispy air by her chariot-team of doves, she came to Laurentia's shores, where Numicus snakes his waters through tall reedbanks to the sea close by. And she commanded him to cleanse Aeneas's body of all death's impurities and on his quiet-flowing waters

carry them out to sea. Then, his body purified, Venus anointed it with divine perfumes, caressing his face with ambrosia blended with sweet nectar, and transforming him into the god the Romans would call Indiges as they worshipped him with altars and a temple.

Later, it was said that Aeneas never died, but was transported alive to heaven, and that days later Ascanius and others saw him transformed, walking by the banks of the Numicus wearing the same clothing he had worn in battle. This proved (says our anonymous source) that he was now immortal, so they consecrated a temple to him as Father Indiges. *Indiges* meant 'indigenous', and the title was bestowed on mythological mortals who performed outstanding deeds and were worshipped posthumously as gods in the belief that in life they had embodied a spark of the divine. Another legendary *indiges* was Romulus, and in historical times the idea that powerful men could be deified was so ingrained that it enabled the apotheosis of recently dead politicians such as Julius Caesar and Augustus.

Aeneas was also thought to be a 'Lar', another type of protecting spirit, but it was as 'Indiges', 'Father Indiges', or even 'Jupiter Indiges' that he was worshipped at Lavinium's fourth-century BC heröon (hero shrine), which abutted a seventh-century BC grave, anachronistically believed to be that of Aeneas. As Dionysius of Halicarnassus wrote:

> The Latins built a hero shrine for Aeneas together with the inscription: 'To the god and father of this place, who protects Numicus's waters'.... There is a small mound [covering both grave and heröon], around which trees have been planted in regular rows. They are well worth seeing.

So important was Lavinium's heröon that following the town's inclusion in the Roman federation in 338 BC, for centuries Rome's most important magistrates came here each year to offer sacrifice to Aeneas, as well as to Vesta and her fellow Penates, at the beginning and end of their period in office. Indeed, the heröon itself may well have been thought so iconic that it influenced the design of Augustus's Mausoleum in Rome (though Cleopatra's tomb in Alexandria may have inspired it, too).

An Offering of Wine

It was left to Aeneas's son, Ascanius, to end the war, and he did so not by force but by piety and guile. One day, when the Latin army was occupied elsewhere, Mezentius's son, Lausus, seized the city. With Lavinium at the Etruscans' mercy, surrender seemed the only option, but when he heard that Lausus's terms included a demand that all local wine be surrendered as tribute for many years to come, Ascanius demurred. This was a clause too far.

Instead he made a proclamation to his army: if, with Jupiter's support, the Latins were victorious, the people of Lavinium would not only consecrate their city but dedicate the wine from every vintage to him for all future time. Then they donned their armour and poured out from their camp, killing Lausus, scattering the Etruscans and forcing Mezentius to flee. When negotiators met a little later, they managed to thrash out a treaty. Shelving their differences, the Latins and Etruscans swore friendship and alliance.

Ascanius and Lavinia

Relations between Ascanius and his stepmother Lavinia were fraught, especially when, shortly after Aeneas's death, she was discovered to be pregnant. She was so terrified that, if she bore a son, Ascanius might consider him a rival and attempt to kill him, that she stole out of Lavinium to the forest house of a trusted servant, Tyrrhus. He had been master of her father's herds, and he loathed Ascanius for killing his pet stag.

This superb creature had been hand-reared by Tyrrhus, whose daughter Silvia loved it dearly, combing its coat until it shone and festooning its magnificent antlers with garlands. It was so tame that by day it grazed in meadows, but came home at dusk to its stable, until one hot afternoon, as it was wandering dreamily down river, Ascanius and his comrades, who had only just reached Italy, went hunting. Ascanius's arrow pierced the poor beast's flank, but failed to kill it. Instead, it staggered, bleeding, back to Tyrrhus's stables, where it collapsed, weakened and whimpering. Silvia was distraught, her father furious, and the whole household was so moved by the dying stag's plight that they swore vengeance on its killers.

Now, when the Latins realized that Lavinia could not be found, they feared the worst. Surely Ascanius had murdered her. As an angry mob poured out into the public square and bayed for vengeance, Ascanius leapt onto the Speaker's Platform and addressed them. She was alive, and he would richly reward anyone who found her. At this Tyrrhus, who happened to be present, stood up and promised that if Ascanius swore to guarantee the safety of Lavinia and her child, he would conduct them home. Ascanius did swear this, and with the family reunited, he held Lavinia in highest honour, treating her new son, Silvius (the 'Woodsman'), like a brother.

The Killing of Titus Tatius

Lavinium features in another myth set slightly later, when Romulus and the Sabine king, Titus Tatius, ruled jointly over newly founded Rome. Tatius's friends raided Lavinium's lands, so ambassadors arrived in Rome to demand retribution. Romulus supported them, but Tatius, refusing to punish Romans for crimes against foreigners, dismissed the Lavinians. On their way home, his henchmen attacked them, leaving many dead. When more ambassadors arrived, protesting this fresh outrage, Romulus rounded up the perpetrators, set them in chains and handed them over to the Lavinians. This was more than Tatius could bear. So with a hand-picked band he galloped out, cut down the guard and freed the prisoners.

The situation was not yet resolved when Romulus and Tatius had to travel to Lavinium to make annual sacrifice to Rome's ancestral gods. Despite its being a solemn ritual, friends and family of Tatius's victims were so outraged that, seizing sacrificial knives and ceremonial spits, they stabbed and bludgeoned him to death. His corpse was removed to Rome, where even in imperial times annual rites were performed in his honour.

Lavinium in History and Today

Iron Age graves in fields above Pratica di Mare suggest that Lavinium was occupied from perhaps around 1100 BC, but it was four centuries later that the site began to assume importance. By the seventh century BC, the walled town was part of the Latin League led by Alba Longa, which (at the end of the sixth century) fostered military ties with Rome. By now Lavinium was thriving: a bronze plaque dedicated to Castor and Pollux suggests trade with Greece, and the town was attractive enough for the aristocratic Lucius Tarquinius Collatinus to go into voluntary exile there, following the expulsion of Rome's last king. A Roman–Latin alliance was formalized in 493, but five years later Lavinium was attacked by the renegade Roman general Coriolanus, as he and the Volsci cut a swathe of destruction through Latium prior to an unsuccessful siege of Rome. By the mid-fourth century, increasingly strained relations led to the brief Latin War, which saw Rome defeat the League in 338.

Lavinium was already a religious centre, the spiritual heart of Latium, and it was probably at this time that victorious Rome caused the heröon to be built abutting the grave, believed (wrongly) to be that of their founding father, Aeneas, and already considered so significant that it was reopened at least once in the sixth century, when gifts were placed inside it. Perhaps it was the Romans, too, who caused the thirteen altars, once central to Lavinium's rites, to be deconsecrated and covered over.

While in 82 BC Lavinium suffered at the hands of Marius's army in the civil war with Sulla, the rise of the Julian dynasty, who claimed descent from Aeneas, undoubtedly lent the town renewed significance, and contemporary authors describe its glittering shrines and temples (some believed to have been built by the Trojan settlers). As well as Aeneas's heröon, they included the Temple of Vesta, housing Troy's Penates, with others dedicated to Venus, Liber, Ceres, Anna Perenna and Juturna. Rich villa remains attest to the site's continuing importance throughout the empire, but with the coming of Christianity Lavinium declined. In the fourth century AD, Constantine presented Lavinium and its territories to the Church, and the fifth-century AD Santa Maria della Vigne near the heröon shows the new religion superseding the old. Since the twelfth century, when Pratica's castle was built, the land has been owned by powerful families. Today Pratica di Mare, designed by the sixteenth-century architect Antonio da Sangallo the Younger, belongs to the Borghese family.

· ·

LAVINIUM Some Important Dates and Remains

c. 1100 BC	First settlements.
C7th BC	Heroic burial (later identified as Aeneas).
C6th BC	First of thirteen altars dedicated. Lavinium expands south and west.
c. 500 BC	Dedication made to Castor and Pollux.
488 BC	Lavinium captured by Coriolanus and Volsci.
C4th BC	Heröon constructed.
338 BC	Lavinium recognized as part of Roman federation.
C3rd BC	Altars deconsecrated.
82 BC	Lavinium suffers at Marius's hands during civil wars.
late C1st BC	Lavinium remains an important religious centre.
? AD 320s	Constantine presents Lavinium to Rome's Basilica of the Holy Cross of Jerusalem.
AD C5th	Church of Santa Maria delle Vigne (of the Vineyards) built on the site of a Roman villa.
AD 1017	Lavinium mentioned in Papal Bull as belonging to Rome's Benedictine abbey of St Paul outside the Walls.
c. AD 1530	Pratica di Mare built by Antonio da Sangallo the Younger.
AD 1617	Lavinium (and Pratica di Mare) sold to Borghese family.
AD 1939	Nearby Pomezia built for workers draining the Pontine Marshes.

Lavinium lies 30.5 km (19 miles) southeast of Rome between Pomezia and a military airport. Little remains of the ancient city. Part is occupied by the village of Pratica di Mare, entrance to which is through a **Roman gate**. The real treasures (for access to which contact the Archaeological Museum) lie a little way south off the via del Mare beyond the Johnson and Johnson Medical Facility.

Here are situated foundations (excavated in 1968) of the fourth-century BC **heröon of Aeneas** and the adjoining seventh-century BC **grave**. About 100 m (330 ft) to the west lie **thirteen altars**. Discovered in 1957, these are arranged in an almost straight line running for around 50 m (165 ft) roughly from north to south. The earliest (at the northern end) is lower than the rest and, being near a sacred well, is prone to flooding. The rest sit on a platform of tufa blocks, apparently dedicated in no logical order, from the sixth to third centuries BC, when earlier votive offerings were piled onto the altars and the sanctuary deconsecrated and buried. Which god or gods were worshipped here is unknown. Some suggest Venus (who, Strabo writes, possessed an important temple at Lavinium), others Indiges. Still others believe the sanctuary was shared by the Latin federation, with each city possessing its own altar. Another suggestion connects the thirteen altars to the months of the Lavinian calendar. A bronze plaque discovered here with a dedication to Castor and Pollux is seen as evidence of ties with Greeks. Close by, beyond the spring, a rectangular **archaic building** was destroyed by fire and rebuilt in the fifth century BC. Remains of **two kilns** can be seen nearby.

Less than a kilometre (half a mile) to the north, on the via di Pratica, Lavinium's **Archaeological Museum** is modern in feel, with audiovisual displays exploring topics such as Aeneas's voyages and Lavinium's religions. Highlights include a fifth-century BC terracotta **statue of Minerva** accompanied by Triton, fifth- to third-century BC **female votive statues** and the original **false double tufa door** from the heröon.

On the coast, the mouth of the River Fosso di Pratica (the ancient River Numicus) marks the Trojans' landing place (though the coastline may have advanced since antiquity). It was once known as Troia, and boasted a sanctuary of Jupiter Indiges, but today there is nothing to see save a beach and an unlovely seafront.

* *

CHAPTER 7
ARDEA: CENTRE OF RESISTANCE

[Allecto, the grim Fury] swooped down on jet black wings to the bold Rutulians' ramparts, the city said to have been founded by Danaë for her Argive colonists, when she was shipwrecked here by southern gales. The place was once called by our forefathers 'Ardea', and still 'Ardea' is its mighty name, though fortune has deserted it.

Virgil, *Aeneid*, 7.408–413

On this warm afternoon Ardea has a pleasant feel. Cats lounge, well fed, in shadows, while oleander bushes burgeon in the public square. On street-side pavements men in work clothes sit at plastic tables crowding round intriguing bakeries and cafés, whose counters and displays are cornucopias of loaves and pies, calzone, pizzas, stuffed tomatoes with a side order of roast potatoes, chicken casseroles in metal trays. Meanwhile, a little way along the road women wait patiently on benches for the moment when the jarring bell will ring and an exuberance of children will rush yelling from the schoolhouse to celebrate the end of lessons and the real start of the day.

Further still, the road descends. Stonework becomes older. A stretch of ancient walls gives on to fields, while across the via dei Rutuli masonry juts up amid a desert of abandoned excavations. Now can be seen the sheer tufa rock on whose edge modern houses, pink and cream and orange, perch, its glowing walls a network of deep crevices, pockmarked with caves. And over there, where houses end, what look like crumbling ramparts rear high above the cliff face, taking the eye further to the cloudless sky and causing thoughts to drift to older times, when these imposing battlements secured an ancient city.

Ardea's Foundation

Romans believed that Ardea was founded by a Greek – but precisely who was subject to debate. Some maintained that, during his wanderings, Ulysses visited enchanting Circe on her mountain promontory nearby and fathered three sons – Latinus (whom we met at Lavinium), Rhomus (who gave his name to Rome) and Ardeias (who founded Ardea). While this provided a neat explanation for three early Latin cities' close relationship, it needed just a little thought to realize that it could not possibly be true: a rather more important myth described Ardea as the centre of resistance to Aeneas and his Trojans, and since Aeneas and Ulysses were not just contemporaries but travelling at roughly the same time, Ulysses' son would never have been old enough to found Ardea before the Trojans got there, let alone in time for it to grow into the thriving settlement that opposed Aeneas. Clearly its origins must be far more ancient.

So another tale gained traction, this time involving Danaë, princess of Argos. Danaë was beautiful beyond compare, and when Acrisius, her father, learned of a prophecy that her son would kill him, he tried to cheat Fate by locking her in a bronze-walled cell with just one tiny window. But, looking through the tiny aperture, Jupiter was smitten with desire. So he transformed himself into a shower of gold that dripped gloopily into the cell

A fresco from Pompeii shows Danaë
cradling baby Perseus beside her
wooden box, after fishermen have
rescued her from the waves.

and impregnated Danaë. When Acrisius discovered that she was pregnant,
he was appalled. Again he tried to outdo destiny, this time by locking Danaë
in a wooden casket, which he threw into the sea. Again his scheme failed.
The casket came ashore, Danaë and her son were saved, and years later the
young man, Perseus, accidentally killed Acrisius with a mis-aimed discus.

While Greeks maintained that Danaë's casket was washed up on
Aegean Seriphos, Romans knew differently: it came ashore in Latium, where
the local king, Pilumnus, fell in love and married Danaë – and together

they founded Ardea. In another account, when she reaches Italy, Danaë is already the mother of two sons, Argus and Argeus. However, it is the Argive connection, not the detail, that is important. For this establishes Ardea not only as a rampantly Greek town but one that, like Argos itself, is especially favoured by Juno, Troy's mortal enemy. This was a godsend for a poet such as Virgil, presenting the clash between Ardea's King Turnus and Aeneas as a second Trojan War. (It is a sad truth that there is no archaeological evidence whatsoever to suggest an early Greek link with Ardea.)

Danaë's new husband, Pilumnus, as well as being a king was a local agricultural god, who (not entirely unsurprisingly, since his name meant 'pestle') taught humankind to grind grain. His brother, Picumnus (an incarnation of the woodpecker god Picus), was another farming deity, who was responsible for weddings and young children, and in his capacity as Sterquilinus ('Shitty') presided over the collection and spreading of manure.

Turnus

In mythology Ardea is the capital of the Rutulians, people closely linked with the Etruscans. Indeed, while its most famous ruler is called in Latin 'Turnus', Greeks knew him as Tyrrhenus, 'The Etruscan'. His family was divine. Not only was his mother the nymph Venilia (goddess of winds and sea), his sisters were nymphs too: sweet-voiced Canens (the wife of Lavinium's King Picus) and Juturna, goddess of fountains. His father was equally illustrious, if less certain – some said he was Janus, god of doorways and new beginnings, others that he was Daunus, King of Ardea, the son of Danaë and Pilumnus. In any case, it was his aunt's family that caused his downfall. She was Amata, wife of King Latinus, and together they had one daughter, Lavinia.

Many kings and chieftains sought Lavinia's hand, but Amata was determined that she should marry her handsome cousin Turnus, and so unite two families and kingdoms. Lavinia's grandfather, the god Faunus, had other ideas. He appeared to his son, Latinus, in a dream and instructed him not to pursue this marriage, but instead choose as his son-in-law a foreigner who would (in Virgil's words):

> join his blood with ours to raise our family to the stars, while our descendants shall see the whole world at their feet – from the eastern bounds of Ocean to the west, wherever the sun shines – all nations subjected, ruled by them.

The foreigner was Aeneas, and Amata's fury at her husband's change of heart was whipped up further by Aeneas's sworn enemy, Juno. She despatched an agent of her own to Ardea – the torturess Allecto, who thrived on pain and misery, a savage Fury, her scalp writhing with a crawling mass of blue-black snakes. Appearing to Turnus, she fixed him with her blazing eyes and goaded him to battle. The die was cast; the stage was set; war with Aeneas was inevitable.

In Virgil's sprawling account, despite assuming the anti-hero's role, Turnus possesses heroic magnificence. Riding a piebald Thracian horse and wearing a golden helmet with a scarlet crest, he gallops up to the Trojans' walls, hurls the first javelin and begins the war; he fights his way into the Trojan camp (imagined by Virgil as abutting the Tiber) to battle – single-handed and lion-hearted – until, almost surrounded, he is forced to jump into the river and swim to safety. Declaring that 'Fortune favours the brave', he cuts down Aeneas's friend, Pallas, in a murderous mêlée from which he escapes only when Juno persuades Jupiter to let him chase a phantom onto a ship that then drifts out to sea before miraculously depositing him back at Ardea; there he meets Aeneas for the last great battle.

As the moment of conflict approaches, Turnus's sister, the virago (Virgil's word) Juturna, takes hold of his chariot's reins and drives him (in Virgil's extraordinary image):

> like a blue-black swallow that flies back and forwards through the great halls of some rich master, her wings flashing through high rafters, as she gathers tiny flakes of food to feed her chirping chicks, her cry echoing round empty rooms and mirrored pools.

Even as he wreaks havoc on the Trojans, news comes to Turnus that his greatest mortal ally, Amata, believing he has died, has hanged herself. It is the beginning of the end. Descending from his chariot, Turnus meets Aeneas. Spears fly. Turnus's sword-blade shatters, and he turns and flees, Aeneas hot on his heels, until, Jupiter, tired of war, sends a Fury in the guise of a screech owl to beat its wings in Turnus's face, and cause his will to falter. Juturna knows the end is near, and, covering her head in a grey veil, plunges lamenting into the nearby river. Bleeding from a thigh wound, Turnus falls wounded at Aeneas's mercy. No mercy is forthcoming. Ardea's king is cut down, a blade deep in his breast.

Engraved on an Etruscan mirror, Mercury, Lara and
two other gods watch as a she-wolf suckles the Lares.

Juturna, Lara and the Lares

Turnus's passing was especially mourned by his sister Juturna. Aside from her brief foray into battle, her fate had been sadly predictable: nubile and beautiful, she was beloved by Jupiter, but despite his most ardent overtures she shunned his advances, hiding trembling in hazel thickets or immersing herself in pools. Sympathizing, her sister nymphs did all they could to help, until Jupiter summoned them to a meeting, and pointing out the error of Juturna's ways – 'to sleep with one another is in both our interests: I'll enjoy the greatest pleasure; she'll reap the greatest benefits' – he commanded them no longer to let her take refuge in their waters.

One nymph still tried to save her: Lara, the loquacious daughter of a local river god. Since childhood she had been a gossip, and now her love of tittle-tattle proved her ruin. For she not only warned Juturna (fruitlessly) to avoid the river banks, she told Juno of Jupiter's intended infidelity. When the god found out, he was incensed. He tore out Lara's tongue and commanded Mercury to take her to the underworld, there to haunt a gloomy lake. But Mercury was seized with lust, and in a thicket by the roadside raped her.

Poor ill-used Lara, the silent goddess, bore twin sons, protecting gods of homes and crossroads, called by the Romans 'Lares', though their name in fact derives from *lar*, the Etruscan word for 'lord'. A fourth-century BC mirror back shows them, watched by Mercury, Lara and two other gods, as they are suckled by a she-wolf, an image so familiar that we might easily mistake them for Romulus and Remus. Yet worship of the Lares pre-dated stories of Rome's founding twins by centuries. It was these Etruscan lords that the she-wolf suckled first. It was they who inspired Rome's later civic myth and iconography.

Having ravished Juturna, Jupiter kept his promise to advance her career. He set her in charge of all Latium's rivers, springs and lakes, and gave her as wife to two-faced Janus. Together they had a son, Fons, god of fountains, but at Rome the nymph won approbation in her own right. Water from her sacred pool, the source of the River Numicus, between Ardea and Lavinium, was used for purifying rites, while in Rome's Forum a fine fountain-house, Juturna's Spring, can still be seen, and a little to the north, in what was once the Campus Martius, one of three temples in Largo di Torre Argentina is believed to have been dedicated in her honour.

Violence against women plays a crucial, if uncomfortable, role in myths associated with Ardea. Perhaps the most famous and far-reaching episode is said to have occurred in the late sixth century BC. By now the Rutulian capital had been rebuilt following its defeat by Aeneas, and Ardea was once more enjoying great prosperity. So much so, in fact, that Rome's acquisitive King Tarquin the Proud resolved to conquer it, and, when his first attack was repulsed, he ordered his army to settle in for a siege.

To while away the hours, some senior officers, including the king's son, Sextus, took to drinking and discussing the merits of their wives. Each claimed his own was the most virtuous, until Lucius Collatinus suggested they should put the matter to the test by unexpectedly visiting each wife in turn to see what they were doing. So they saddled up and rode first to Rome only to discover that, instead of sitting at home pining, their wives were partying and entertaining. The last to be visited was Collatinus's wife, Lucretia. The lengthy gallop to Collatia was not wasted – although it was now late at night, they found her demurely working at the loom with her maidservants. Bashfully she welcomed Collatinus and his colleagues. Triumphantly he insisted they all stay to dinner, and in the morning they all trotted back to Ardea to resume the siege.

But Sextus Tarquinius did not stay at Ardea. He ached with lust for Lucretia and meant to have her. That evening he returned with some excuse to Collatia, where Lucretia, as his rank deserved, gave him dinner and a bed in the guest-quarters. In the darkness, Sextus crept through the corridors to Lucretia's room, where, sword drawn, he pinned her roughly to the bed. She struggled, and would have screamed, but the young man whispered threats: resist him and he would first kill her, then kill a slave and place his naked body next to hers, so that whoever found them would conclude they had been caught in flagrant adultery. Terrified, Lucretia submitted to Sextus's lecherous demands, but in the morning when he had slunk away she sent a letter to Ardea, begging Collatinus to come as quickly as he could. He did, and brought with him not just her father but also Lucius Junius Brutus, the king's nephew.

When Lucretia told them what had happened they were outraged. When she made them swear an oath of vengeance, they did so willingly. When she seized a dagger and plunged it deep into her heart, they were incensed. Why should she suffer? She had not submitted willingly! As husband and father wept uncontrollably, Brutus seized the bloody dagger and vowed to rid Rome of the Tarquins' tyranny. Too long had the city suffered under them. (Too long had Brutus suffered, too. Tarquin's sons had bullied him, and, giving

Believed to show Lucius Junius Brutus, this fine portrait head (perhaps dating to the fourth century BC), with glass-inlaid bone eyes, is now housed in Rome's Capitoline Museum.

him his nickname, *brutus*, 'stupid', made him tag along to Delphi, when they went there to consult the oracle. Yet when they heard the prophecy, that whoever kissed his mother first would end up ruling Rome, only Brutus understood. He fell to the ground and kissed Mother Earth, and now the divination was coming true.)

First to Rome, whose citizens they roused to anger, then to Ardea at the head of a popular army, Brutus and Collatinus brought their freedom cry. At Ardea they discovered that Tarquin had already fled to Caere in the heart of his Etruscan homelands to the north. Meanwhile, his son Sextus, seeking refuge in nearby Gabii, wrongly believing that the town supported him, was murdered by his enemies. In recognition of their services, the Roman people appointed their liberators, Brutus and Collatinus, as the first of their two annual consuls. Their fame resonated through the ages. More than four centuries later a descendant of this Brutus would feature large in a conspiracy to kill another would-be tyrant, Julius Caesar.

Camillus and the Gauls

Despite its relative obscurity, Ardea still had a part to play in Roman history. In 390 BC, it was home to Rome's exiled dictator, Marcus Furius Camillus, the brilliant general who defeated powerful Veii only to fall foul of factional politics. Now, though, his skills were needed once again, for the Gauls had marched into Italy and were ravaging Latium. Soon a detachment was encamped outside Ardea's walls, and the citizens were rightly nervous. Not Camillus, however. After a rousing speech, he led Ardea's men at night into the Gaulish camp, where (just as he had promised) they found the enemy unprepared for battle. It was a massacre, and by morning the surviving Gauls were fleeing for their lives.

Yet the Gauls still occupied Rome. With great daring a messenger was sent to the besieged Capitol to gain permission to recall Camillus, and, when he learned of the Senate's decree, the general returned to take command. He reached Rome in time to launch a devastating attack that saw the Gauls routed, and their threat removed. Once more Ardea had witnessed a turning point in history, but miscalculations and continued hostility to Rome led in time to its abandonment. As new landowners took over its rich pastureland, the only natives still on the land were Pilumnus and Sterquilinus.

A City Transformed

Defeated by Aeneas, and subsequently by Rome, Ardea became a byword for a vanquished city. It even appeared in a Latin proverb, reminding people that not even the capital of empire (overrun by Gauls in 390 BC) was invulnerable: 'even Rome was captured once – just like Ardea'. According to Ovid's *Metamorphoses*, however, after its sack at the hands of Aeneas, the town was the site of a miracle:

> Turnus fell, and with him Ardea, so famous for its power while Turnus lived. But when the foreigner's sword had done its work, and homes sank deep into warm cinders, a strange bird soared high from the wreckage, churning the ashes with its beating wings. In its screams and ravaged, grey appearance, everything that marked the city out – even its name, Ardea – is still preserved in that bird. The city of Ardea beats its own lament in the bird's feathers.

As any ornithologist will know, from the ashes of the fallen town had sprung a heron (*Ardea*).

Ardea in History and Today

The area around Ardea has been inhabited and farmed since the second millennium BC, but the foundation of the town itself appears to date only to the eighth century, when it became the capital of the Rutulians. Hints in fragments of lost Greek historians, and the tradition that Latinus, Rhomus and Ardeias were brothers, suggest that in the sixth and fifth centuries BC Ardea's power rivalled that of Rome, but much current knowledge derives from brief (unreliable) material in Livy's first book. Here we read that Rome's last king, Tarquin the Proud, attracted by Ardea's wealth, tried to reduce the town by siege in 510 BC, before himself being deposed by the besieging army led by Lucius Junius Brutus. Fine sixth-century BC defensive walls perhaps go some way to corroborating the historian's account. Whatever the outcome of the siege, in the fifth century Ardea and Rome were allies – in 443 BC, when the Volsci attacked Ardea from the south, it was a Roman army that defeated them.

Two centuries later the favour was not repaid, when Ardea refused to support Rome in its existential struggle against Hannibal. At the end of the Second Punic War in 201 BC, Rome responded by bringing the town under direct control. In many ways this marked Ardea's demise. By the first century AD, the town's population had dwindled, though the agricultural writer Columella owned estates in the vicinity. From AD 476, Ardea was virtually uninhabited for five hundred years, when a castle was built that would pass into papal hands. It was only in the twentieth century, with the draining of its surrounding marshes, that Ardea returned to prosperity. Today it is a thriving agricultural town.

C8th BC	Foundation of Ardea: burials and traces of huts discovered.
C6th BC	Defensive walls constructed.
510 BC	Ardea besieged by Tarquin the Proud.
509 BC	Ardea mentioned as Roman ally in treaty with Carthage.
443 BC	Roman army beats back besieging Volsci from Ardea.
C4th–3rd BC	Sanctuary dedicated at nearby Fosso dell'Incastro.
390 BC	Camillus defeats the Gauls outside Ardea.
348 BC	Ardea again listed as Roman ally in treaty with Carthage.
218–201 BC	Ardea refuses to back Rome in Second Punic War, leading to imposition of Roman direct rule.
C1st AD	Columella owns estates at Ardea.
AD 1118	Pope Gelasius II stays in castle at Ardea.
AD 1932	With draining of marshes, Ardea begins again to prosper.
AD 1991	Sculptor Giacomo Manzù dies at Ardea. Museum erected in his honour.

Although Ardea should be visited chiefly for its associations, there are some remains still to be seen. These include stretches of the seventh-century BC **defensive walls** with fourth-century BC additions. Elsewhere, foundations of four temples have been discovered, while in the Casarinaccio area near via dei Rutuli, site of Ardea's forum, are remains of a sixth-century BC temple (perhaps dedicated to Venus) and a first-century BC basilica (one of the earliest in the Roman world). Here, too, an early **Christian Oratory** with fine **frescoes** can be visited by prior arrangement. At the mouth of the nearby River Incastro are remains of both a fourth-century BC to third-century AD **port** and a sixth-century BC to second-century AD **sacred area** dedicated to Venus Marina.

Nothing remains of ancient **Collatia**. Its presumed site lies in the village of Lunghezza astride the via Collatina, 24 km (15 miles) northeast of Rome beneath the Castello di Lunghezza, a fortified medieval farmhouse with impressive walls, whose grounds are now a fun park.

CHAPTER 8

ALBA LONGA:
HILLTOP HOME OF KINGS,
EMPERORS AND POPES

Alba was built between the mountaintop and lake, occupying
the space between the two. These two natural features, which
made it difficult to capture, served as city walls. For the mountain
is both strong and high, and the lake is wide and deep, and by
opening sluices its waters can be diverted to the plain, so that
citizens can regulate its flow at will.

Dionysius of Halicarnassus, *Roman Antiquities*, 1.66

The air is cool and clear, the long-dead crater's steep slopes dense with dark-leaved trees, while through their branches sunlight pours in cataracts to break in dappled splashes on the vivid, verdant, lush green grass. Down at the lake's edge on a shrub-studded beach bathers wade into the water. Close by, white yachts are drawn up on springy turf or moored a short way out, the sunlight rippling against their perfect hulls, their rigging slapping softly in the warming breeze. The lake itself is myriad shades of blue, with phosphorescent trails of silver sunlight dancing over it, careening, bursting into countless pinpoints of pure light.

Sometimes (though not today) the surface is so motionless that it is like a mirror. Stand on the hillside then and it seems that you are standing on the edge of a great ring, the only solid point between the sky and lake, each wispy with pale clouds, each an unbearable intensity of blue, each stretching to infinity. Against that blue, upright against the sky, inverted in the lake, each dark green needle of the stark umbrella pines seems visible on the horizon, amid the mass of roofs and domes and whitewashed buildings stretching, confident in their authority, across the undulating ridge. The beauty is breathtaking, and although Rome with its traffic and its bustle and its fumes is only half an hour away, it could be another world.

Founding Alba Longa

Thirty years after Aeneas reached Italy, his son, Ascanius, founded Alba Longa ('White Long Town'), so called because of its position, extended across a ridge of Mount Albanus ('White Mountain'). Or so most Romans said. In fact, Alba Longa's mythology is never easy, and Livy sets out the present problem:

> It is not entirely certain – indeed, who *can* be certain about such ancient history – whether it actually *was* Ascanius or an elder brother, born of Creusa while Troy was still unharmed, who [also] fled with his father. I mean the man the Julii call Julus, after whom they take their name.

Confusion grew. Dionysius of Halicarnassus (writing when kings were anathema to Romans) knew another story in which the Julus from whom the Julii were named was Ascanius's son. According to him, while Julus did not inherit the throne, the Latins conferred on him an august dignity that was even better than kingship, and which the family preserved to his day. Meanwhile Virgil solved the problem by claiming that Ascanius himself was sometimes called Julus.

Preserved in the House of the Vettii, Pompeii, a lararium's
fresco shows the householder flanked by two cornucopia-
holding Lares, while a snake, symbol of good fortune,
slithers beneath them.

No matter its founder's precise identity, Alba Longa immediately became
capital of the Latin peoples (though, thanks to the Penates' reluctance to
move here, Lavinium remained their spiritual home), and, after many centuries, its princes would in turn found Rome. The two cities' relationship
was always uneasy: in time Rome would destroy Alba Longa, obliterating
it completely from the map, which is possibly why there are so few myths
about its very early history.

Indeed, most of Alba Longa's myths appear to have been deliberately
invented, when chroniclers discovered an awkward gap between Aeneas's
arrival in Italy (traditionally around 1185 BC) and Rome's foundation (confidently claimed to have occurred on 21 April 753 BC). While previously there
had been a host of contradictory and time-bending theories about who
founded Rome – either Aeneas himself (there was even one tradition that

he did so with Ulysses, naming it after Romē, one of the Trojan women), or Aeneas's son Romus (brother of Ascanius plus two others, Romulus and Euryleon), or Ascanius's son (also called Romus), to name but three – for the sake of scientific neatness a scheme was now drawn up that would be universally approved: the dynasty of Alba Longa's kings was born.

Alba Longa's Dynasty

These kings were a motley bunch, many of whom are little more than names, but despite this they were considered so central to Rome's national identity that they appeared in a key group of statues in Augustus's Forum (opened in 2 BC) flanking Aeneas on one side, with on the other statues of the Julii, Augustus's ancestors.

What distinguished each was the extraordinary (and unlikely) length of his reign. Ascanius himself ruled for thirty-eight years, after which the Latin people voted that he should be succeeded not by his son, Julus, but by his half-brother, Silvius (Aeneas's son by Lavinia), who ruled for twenty-nine years and gave his name to the rest of the dynasty. He was followed by a shadowy array of long-ruling monarchs (Aeneas Silvius, thirty-one years; Latinus Silvius, fifty-one years; Alba Silvius, thirty-nine years; Capetus Silvius, twenty-six years; Capys Silvius, twenty-eight years; Calpetus Silvius, thirteen years) until the first king of any real interest, Tiberinus Silvius.

Tiberinus's reign was exceptional not only for its brevity (a mere eight years), but also for how it ended. Back when Ascanius made peace with the Etruscans, they agreed that the border of their territories should be the River Albula. Over time, skirmishes broke out along the river banks, during one of which Tiberinus was killed, and his body washed away in the current. So distraught were the Latins at his untimely death that they renamed the river after their dead king, which is why it is now called the Tiber. (Another myth known to Virgil claimed that the river was named after a giant, Thybris, in the period before Aeneas reached Italy.)

Next came Agrippa Silvius (forty-one years), and then the terrifying Allodius, also known as Romulus Silvius. Dionysius writes:

> He was a tyrannical character, hated by gods, and he reigned for nineteen years. He was sceptical of divine powers, and found ways to imitate thunder and lightning, with which he meant to frighten mortals and persuade them that he was divine. But heavy rain and lightning battered his house, and the lake, on whose shores it stood, became so full that he and all his household were engulfed

and destroyed. Still today, when the water level subsides and the lake is still, there is a place where you can still clearly see the ruins of his portico as well as other remains of his palace.

Sadly (leaving aside any physical evidence that Dionysius may have seen, and dismissing the possibility of lightning striking twice in the same place) we must discount the tale – it comes straight from Greek mythology, where precisely the same fate befell Salmoneus, King of Elis.

Curiously, a Victorian visitor heard a similar tale, that in Albanus's crater there was once a thriving city. When Christ came to Italy begging alms, not one of its rich citizens would show him kindness. Only an old woman gave two scoops of precious meal. So Christ told her to gather her belongings and leave quickly. Then, when she was safe, he made the city sink into the crater and the waters rise to cover it.

It took just two more Alban kings (Aventinus Silvius, thirty-seven years, from whom Rome's Aventine Hill, the site of his burial, was named; and Proca Silvius, twenty-three years) before the stage was set for the main event: the birth of twins that heralded the great foundation myth of Rome.

Numitor, Amulius and Rhea Silvia

Proca had two sons, but although he intended the throne to pass to the elder, Numitor, the younger, Amulius, seized it by force and did all he could to hold onto it. Key to this was neutralizing Numitor's two children, a boy and a girl: the son's death he engineered in an 'ambush at the hands of robbers unknown'; the daughter (Rhea Silvia, aka Ilia) he made a Vestal Virgin, intending to prevent her bearing children, who as adults might claim their true inheritance. Loath to provoke civil unrest, Numitor watched helplessly. The gods, however, thought otherwise. For (as Livy patriotically puts it):

> In my opinion Fate had already decided to found our mighty city, and set on course the greatest empire in the world, second only to the gods'.

Which was why in the fourth year of Amulius's reign, as Rhea went to fetch water from Mars's sacred grove, one of the gods took it on himself to rape her. His identity was endlessly debated. Was he Mars himself? Was he a local spirit, the genius of Alba Longa? Was he even one of Rhea's mortal admirers? Was he, indeed, Amulius dressed up as a god? Whoever it was, the deed was accompanied by portents – a solar eclipse, darkness spreading over the earth – and Rhea swore that before the god vanished he promised that she would give birth to twins who would surpass all men in bravery.

When Amulius discovered that Rhea was pregnant, he placed her under armed guard, and reported her condition to a meeting of his elders. Desperately Numitor managed to convince the assembly to spare her, at least until they saw if the prophecy was true and she did indeed bear twins. In the end, even this did not save Rhea. When she was delivered of two sons – Romulus and Remus – Amulius claimed that one had been smuggled into the birthing room by an accomplice, and such was his anger that the cowering council agreed to his demands: as a lapsed Vestal, Rhea must be imprisoned (or in some versions beaten to death), while the boys must be set adrift in a basket on the river.

Some believe that the central figure in this panel from the Ara Pacis Augustae (Altar of Augustan Peace) is Rhea Silvia (with Romulus and Remus), others that it is Ceres, goddess of fertility.

Romulus and Remus

In myth such plans habitually fail, and the condemned babies were rescued by a kindly herdsman, Faustulus, who brought them up on Rome's Palatine Hill, where they helped him graze his flocks. By the time they were eighteen, they quarrelled so violently with shepherds on the nearby Aventine that their rivals resolved to bring them to Amulius for trial. The Aventines laid an ambush, but captured only Remus. For the time being Romulus, celebrating a religious festival in a nearby Sabine town, Caenina, remained at liberty.

When he heard what had happened, Romulus rallied his fellow herdsmen, but already in Alba Longa Remus had been dragged before the king. Scornfully Amulius pronounced him guilty, but he left it to Numitor (whom he was now trying to appease) to decide the sentence. However, something about Remus's demeanour struck a chord with Numitor, and, when the young man told him all he could about his childhood, it became apparent who he really was. Delighted, Numitor sent a trusted servant to make contact with Romulus, too, and before long loyal herdsmen thronged the streets of Alba Longa – among them Faustulus, clutching beneath his cloak the basket from which he had once saved the babies, and which he now hoped would prove their story.

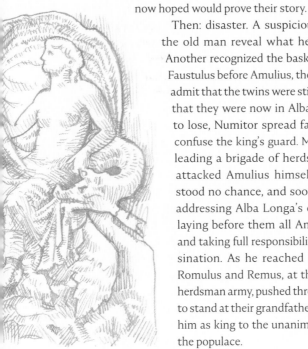

Then: disaster. A suspicious guard made the old man reveal what he was carrying. Another recognized the basket, and, hauling Faustulus before Amulius, they forced him to admit that the twins were still alive – but not that they were now in Alba. With no time to lose, Numitor spread false rumours to confuse the king's guard. Meanwhile, each leading a brigade of herdsmen, the boys attacked Amulius himself. The usurper stood no chance, and soon Numitor was addressing Alba Longa's citizens, at last laying before them all Amulius's crimes, and taking full responsibility for his assassination. As he reached his peroration, Romulus and Remus, at the head of their herdsman army, pushed through the crowds to stand at their grandfather's side, saluting him as king to the unanimous approval of the populace.

With Numitor now safely back on Alba Longa's throne, his grandsons' thoughts turned to founding their own city. So they returned to the grassy Palatine with a crowd of herdsmen, Latins and such Alban citizens who wished to start new lives – in Livy's words, 'so many that it seemed natural to hope that Lavinium and Alba Longa would seem insignificant compared to the new city that would soon be built'.

The Horatii

Despite their ties, relations between Rome and Alba Longa collapsed early in the reign of Rome's third king, Tullus Hostilius. When each city accused the other of border raids, both sent ambassadors to discuss reparations. Once at Alba, Rome's envoys, following Tullus's instructions, came straight to the point, demanded compensation and were immediately refused. Meanwhile at Rome, wined, dined and delayed by conniving hosts, the Albans could not bring themselves to discuss unpleasant business. As a result, when they eventually did, Tullus was able to inform them that Alba, not Rome, had already rejected terms, that Alba was thus in the wrong, and that Rome was justified in declaring war.

At once, Alba Longa's warlike King Cluilius led his army close to Rome, excavated an impressive trench, faced off the Romans (who were similarly dug in) – and promptly died. Whether this was the result of poison, age or divine intervention no-one knew, but naturally Tullus proclaimed it was the latter, and, rousing his men, led them at night past enemy lines into Alban territory. Next day, the Albans, now led by their vacillating but canny general, Mettius Fufetius, pursued them. While they were preparing for battle, disturbing reports arrived. Their mutual enemy, the Etruscans of Veii and Fidenae, were lying in wait, ready to attack in the aftermath of battle, when the two warring sides were exhausted.

So, they reached a compromise: to let the issue be decided by three champions from each side. Whichever city won would forever rule the other. It happened that (miraculously) each army's ranks contained a set of triplets: Rome's Horatii and Alba's Curiatii. Even more miraculously both sets were born on the same day. As if this were not enough, the mothers of each set were sisters, and the boys had grown up together from birth. Nonetheless, despite deep ties of blood and friendship, despite Alba Longa being Rome's mother city, and despite this being a contest to the death, all readily agreed to fight for honour and supremacy.

To their armies' cheers, the champions, matched equally, strode into no man's land. The fight was long and bitter. One Roman fell, and then another,

Near Lake Albano on the Via Appia Nuova stands a massive Etruscan-style tomb, said to be that of the Horatii and Curiatii.

until, surrounded by the Curiatii, it seemed the last Horatius would be cut down. Then, choosing his moment carefully, he dodged and ran. Though wounded, the Curiatii pursued him. One almost caught him, but, before he did, Horatius swung round and attacked him. Taken off guard, the Alban fell. One of his brothers was already near. Before he could draw breath, Horatius had killed him, too. Now only one remained on either side, but the last Curiatius was so badly wounded in his thigh that he could hardly stand. He was no match for the Roman. He was easily despatched.

As Tullus accepted Alba's surrender, and the two sides signed a treaty, Horatius was carried back to Rome in triumph. It was not an altogether happy homecoming. His sister was betrothed to one of the Curiatii, and when she recognized the wedding robe that she had woven for her beloved, now slung, torn, across her brother's shoulder, she broke down and wept. For Horatius this was intolerable. Furious that she put an enemy's welfare before her brother's and her city's, he ran her through with his still-bloody sword, exclaiming: 'Love your lover in the underworld! So die all Roman women who shed tears for an enemy!' Her murder cast a pall over Rome's victory, and Horatius would have been executed, had not his father appealed the sentence. Instead, he was purified of his guilt, and made to pass beneath a 'yoke' – a wooden beam supported on two uprights – still said to be surviving at the end of the first century BC. Fate would not be so lenient with Mettius Fufetius and Alba.

Alba's Destruction

Rome's hostilities with Veii and Fidenae erupted into war. Citing their treaty, King Tullus summoned Alba Longa's army, and together they met the enemy at the confluence of the Anio and Tiber. There, in the heat of battle, and contrary to orders, the treacherous Fufetius withdrew his cohorts to the safety of a nearby hill. Tullus's ally was deserting him. The effect on morale could be disastrous. Ordering his cavalry to hold their spears vertically to screen Fufetius's manoeuvres, Tullus proclaimed he was deliberately sending Alba Longa's army to outflank the enemy. While his words inspired the Romans, the Veientines and Fidenates tried desperately to escape across the rivers. Weighed down by armour, they made easy targets. It was Rome's greatest victory to date.

What was to be done with perfidious Alba Longa? Clearly Fufetius's tactic had been to sit out the battle, see who won, and ally himself with the victor. His wish had been to have a foot in both camps; his punishment must fit his crime. So, he was strapped, spread-eagled, to two four-horse chariots, whose teams galloped off in two opposite directions, tearing him apart, leaving only 'bits of mangled flesh still bound by ropes'. As for Alba, Horatius was sent with orders for its citizens. They were to leave their homes immediately with anything they wished to bring and come to Rome, where they would find new houses on the Caelian Hill. In Livy's imaginative description:

> An unbroken column of refugees filled the roads, and as they recognized each other they wept at their shared misery. Cries of grief were heard (especially from women) as they passed their temples, guarded now by armed men, as if the gods themselves were captives. When every Alban was gone, the Romans levelled all their buildings to the ground – public and private alike. In one hour four centuries of Alba's history were destroyed. The temples were spared, however, in accordance with the king's command.

Nonetheless, the rituals associated with these temples were gradually neglected, and this provoked Jupiter's anger. In wrath he rained down boulders onto Mount Albanus, in fear of which Tullus Hostilius scrambled to re-establish the abandoned sanctuaries; but nothing could save the warlike king. When he bungled Jupiter's rites in Rome, the god unleashed a lightning bolt, destroying both Tullus and his palace.

Managing the Lake

Just over 300 years later, in the early fourth century BC, Rome learned that Lake Albanus (modern Lake Albano) held the key to victory in her war with Veii. Lying in the crater of an extinct volcano, the lake has no natural outlets, and when during a drought its waters rose inexplicably, all thought it a great omen. What did it signify? Normally Romans would consult Etruscan haruspices, entrail-inspectors, who were experts in interpreting such prodigies, but since the war they had all been sent away. So an urgent mission was despatched to the Delphic oracle in Greece.

Its reply was clear: Rome would not prevail until the lake was drained, and its waters diverted into irrigation channels before reaching the sea. Moreover, the Romans must ensure that the pan-Latin festival on Mount Albanus be conducted with proper attention to ancestral ritual. So rites were performed, a tunnel dug, and Veii fell (thanks to mines excavated beneath its acropolis). In fact, archaeology suggests that all the Romans

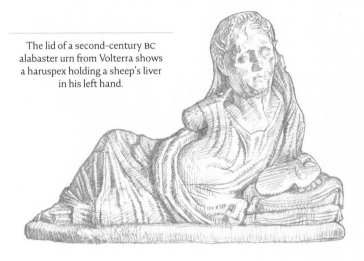

The lid of a second-century BC alabaster urn from Volterra shows a haruspex holding a sheep's liver in his left hand.

needed to do was repair an existing sixth-century BC overflow tunnel that had fallen into disrepair. What lies behind the myth may be the genuine political realization that only by reinvigorating a sense of unity within the Latin League (which Alba Longa had once headed) through honouring its sanctuary on Mount Albanus and improving irrigation on the plain could Rome hope to defeat the Etruscans. The experience of tunnelling was an added bonus.

Alba's Foreign Foundation

Rome was not the only city said to have been founded from Alba Longa. According to the medieval chronicler, Geoffrey of Monmouth, when the wife of King Silvius (here Aeneas's grandson) was pregnant, a soothsayer predicted that the child would grow up to be the bravest, best-beloved man in Italy. Furious at the prospect of being usurped, Silvius slew the prophet, but, when his wife died in childbirth, he nonetheless brought up his son, Brutus, in his palace. However, Fate intervened on a hunting expedition, when Brutus's misfired arrow accidentally killed Silvius, and the boy was forced into exile.

After many adventures, Brutus and a brave band of Greeks and fellow Trojan exiles fought their way through Gaul (where they founded the city of Tours) before sailing north, and landed at Totonesium on the island of Albion. A mighty battle with resident giants resulted in such a convincing victory that the wanderers renamed the country 'Britain' after their leader, and the county 'Cornwall' after Corineus, one of their generals, while Totonesium became Totnes. The victors then marched east until they reached the banks of the River Thames, where they founded a new city, Troia Nova or Trinovantum. Today we call it London.

Alba Longa in History and Today

Alba Longa's importance lies not so much in its ancient history (which is short) as in its spiritual associations as Rome's mother city. It was the powerful head of the Latin League until the middle of the seventh century BC, when it was so utterly destroyed by Rome that few, if any, traces survive. In around 396 BC, however, Romans helped repair an existing drainage tunnel, allowing water from Lake Albanus to irrigate the nearby plains. Following the Latin League's ultimate defeat in 338 BC, the Alban Hills continued to help define Rome's spiritual identity. The sanctuary of Jupiter Latiaris remained symbolically important: during the *Feriae Latinae* (Latin Festival), attended by both of Rome's consuls, meat from a white heifer sacrificed here was solemnly distributed to each of the Latin peoples. Here, too, Rome's generals celebrated lesser victories that were not considered worthy of a full-blown triumph.

The tranquil Alban Hills, so close to the hubbub of the city, became a favourite haunt for the urban rich, including first-century BC politicians Clodius and Pompey, and the first-century AD emperor Domitian, whose huge villa probably straddled the site of Alba Longa. Just over a century later, in 202 the emperor Septimius Severus quartered the Legio II Parthica at nearby Albanus. In the twelfth century AD the area became the preserve of the Gandolfi family, from whose palace (the successor to Domitian's) it now took the name Castel Gandolfo. Bought by the Vatican in 1596, the castle was rebuilt and refurbished in 1624, since when it has been the Pope's summer residence.

· ·

ALBA LONGA Some Important Dates and Remains

C9th–7th BC	Alba Longa is capital of the Latin League.
mid-C7th BC	Rome destroys Alba Longa.
396 BC	Romans help repair drainage tunnel from Lake Albanus.
C2nd–1st BC	Alban Hills become a popular resort for Rome's elite.
AD 81–96	Domitian has palace built at Alba Longa.
AD 202	Septimius Severus quarters Legio II Parthica nearby.
C12th	Gandolfi family build palace on the site of Domitian's.
AD 1596	Castel Gandolfo bought by the Vatican.
AD 1624	Castel Gandolfo redesigned as Pope's summer residence.

Thanks to its violent prehistory, nothing remains of legendary Alba Longa. Its site is debated. Some place it at Castel Gandolfo at Lake Albano's western side, while others site it to the east. More certain is the location of the archaic **emissarium** or **drainage tunnel**, 1,450 m (4,757 ft) long with an average width of 1.2 m (4 ft), a maximum height of 2.5 m (8 ft) and a slope gradient of about 0.14 per thousand. Its entrance lies below Castel Gandolfo, with an exit at Le Mole.

South of Castel Gandolfo, remains of Domitian's villa, originally built on three narrow terraces each 500 m (over 1,640 ft) long, are situated within the papal palace grounds and closed to visitors. Those in search of antiquities should head for Albano with its remains of the legionary camp,

Castra Albana. These include (half) an **amphitheatre**, the **Porta Praetoria** (an imposing gateway) and the **Baths of Cellomaio**, built by Caracalla after murdering his brother Geta. A **nymphaeum** originally belonging to Domitian's villa has been converted into the Church of **Santa Maria della Rotonda**. To the southeast can be found the so-called (heavily restored) **Tomb of the Horatii and Curiatii**: a first-century BC construction with four truncated cones at each corner, its architecture is unique. West of Albano in the park of Villa Doria Pamphili, bordering the ancient via Appia, lie foundations of the so-called **Villa of Pompey**, while a little to the northeast is a large **tower-shaped tomb**, also associated with Pompey.

Nearby, Lake Nemi with remains of the **Temple of Diana** is well worth visiting. The **Museo delle Navi Romane** on the shore is particularly poignant. From 1932 it housed Caligula's two massive pleasure barges, painstakingly retrieved from the lake bed, but in 1944 they and the museum were deliberately burnt by German soldiers. Scale models are now on show, as well as other boat-related artefacts.

• •

CHAPTER 9

THE PALATINE HILL:
PALATIAL SEAT OF POWER

Descendants of Pallas, the Arcadians, who followed where
their comrade, King Evander, led them, chose this location
and built their city on these hills, calling it Pallanteum after
their ancestor, Pallas.

Virgil, *Aeneid*, 8.51–54

Leave the crowds that swirl around the Colosseum, the ticket touts, the street musicians. Leave the hustling street artists who crouch over spray-painted stencils of Rome's ruins in a haze of mind-bending solvent. Leave the buses that disgorge or swallow freights of dazed, surfeited tourists ticking one more landmark off their bucket list. And climb onto the Palatine.

Trees line the path, leaves sighing gently in the summer breeze. Crows call. Insects rustle in the grass. Peace has returned, and sanity. How romantic this place is! Masonry rises from the undergrowth and roses bloom. Walk over there, and we could look down on the Forum spread out like an architectural model or child's toy. Walk there instead, and we could contemplate the Circus Maximus stretching out towards the skeleton of Caracalla's Baths. Or there, and we could gaze out over Rome towards the Alban Hills.

It is as if we have been elevated far above the hubbub of reality, as if we are standing in a blessed special place. As indeed we are. For this was where Rome's rich and powerful had their houses, from kings of myth and early history, to lawyers, generals and politicians of the Republic, to all-powerful emperors, whose sprawling mansions and extravagant estates became so famous that they were named after the Palatine: the world's first palaces.

Enter Evander

Mythical Rome was a city of refugees and immigrants. Two generations after its first king, Saturn, was banished here by Jupiter, another Greek landed near the Tiber's mouth: the young Arcadian prince Evander (whose name in Greek means 'good man') from the city of Pallantium. Although he played a doughty role in Rome's prehistory, his genealogy and why he came to Italy were debated.

Some maintained that Evander's great-grandfather, Lycaon, Arcadia's fierce king, sacrificed young children and tried to feed their flesh to Jupiter, and so the god made him a werewolf. They said, too, that Evander's mother somehow persuaded him to kill his father, which was why he had to flee the country. Others, loath to make Rome's ancient king a parricide, wove a different tale: here the noble Evander was Mercury's son by the prophetic nymph, Carmenta, the victim of a power grab when a civil uprising in Pallantium drove him, his mother and his followers into exile.

Even details of his arrival in Italy were uncertain. One story saw him fighting for possession of the land around the Tiber, seeing off stiff opposition from the army of Praeneste (modern Palestrina), leading his Arcadians to glorious battle, and slaying the enemy king, Herilus (or Erulus), in heroic combat. (Herilus's mother, Feronia, a prophetic goddess of fertility and the wild, gave him three lives. So three times Herilus died in battle beneath Praeneste's crag, and twice he was regenerated before Evander could finally kill him.)

The more common myth imagined Evander mooring his ships benignly by the river bank, its shores dotted with simple wooden huts, while his mother prophesied great things for his new settlement, and the local ruler, Faunus, welcomed him with open arms. Into this idyll, Evander brought civilization: the alphabet and writing; stringed instruments and flutes; the worship of a panoply of Greek gods; laws; the Arts; and 'many other things of benefit to public life'.

Dionysius of Halicarnassus describes how Evander's mother bade him choose a local hill:

> a little distant from the Tiber, which is now right in the middle of Rome's city, where he built a little village. It was just big enough for the crew of the two ships in which they sailed from Greece, but in time it would become greater than any other city, Greek or barbarian, in size, power and fortune, praised above all others for as long as mankind shall live. They named it Pallantium after their mother city in Arcadia, but now, corrupted over time, Romans call it Palatine, a name that has inspired many absurd etymologies.

One of these etymologies claimed that, since the hill was once used as pastureland for sheep, its original name was 'Balatium', 'The Place of Baa-ing'.

Hercules and Cacus

Virgil's *Aeneid* has Evander himself narrate one of early Rome's key civilizing myths, the destruction of malignant Cacus (whose Greek name means 'Evil One'). Vulcan's son, Cacus was a monstrous fire-breathing ogre, lawless and ugly, who lived deep in a cave, its doorway decorated with decaying heads, and its floor slick with blood. For years Cacus had terrorized the local countryside, the bane of its new settlers, who prayed constantly for a saviour.

While early myth identified the saviour as an Italian shepherd, Recaranus, later Romans agreed that he was none other than Hercules, returning to Greece from one of his twelve labours with cattle stolen from Geryon, the triple-bodied giant who lived in far-off Spain. As evening fell Hercules let the beasts graze on the Palatine's high grasses, while he lay down to sleep. That night Cacus crept up onto the hill, seized as many of the creatures as he could, and dragged them by the tail backwards to his cave.

Next dawn, Hercules discovered several beasts missing, but (thanks to Cacus's ruse) he found no tracks leading off the Palatine. Resigned to his loss, he was about to recommence his journey when one of his oxen set up a plaintive lowing – which was answered by a bellow deep below the earth. At once Hercules understood. In fury he seized his knotted club and thundered off to find his cattle. Even gross Cacus was terrified. He had been watching, gleeful and concealed, but now he ran back to his cave and, cutting a cord, caused a boulder to crash down and block its entranceway. Incensed, Hercules paced back and forth across the Palatine, looking for a way inside, but, finding none, he resorted to force.

> There was a steep flinty pinnacle that towered sheer from the ridge above the cave, a ready nesting-place for vultures. It slanted from the hilltop left above the river, but Hercules threw his weight against the right side and ripped it from its very roots. Then suddenly he pushed the other way, and as he did the air ripped with a crack of thunder, the river banks recoiled and the river flowed backwards in terror.

Exposed, Cacus cringed on the cavern floor, breathing fireballs as Hercules shot arrows into the smoke-filled hollow, before, leaping down into the cave, he throttled the ogre with his bare hands. As Hercules dragged Cacus's cadaver into the daylight, Evander and his fellow settlers crowded round delightedly to gloat over their tormentor's twitching corpse.

In historical times, a steep path leading up onto the Palatine was known as Cacus's Steps, though both Virgil and Ovid place his cave across the valley on the Aventine, a hill traditionally associated in Romans' minds with the urban poor. However, it was the rich and powerful who (initially at least) identified with Hercules, the son of Jupiter and a Greek princess.

Romanizing Hercules

Canny, rationalizing Romans believed that myths of Hercules' travels were fictionalized accounts of early military expeditions mirroring the imperial expansion of their own age. Dionysius was not alone in seeing him as a proto-Augustus, marching at the head of a great army, defeating aggressive states, overthrowing tyrants, imposing law, order and legitimate monarchies, founding cities, building roads and draining swamps, while deliberately intermingling the various peoples of his new empire. This, he believed, accounted for Hercules' numerous sanctuaries throughout Italy, 'with so

A late second-century AD marble portrait bust of the Emperor Commodus dressed as Hercules, complete with lion-skin and club, now resides in Rome's Capitoline Museum.

many altars in cities and at roadsides, that it would be hard to find anywhere he is not honoured'.

His Cacus was a robber baron, who set thieves to pillage Hercules' great army's baggage train. After a lengthy siege the Greeks defeated him, and, when Hercules moved on, he left behind two trusted lieutenants – Faunus and Evander – to rule over the land. Later, Hercules travelled south to the Bay of Naples to meet up with his fleet, which had been fighting off Spain, and were now moored in a harbour that Dionysius (with no prescience of the disaster that would soon unfold) described as 'at all times safe and secure': Herculaneum.

Before Hercules left Rome, Evander, forewarned by his mother Carmenta that 'because of his great virtue' his Greek guest would in time become a god, erected a massive altar near the Tiber, where he sacrificed cattle in Hercules' honour. Its location was later called Forum Boarium ('Cattle Market'). Here in historical times, at Hercules the Victor's round temple, members of two ancient families, the Potitii and Pinarii, self-proclaimed descendants of Evander's priests, made annual sacrifice of a young heifer. (Another legend said that, because the Pinarii arrived late for the first ceremony, they were subordinate to the Potitii and not allowed the dubious honour of eating the beast's entrails.)

Hercules and Acca Larentia

Years later, during the reign of Ancus Marcius, Rome's fourth king, Hercules' priest was bored. So to pass the time he played a game of dice with himself, claiming his left hand's throws for himself and assigning those of his right to Hercules. His right hand won, and as the god's prize the priest arranged for a gourmand meal to be delivered to the temple along with a stunning Etruscan girl called Acca Larentia, who spent the night inside alone – during which time (writes Plutarch) Hercules visited her, consorted with her 'not in the manner that a mortal would', and told her to waylay the first man she met next morning.

It happened that he was a fellow Etruscan, the fabulously wealthy Tarutius, who fell in love with her, married her and died shortly afterwards. This was not the end of Larentia's good fortune. Some years later in the Velabrum market near Hercules' temple, she vanished into thin air. The god had claimed her as his own. When her will was read, it was discovered that Larentia had left her money and possessions to the Roman people, in gratitude for which the king recognized her as a goddess and instituted an annual festival, the Larentalia, with sacrifices to both her and the Lares, protecting fructifying deities of homes and countryside.

Evander and Aeneas

When Aeneas reached Italy, he found in Evander a staunch ally. By now the king was very old – he had been exiled sixty years before the Trojan War. Nevertheless, he still remembered how, as a young man, he had met Aeneas's father, Anchises, who visited Arcadia with Troy's King Priam and presented him with rich gifts. Now Evander was making annual sacrifice to Hercules beside the Tiber, when Aeneas and his shipmates sailed upriver.

Virgil's *Aeneid* revels in this momentous meeting, inviting his chic urban readers to imagine a time when Rome was little more than fields and pastureland, making Evander take Aeneas on a tour of well-known landmarks mirroring the route followed by real-life Roman generals on their return from war: past the scrubby Capitol 'all golden now', past cattle grazing in the future Forum, up onto the Palatine, and his royal house – a hut, with heaped leaves for a bed and a bearskin for a blanket. The description is more than simply humorous or nostalgic. Romans believed in traditional values, and it did no harm to remind readers of their humble, austere origins.

This was not the only way in which Virgil manipulated Aeneas and Evander's encounter on the Palatine (a stone's throw from the site of

Augustus's palace). Early myths described war between incoming Trojans and native Etruscans, but, with leading Etruscans now in Augustus's court, Virgil needed to show them on the right side of history. So he changed the story. Since the Etruscan nation must now be Aeneas's allies, his enemy must be an Etruscan renegade: the cruel king Mezentius. His depravity knows no bounds. Assuming control of Caere (modern Cerveteri), Mezentius rules despotically, punishing enemies by lashing them alive to decaying corpses, until a popular rebellion drives him to seek refuge with his friend, Turnus of Ardea.

Meanwhile the Etruscans bayed for Mezentius's blood. But, as bad omens prevented their supreme commander, Tarchon of Tarquinia, from launching an attack, his haruspex warned him that it was not fated for an Italian to defeat Mezentius. Rather they must choose a foreign leader. Venus confirmed Evander's conviction that this long-awaited leader was Aeneas by causing a thunderstorm to crash over the Palatine, with spectral weapons flickering in the sky, and the sound of braying Etruscan trumpets. Eager to embrace his destiny, Aeneas, a russet lion-skin draped about his shoulders, led a hand-picked delegation from the Palatine, and rode across the Tiber towards Caere, where Tarchon's army was encamped, to form an alliance that would bring Rome's greatness another step closer. But it was four hundred years more before the city itself was founded, under circumstances both renowned and troubling.

Romulus and Remus Adrift

When Amulius, Alba Longa's usurping king, discovered that (despite his efforts) his niece Rhea Silvia had given birth to twins, he placed the baby boys in a basket, gave it to trusted servants, and ordered them to cast it adrift on the Tiber. Dionysius records what happened next:

> When the servants came nearer, and saw that because of heavy rains the Tiber had burst its banks and flooded the plain, they came down from the Palatine as close to the river's edge as possible (they could get no closer) and placed the basket into the water by the foot of the hill. It floated a little way, but as the water gradually became shallower it hit a rock, capsized and dislodged the babies, who lay whimpering in the mud. But along came a she-wolf, who had just given birth, and whose udder was distended with milk. She gave them her teats to suckle on and licked off the mud.

Some herdsmen saw the wolf and tried to frighten her away, but she waited calmly until the boys were fed, only backing off when she knew that they were safe. Then she tamely loped off to a cave beneath the Palatine, near a fig tree beside a shrine of Pan. Among the herdsmen was Faustulus, the king's swineherd. He alone knew the babies' true identity, but being a kindly man, whose wife was grieving their stillborn child, he resolved to thwart his master's plan and bring them up in secret as his own. And so, as young men, the twins returned to Alba Longa, overthrew Amulius and restored their grandfather Numitor to the throne.

The myth of Romulus, Remus and the she-wolf is so well-known that it is a shock to realize that it may have been a late fourth-century BC invention, created at a time of growing prestige to provide a glorious ancestry for Rome. Similarities with myths such as that of Mercury and Lara's twins, the Lares, also suckled by a she-wolf, or King Tarchetius, a Latin with an Etruscan name, who similarly set newborn twins adrift, suggest that the Romulus and Remus story may have been honed for propagandist purposes: god-fearing, militaristic Rome, it declared, was founded by sons of a virgin priestess and the war-god Mars. Still, some tried to debunk the myth. Since *lupa*, 'she-wolf', could also mean 'prostitute', they claimed that Numitor smuggled the twins out of Alba Longa and gave them to noble Faustulus (a descendant of Evander) to be suckled not by a beast but by his wife, who had once been a working girl – none other than Acca Larentia, whose favours Hercules enjoyed (and who was herself connected to the Lares).

The she-wolf's cave and nearby fig tree became important landmarks in urban Rome, the site of the first rites of the Lupercalia, a fertility festival held annually on 15 February. Here, hides of a sacrificial goat and dog were cut into strips and given to young noblemen, who ran naked round the Palatine, flogging bystanders with their thongs. Women deliberately offered themselves for whipping, since this was believed to improve their chances of an easy and successful pregnancy.

Romulus, Remus and Rome's Foundation

With Numitor established on the throne, Romulus and Remus left Alba Longa with a band of young men to found a city of their own by Tiber's banks. Almost immediately they quarrelled. Unable to agree a site, they entrusted the matter to the gods. Before sunrise each took his stance at his preferred location – some said that Romulus watched from the Palatine, and Remus from the Aventine. As they gazed towards the horizon and the Alban Hills' pale silhouette, Remus was first to see a sign: six vultures flapping across the sky from his right side. Triumphantly he ran onto the Palatine to announce his supremacy, but as he approached Romulus saw not six but twelve vultures flying in from the right. Who, then, had won – Remus, whose portent came first, or Romulus, to whom twice as many birds appeared?

With his supporters' backing, Romulus's claim won out – especially when a spear, which he threw symbolically into the hilltop, miraculously sprouted leaves. A solar eclipse on 21 April found the new colonists making sacrifice on the Palatine, lighting fires and jumping through the flames to purify themselves. Then Romulus yoked a bull and cow together to a plough, before cutting a rectangular furrow round the hill, into which he threw the first fruits of the land. With this ditch he marked the course of the future city walls, only lifting the ploughshare where the gates would be. Meanwhile, he ordered his commander-in-chief, Celer, that from now on, anyone who tried to enter the sacred enclosure by any way other than the gates would be guilty of profanity and treason, punishable by death.

Remus, however, still harboured grudges and did all he could to deprecate his brother, taunting him with the building work's slow progress. 'Call that a city wall?' he sneered, and jumped with ease over the still-low foundations. Celer was nearby, and, true to his orders, seized his spade and smashed it into Remus's skull. When Romulus saw his brother's corpse, he muttered stoically: 'Thus may anyone die, who tries to cross Rome's walls!' The impious invader was dead, but it was a terrifying portent for the city's

Followed by a group of men in togas,
a ploughman (perhaps Romulus)
guides his oxen on this relief.

future. By the late Republic, Romans, now used to fratricidal civil wars, believed an even darker version of the story: it was Romulus himself who slew his twin. Or perhaps (an earlier, more benign interpretation claimed) Remus deliberately sacrificed himself for his city's future good.

Throughout Rome's ancient history, the festival of the Parilia marked its foundation day (in 753 BC) with sacrifices made to Pales, the presiding goddess, whose name may be connected to the Palatine. This was originally a shepherds' festival, when flocks and herds were purified by being led over fire, pens cleansed, and citizens, leaping over flames, were sprinkled with water from sacred laurel leaves. Later a grotesque sacrifice was added: the leading trace-horse from the team that won a special chariot race the previous October was slaughtered, and its blood mixed with the ashes of an unborn calf ripped from its mother's belly. Both were then added to smouldering bean stalks and used for fumigation. In 45 BC Julius Caesar added games to the festival, and in AD 121 Hadrian used the occasion to inaugurate his new Temple of Venus and Rome, whose remains can be seen opposite the Colosseum.

Claudia Quinta

In 204 BC, during the war with Hannibal, priests consulting the Sibylline Books proclaimed the reason for Rome's lack of progress: 'The mother is absent! I tell you, Roman: seek out the mother and when she comes, make sure a chaste hand welcomes her!' The mother in question was the Great Mother, Cybele, a Phrygian fertility goddess whose home was Mount Ida near Troy. At first the local king, Attalus I of Pergamum, was loath to give up the black stone worshipped as the goddess's embodiment. Then, during an earthquake, a voice resounded from her shrine insisting: 'Send me! I want to go! Rome is a worthy home for gods!' As a result of this (and of Attalus's desire to placate the Romans), the stone began its journey west; but, as it came up the Tiber, the ship transporting it became stuck on a sandbar.

There was nothing anyone could do. Not even the most chaste Romans – priests and Vestal Virgins – could find a way to refloat it. The omens seemed desperate – until Claudia Quinta stepped forward. She was not an obvious saviour. Thanks both to her exquisite beauty and her refusal to do what men told her, she enjoyed an unfair reputation for lax morals. Now was her chance to be vindicated. Scooping water from the Tiber, she stretched her open palms to the skies, and prayed to Cybele that if she was, indeed, chaste, she might convey the goddess to the city. Then she grasped the ship's rope and easily pulled it off the sandbar. At last, after sacrifice and

MATRIDEVMETNAVISALVIAE
SALVIAEVOTOSVSCE?TO
CLAVDIA   SYNTHYCHE
      D   D

Claudia Quinta guides the ship bearing the goddess Cybele
ashore on this altar from Rome dedicated by Claudia Syntyche,
dating to around AD 50.

prayers, Cybele's temple was consecrated on the Palatine amid scatterings
of flowers. The event was celebrated in the annual Megalesia held on 4 April
with processions, dances in armour and dramas (including comedies) performed while audiences watched from the temple steps.

The Palatine in History and Today

While archaeology cannot always confirm mythology, on the Palatine it
supports its basic chronology. Twelfth-century BC remains have been uncov-
ered in the northern sector, and eighth-century BC huts in the southwest,
including a two-roomed dwelling identified in Roman times as 'Romulus's
Hut', and considered so significant that it was preserved, fenced off, as a
historic monument. Dionysius describes how it was:

> conserved as a sanctuary by those who look after it. Not even
> the smallest thing is added to it to make it more august, and if it
> suffers damage from storm or the effects of time they repair it and
> restore it as far as possible to its former condition.

Further evidence confirms that city walls were built in the mid-eighth century BC at precisely the time suggested by mythology.

As surrounding low-lying land (including the Forum Boarium, Forum areas and the site occupied by the Circus Maximus) was drained, Rome expanded and even kings moved off the Palatine, but the hill retained its cachet. While the southwest quadrant remained a sacred area (with temples to Victoria, Cybele and Apollo), the rest of the hill became studded with increasingly luxurious urban villas. By the late Republic, it was home to such luminaries as Cicero, Tiberius Claudius Nero (father of the emperor Tiberius) and Mark Antony.

Augustus's conscious decision to commandeer the house of Quintus Hortensius Hortalus (complete with fishpond) changed the Palatine forever. Sited between Romulus's Hut and temples of Cybele and Apollo, this was not just prime real estate but a site of profound religious significance, ripe for exploitation by Rome's first emperor with his discerning understanding of myth's propagandist power. Indeed, imagining Mount Olympus, Ovid drew a telling parallel:

> Here the powerful, famous gods have made their home (plebeian gods live somewhere else). If I might risk a daring phrase I'd scarcely hesitate to call this place 'Heaven's Palatine'.

While Augustus famously led an austere lifestyle, his successors were less restrained. Preserving the homes of Augustus and his wife Livia as heritage sites, immediate successors built increasingly large villas nearby. These included Tiberius (the Villa Tiberiana subsequently housed heirs and potential heirs), Caligula and Nero, part of whose 'Golden House' estate took in the Palatine, while Domitian's sprawling, towering palace combined residences (including a mirrored bedroom allegedly to stop would-be assassins creeping up behind the emperor), audience and reception rooms, and administrative offices – the first time that every aspect of imperial government was brought under the same roof. Nearby in the northeast quadrant of the Palatine, the Gardens of Adonis provided a cool, well-watered pleasure park.

A century later, Septimius Severus further enlarged the palace, possibly linking it to the Caelian Hill with his Septizodium, an enormous structure (parts of which stood until the sixteenth century) 9 m (30 ft) high and 27 m (90 ft) long, built around the Aqua Claudia aqueduct. Such excesses were tame compared to parties held by one of his successors, Elagabalus, from whose ceilings rose petals dropped in such profusion that they suffocated guests, while pools were filled with wine. By the late third century, however, the Palatine's lure was waning, a process hastened when Diocletian split the empire in AD 293. While the early fourth-century Maxentius did build on the Palatine, he chose to site his palace outside Rome beside the Appian Way (though he did bury his imperial insignia for safekeeping on the Palatine).

Christianity increased the Palatine's woes. In AD 394, when pagan practices were outlawed, Theodosius's adopted daughter Serena was seen stealing the necklace from the statue of Cybele. Her subsequent execution was seen as divine justice. Fifth-century incursions by Goths and Vandals targeted the wealthy Palatine, and, although Theodoric restored something of its former greatness, by now only the summit was habitable. Ruinous and abandoned, the Palatine reverted to farmland and vineyards, and many remains were burnt for lime. In the sixteenth century the Farnese family built a villa here, with ornamental gardens in an archaic Roman style, but following his visit to Rome in 1764 Edward Gibbon could still write:

> Cast your eyes on the Palatine Hill, and seek, among the shapeless and enormous fragments, the marble theatre, the obelisks, the colossal statues, the porticoes of Nero's palace: survey the other hills of the city; the vacant space is interrupted only by ruins and gardens.

· ·

THE PALATINE Some Important Dates and Remains

c. 1150 BC	Village settlements and burials.
753 BC	Traditional date for Rome's foundation.
c. 750 BC	Huts and first enclosing walls.
c. 525 BC	Inhabited area expands to north.
294 BC	Temple of Victoria dedicated.
204–191 BC	Temple of Cybele constructed.
C2nd/C1st BC	Home of elite Romans.
c. 30 BC	Augustus takes up residence.
c. AD 15	Tiberius builds villa north of Augustus's villa.
AD 81–92	Domitian's palace built.
AD 191–211	Septimius Severus enlarges palace.
AD 293	Tetrarchy heralds decline of Palatine's importance.
AD 306–312	Maxentius builds palace beside Appian Way.
AD 326	Church of Santa Anastasia built in Gardens of Adonis.
AD 394	Serena steals Cybele's necklace.
AD 410	Alaric sacks Rome. Temples of Cybele and Apollo in ruins.
AD 455	Vandals sack Rome.
AD 526	Theodoric lives on the Palatine.

While several major archaeological surveys have been conducted since Gibbons's time, to layman and expert alike the Palatine can still seem a baffling confusion. A good site map is essential, as are a hat, water and a vivid imagination.

The Palatine is accessed either from the via di San Gregorio near the Aqua Claudia aqueduct or (included in a ticket for the Forum) from near the Arch of Titus, from where a steep climb leads across the impressive **cryptoporticus** (part of the Villa Tiberiana) to the rather desultory Farnese Gardens. From here there is access to a terrace giving superlative **views** across the Forum towards both the Capitoline Hill and Colosseum.

An anti-clockwise route leads via another viewing platform (views embracing St Peter's and the Forum Boarium) to the sacred southwestern quadrant. Here are scant remains of the **Temples of Victory** and **Cybele** as well as (under a metal roof) **Romulus's Hut** and the site of the **Scalae Caci** (Cacus's Steps). More impressive (if open) are the **Houses of Augustus** and **Livia**. Both contain stunning wall-paintings; the **Room of the Masks** may for forty years have been Augustus's bedroom. Attached to Augustus's palace was the Temple of Apollo with Greek and Latin libraries.

A path leads to **later imperial quarters**, whose most significant remains date from the reigns of Domitian and Septimius Severus. These contain a labyrinth of rooms; the use of many is debated. Most notable are the so-called stadium, in fact a late first-century AD sunken garden some 14 m (45 ft) long, and the **Arcate Severiane**, a colossal extension to the Palatine whose substructures extend almost to the Circus Maximus, and which contained the imperial box from which Severus and his family could enjoy chariot races. From its westernmost edge are fine **views** towards the Alban Hills.

The **Palatine Museum** contains a cornucopia of finds, including **painted terracotta panels** from the Temple of Apollo, **statues** from the temple's Danaid Portico, **frescoes** showing scenes from Homer, **portrait busts** and a **scratched graffito** showing the crucifixion of a donkey-headed man with the inscription, 'Alexamenos worships God'.

● ●

CHAPTER 10
THE CAPITOL: HOME OF THE GODS

Next he led him onto the Tarpeian Hill, the Capitol, all golden
now, but once an overgrown entanglement of brambles.
But even then the awe-inspiring spirit of the place struck fear
into trembling country folk, and even then they shuddered as
they looked upon the wood and rock. 'A god lives in the grove
high on this leafy hill', he said, 'though which god I don't know.
Arcadians believe that they've seen Jupiter shaking his black
aegis in his right hand, summoning the clouds.'

Virgil, *Aeneid*, 8.347–54

From the House of the Dioscuri in Pompeii, a fresco
shows Jupiter enthroned in majesty, his eagle at his feet.

Chattering green parakeets dart high above the piazza del Campidoglio, its warm cobbles loud with excited voices. Beside the proud equestrian statue of Marcus Aurelius, his right hand outstretched in a gesture of beatific power, well-tanned *carabinieri* in immaculately pressed blue uniforms lounge self-importantly as they survey the crowds. Look around and you will see more horses: two fine white marble beasts stand proud beside their masters, the Dioscuri, those archetypal riders Castor and Pollux, guarding either side of the steep ramp, the Cordonata, as it climbs from the busy road below. And looming high into the cloudless sky, stark against the sunlight, two teams of horses pull twin chariots of bronze in which ride the winged goddesses of Unity and Freedom, atop the brilliant white confection of the 'wedding cake', the 'Altar of the Fatherland', the eyesore also known as the memorial to Italy's King Victor Emanuel II.

The building excites strong emotions, from proud patriotic fervour to artistic scorn. Nonetheless, its impact on the cityscape is inescapable, its towering chariots glimpsed by chance from unexpected corners, an omnipresent landmark. It speaks of power and authority; and – despite (or perhaps because of) its perceived vulgarity – of irrepressible self-confidence. In part it is its site that lets it preen so shamelessly. For close by there once stood one of the Roman world's most sacred and impressive temples, whose foundations, now protected in a light-filled hall of chrome and glass, can still impress: the Temple of Jupiter Optimus Maximus, Jupiter the Best and Greatest, the most powerful god in all Rome's pantheon.

The Age of Saturn

With steep cliffs and an air of wonder, the Capitoline Hill seems for late Bronze Age Italians to have possessed an aura of divinity, which is why they thought it was from here that Saturn had once ruled. As the first-century BC Varro wrote:

> Authorities maintain that the original name for the Capitoline Hill was Mount Saturnium, from which Latium gained the name 'The Land of Saturn'.... They write, too, that the ancient city of Saturnia once stood upon the hill.

This Saturn was a far cry from his Greek equivalent, Cronus, a ferocious god who ate his children raw so that they would not usurp him, and was eventually overthrown through trickery and war – something that Dionysius of Halicarnassus was adamant no Roman could believe. Instead, Italy's Saturn was considerably more benign. Wielding the thunderbolt (like the Etruscan god Satres, to whom he was possibly related) he was a god of cosmic order, presiding over time and seasons, especially important to farmers who relied on him for ample harvests and called him the god of wealth, the husband of the goddess Ops ('Abundance'). It was no coincidence that Rome's treasury was housed in Saturn's temple beneath the Capitoline Hill.

Saturn – a scythe-bearer like 'Father Time' – was trusted to maintain the year's regular cycle, which was why he was honoured with an annual winter festival, the Saturnalia, straddling the winter solstice. Now woollen bonds that bound the feet of his cult statue (its hollow interior awash with olive oil to help preserve its ivory façade) were ritually untied, and for seven days a party atmosphere gripped Rome. Gifts were exchanged, great quantities of food and drink consumed, and slaves accorded extraordinary licence, temporarily lording it over their masters. For, as the second-century AD historian Justin observed:

> Under Saturn there were no slaves, and no-one owned private property. Rather everything was shared in common, undivided, a joint inheritance. This is why during the Saturnalia slaves sit with masters at banquets.

A century earlier, the poet Statius described the Saturnalia's extraordinary atmosphere:

> Saturn lavishes generous gifts upon us! On this day all dine together at one table indiscriminately – old and young, men and women, rich and poor. Here is where Liberty trumps rank!

In time, however, the cruel, consuming nature of Saturn's Greek counterpart infected the Roman god's festival. Ten days of games, in which gladiators fought to the death, were introduced into the Saturnalia, and Romans began to wonder whether certain rites (including those in which straw effigies were thrown into the Tiber) once involved human sacrifice.

Somehow the original Saturn still cast his spell over the Capitol. His fate, being banished from Greece by his usurping son Jupiter, chimed with the notion that Rome's founders were exiles. Virgil imagined him gathering untamed peoples from their homes, teaching them laws and calling the region 'Latium' because he had safely hidden here (*lateo* means 'I hide'). Although in historical times the hill was more closely connected with Jupiter, associated myths regarded it as not just a centre of justice but a place of safety.

Asylum

Romulus and Remus brought to Rome a crowd of loyal supporters, but even they could not populate the city quickly rising on the Palatine. So, following Remus's death, Romulus issued a proclamation. In a saddle of the Capitol between two groves there was a clearing, the 'Asylum' sacred to the god Asylaeus; now, Romulus announced, an oracle demanded that any man who came here, whatever his past misdemeanours, should be automatically enrolled as a Roman citizen and offered every protection that this afforded. Soon a motley band of vagabonds and ne'er-do-wells was clambering up the steep sides of the Capitol – escaped slaves, debtors, even convicted murderers – all fervently clinging to the hope of a new life.

As Rome's population swelled, Romulus began to turn his mind to how it should be governed. So he chose her hundred most senior men and appointed them elders – *senatores* in Latin – to guide him and advise on policy, while acting as the 'fathers' of the constitution. And since the Latin for 'fathers' is *patres*, they and their upper-class descendants became known as patricians.

This myth of early Rome attracting men from across the earth, no matter what their background, nurturing them and making them citizens, who would in turn advance Rome's cause, was potent, especially in the rapidly expanding Republic and early Empire. It also brought ugly consequences. One was that part of what Romulus promised these first asylum-seekers was a share of all land seized in war: prosperity, freedom and the Roman way of life were to be built on the conquest of others. Another was more immediate but equally violent. Most of the asylum-seekers were men, but without women Rome risked dying out within a generation – which led to one of the most controversial of all early Rome's myths.

The Sabine Women

Advised by his new Senate, Romulus sent ambassadors to local cities, requesting that they grant the right of intermarriage to Rome's citizens. Despite the diplomatic terms in which these requests were couched, however, not one agreed. What decent freeborn man would choose a runaway slave or convicted felon as his son-in-law? Besides, it was not in their interests to help Rome, for, if she became established, they worried that she might defeat them. So they dismissed the ambassadors, scornfully suggesting that they should consider offering asylum to shady women, too, since only then could they ever hope to marry.

While Rome's bachelors ground their teeth in growing frustration, Romulus hit on a bold (if unsavoury) plan. He claimed to have found an altar hidden in the earth in the valley between the Palatine and Aventine Hills. Sources disagree about which god was worshipped here – Consus (a god of grain) or Neptune – but since both had connections with horses it did not really matter. For Romulus announced that on 21 August, four months after Rome's foundation, he would hold a horse race and festival, a celebration of his miraculous discovery, and he invited the great and good from all around to come and enjoy the fun.

Few could resist the opportunity to travel to the Tiber and admire the newly rising walls, and entire families poured in from nearby Latin and Sabine cities. Food was eaten, wine consumed and merrymaking guests lulled into a pleasant sense of torpor. Then Romulus gave the signal. At once young men ran through the crowds, seizing the most beautiful young women and making off with them. Some took them to their own homes, others to houses of patrician overlords. One girl in particular was so beguiling that all who saw her asked where she was being taken. 'To Thalassius!', the cry went up, and, shouting this, they brought her to the young patrician's door. (So write both Livy and Plutarch, attempting to explain why guests chanted 'Talassio' during the procession to a bride's new home.)

The festival collapsed in acrimony, as fathers rounded up remaining family members and drove off in wagons, cursing Rome, convinced that the gods would avenge them, since the outrage occurred at a religious festival. Meanwhile, Romulus toured the houses where the women were imprisoned, assuring each that his Romans would never have behaved like this if they had been accorded marriage rites, and even now their intentions were honourable: they would grant the women marriage, citizenship, property and children; they would be good husbands; they would more than make up for their loss of homes and parents. Livy (chauvinistically) avers:

His words were backed up by the men's honeyed words. They excused their behaviour as motivated by passion and love, the most effective way of all to win a woman's heart.

Historians debated the number of women seized. One cited a round number (30); two others were surprisingly specific, claiming 527 and 683 respectively.

Spolia Opima

The women's families were not so easily won over. With no help forthcoming from Alba Longa, where Numitor still reigned, they converged on Cures in the Sabine Hills, the city of King Titus Tatius, whom they made war leader. His response was too slow for the city of Caenina. Ablaze with impatience, her men launched their own attack on Roman territory, burning crops and homesteads. They did not prevail for long. Rome already possessed a well-drilled force: Romulus routed the invaders and slew their leader. Then he chased the fugitives back to their walls, and by nightfall Caenina was in Roman hands. The conquest had begun.

Romulus had stripped Caenina's king of his armour, and now for a solemn procession he arranged it on a frame, which he heaved onto his shoulder and carried up onto the Capitol. Here, garlanded with laurel leaves, he dedicated it in front of a sacred oak tree. It was the first Roman triumph in history.

Now Romulus marked out the foundations of a new temple, which he consecrated to Jupiter Feretrius (God of Trophies), declaring that here should be dedicated *spolia opima*, 'spoils of honour', won by generals who killed enemy kings or commanders. Only two other Romans achieved this: Aulus Cornelius Cossus, who defeated Veii's king in 437 BC, and Marcus Claudius Marcellus, who killed the Celtic king Viridomarus in 222 BC. Romulus's consecration of the temple was significant on two counts. Not only was it was Rome's first temple, it also marked the coming to the Capitol of Jupiter, the god who would dominate the hill, the city and the Roman world for centuries to come.

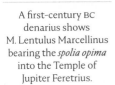
A first-century BC denarius shows M. Lentulus Marcellinus bearing the *spolia opima* into the Temple of Jupiter Feretrius.

Tarpeia's Treachery

As a Sabine army massed to the north, Romulus deployed his men to strengthen the walls round the Palatine and build others round the Aventine and Capitoline Hills. The attack came in early spring. Dionysius (improbably) describes 25,000 Sabine infantry marching with 1,000 cavalry against an almost equal force of Romans and their allies from Alba Longa and Etruria. With three of Rome's seven hills well fortified, Romulus encamped on the Esquiline, posting his Etruscan ally Lucumo on the Quirinal, while entrusting the Capitol's defence to his officer, Spurius Tarpeius.

By daybreak King Tatius was encamped on low ground east of the Capitol, nervously surveying the landscape, while the Romans watched from their high vantage points. Among them was the commander's daughter, Tarpeia. She looked in wonder at the bracelets of solid gold that the Sabines wore around their left wrists, now shimmering in the sun. What she would give to own them! So that evening, pretending to fetch water, she slipped through a narrow gate to Tatius's tent. If the Sabines gave her what they wore on their left arms, she said, she would lead them to the Capitol. And so she did. Under cover of darkness Tatius and a hand-picked force followed Tarpeia through the gate and up onto the citadel. But when she demanded her reward, Tatius threw her not just his bracelet but also his shield – for this, too, he wore on his left arm, and, as his soldiers did the same, treacherous Tarpeia was crushed to death under their weight.

Such is the best-known version of the myth. Some, however, insisted that Tarpeia lured the Sabines to the Capitol, all along intending to deprive of them their shields, so that Rome's garrison could easily defeat them, and that Tatius killed her only when he realized her trickery. In historical times there was a shrine to Tarpeia at her grave on the Capitol, where annual libations were poured in her honour – decidedly not how a traitor would be remembered. Indeed, the Capitol itself may have originally been called the Tarpeian Hill. Even when its name changed, one of its steep cliffs (from which certain criminals were thrown to their death) was called the Tarpeian Rock.

Reconciliation

With the Capitol in Sabine hands, the Romans were wrong-footed. Try as they might, they could not dislodge them. Tatius remained confident, and as Romulus led his men up the slopes, the Sabine king ran out to meet them, beating the Romans back into the valley (where now the Forum is located). There, recent spring rains had caused flooding, the ground was hazardous and muddy, and many became bogged down and trapped – among them a

Sabine cavalryman, Mettius Curtius, who was forced to abandon his horse in the quagmire (and who, some said, thus gave his name to the Forum's Lacus Curtius, the 'Curtian Lake').

The Romans retreated towards the Palatine, until Romulus, concussed from a head wound and distressed to see his dream of a new city evaporate, raised his hands to heaven and prayed to Jupiter to come to his assistance. When the Romans heard his words, they stood their ground with greater resilience. Now the battle hung in the balance. The Sabines faltered. Then, as casualties mounted something altogether unexpected happened: into the valley rushed the abducted Sabine women, many carrying newborn babies.

As the warring sides looked on in wonder, the women forced themselves between the fighters, and demanded order. Then one, Hersilia, who had seen her husband killed, made a remarkable speech. Yes, their kidnap had been shameful, but they were now happily married, and many had children in whom Roman and Sabine blood was intermingled – and they would be the victims if the war continued. At these words, so noble in their simplicity, the armies were shamed into silence. Romulus and Tatius stepped forward and agreed to make peace and unite their nations, with both men ruling jointly (like later Roman consuls). As for Hersilia the peacemaker, Romulus took her as his wife and queen, building a temple to Jupiter Stator (Jupiter the Stayer) in the Forum. It was believed to have survived until the great fire in AD 64 (and in it Cicero delivered the first of his famous speeches against Catiline).

Head of the World

Two and a half centuries after Romulus, under Rome's last king, Tarquin the Proud, the Capitol truly came into its own. Previously its summits had been home to minor shrines and temples, many of which (it was said) were the work of Titus Tatius, who had previously vowed to build them during his brief capture of the hill. When Tarquin returned to Rome, however, victorious in war over his recalcitrant Latin neighbours, he dismantled many of these buildings and removed tombs (including Tarpeia's) from the southern summit in order to construct a magnificent new temple to Jupiter Optimus Maximus.

So that the ground be cleared propitiously, augurs prayed for favourable signs. While all other gods sent omens showing their willingness, one declined to move. He was Terminus, guardian of boundaries and ownership, and his refusal sparked great excitement. For the augurs interpreted it as showing his commitment to keep Rome secure – and they commanded that his shrine be left exactly where it was, incorporated into the new temple, with an opening in the roof above to let Terminus see the sky.

A second sign was equally auspicious. Workmen digging foundations unearthed a human head, its features perfectly intact. Now no-one was in any doubt: here was proof, if proof were needed, that Rome would be head of a great empire. And from the Latin *caput* ('head') they renamed the hill Capitoline. In time Rome herself was known as *Caput Mundi*, 'Head of the World'. In fact the temple was dedicated to three gods, the Capitoline Triad: Jupiter, his daughter Minerva and his wife Juno.

Saved by Geese

It was Juno who saved the Capitol during one of the most dangerous episodes in Rome's history. In the early fourth century BC a Gaulish army led by the formidable Brennus swept from the Alps into Italy. At the Battle of the River Allia (about 18 km or 11 miles north of the city) they were victorious, and, when the Roman army fled to nearby Veii, the Gauls marched on Rome. They found it almost deserted. Only the Capitol was garrisoned, for here the able-bodied had barricaded themselves behind high walls with their wives and children.

As their city burned, the Romans settled down for a long siege. Yet even now it seemed their faith might save them. Gaius Fabius Dorsuo was particularly god-fearing. His family was charged with making annual sacrifice on the Quirinal Hill, and he was determined not to shirk his duty. So he made his way down from the Capitol and through the threatening Gaulish ranks, performed the rites and returned unharmed, his piety his protection. It was the sort of story Romans loved, proof that, for righteous men like them, nothing is impossible.

Soon afterwards, a messenger arrived from Veii. He had floated down the Tiber on a barrel and scaled the Capitoline cliffs unseen, his mission to persuade the senators to recall their general Camillus from exile in Ardea, and appoint him their supreme commander. The senators agreed, but, before Camillus could help them, their situation deteriorated further. One starlit night the Gauls began silently to pick their way up the southwest rock face, nearing the top so stealthily that not even guard dogs heard them. The sacred geese in Juno's temple had keener hearing. Alert, they flapped their wings and cackled so raucously that they awoke the commandant, Marcus Manlius, who roused the garrison. Racing to the cliff edge, they dislodged the Gauls before they swarmed onto the Capitol, shoving them off the rock to plunge into the darkness. The threat was averted. The guard who had failed to raise the alarm was flung from the Tarpeian Rock, and for centuries Romans observed an annual festival in which geese, adorned in gold and purple trinkets, were carried in parade throughout the grateful city accompanied by crucified but still-living dogs.

As days dragged on, however, supplies ran out, and at last the Capitol surrendered. Brennus set terms – a thousand pounds in weight of gold – and when the Romans complained that his weights were heavier than standard, he made them heavier by throwing his sword on top. Even as he snarled '*vae victis*' ('woe to the conquered'), Brennus was disturbed by trumpets. Camillus had arrived. Drawing his sword from its scabbard, his riposte to Brennus was both pithy and memorable: 'The fatherland must be recovered with not gold but iron.' The Gauls fought bravely, but soon they were fleeing east to Gabii and defeat, while Camillus rode in triumph to the Capitol, his face painted red like the statue of Jupiter Optimus Maximus, at whose temple the procession ended.

A footnote shows how fluid Roman history (or myth) could be. At least one poet, Simylus (quoted by Plutarch), claimed that the Capitol was betrayed to Brennus by none other than Tarpeia, who was besotted by him. However:

> The countless tribes of Gauls did not bring her back in triumph to the banks of the Po. No, they threw shields from their warlike arms onto the shameless girl and made these ornaments her death.

The Capitoline Hill in History and Today

The Capitol is not a towering hill. Its higher peak, the northern Arx ('Citadel'), is only 46 m (150 ft) above sea level, but it is surrounded on almost every side by steep cliffs, and it was its relative impregnability that (initially at least) made it important. Beneath its eastern slopes, fourteenth-century BC dedications at Saturn's altar coincide with a Bronze Age settlement to the south. In the ninth to eighth centuries a village sprang up on the saddle of the Capitol, the area 'between two groves' subsequently known as 'Asylum' (now the piazza del Campidoglio), where Romulus offered safe haven.

The southern peak, the Capitolium itself, was most sacred. Here Tarquinius Priscus began, Tarquin the Proud completed and one of the first consuls, Horatius, consecrated the Temple of Jupiter Optimus Maximus, with three *cellae* (inner chambers), each allocated to one of the Capitoline Triad. The central chamber, dedicated to Jupiter, contained a terracotta statue of the god wielding a thunderbolt and wearing a tunic and gold-embroidered purple toga, while those on the right and left were dedicated to Minerva and Juno respectively. This was the heart of Roman state religion, where for centuries the Sibylline Books were housed in a stone chest, and where generals (their faces painted red like that of Jupiter's statue) dedicated spoils of wars at the climax of their triumphs.

Other temples, too, adorned the hill, including that of Jupiter Feretrius (traditionally founded by Romulus), which also played a role in victory celebrations, the Temple of Veiovis (a primitive god of death and reincarnation) near the Asylum, and the Temple of Juno Moneta ('Warner') on the Arx, dedicated in 344 BC, its site previously occupied by the house of Marcus Manlius, who repulsed the Gauls in 390. One of Rome's nearby mints became known by association as *moneta*, the source of the words 'money' and 'mint'. Other non-religious buildings stood on the Capitol. In 78 BC Sulla had the sprawling Tabularium, civil service offices, constructed east of the Asylum.

The Capitol witnessed many great moments in Roman history. As well as attacks, consecrations and triumphal processions already mentioned, the revolutionary Tribune, Tiberius Gracchus, was killed near the Temple of Jupiter in 133 BC; fire swept the hill in 83, destroying many buildings; in 44 Caesar's assassins barricaded themselves into the newly rebuilt Temple of Jupiter, which Caesar himself had approached humbly on his knees during his triumph six months earlier. In AD 69 Vespasian's supporters, taking refuge here, were involved in fighting with his rival Vitellius's partisans; and in AD 80 there was another devastating fire. For much of the imperial age, though, the renovated Capitol stood proud, its temples golden in the sun. The fourth-century Ammianus Marcellinus lauded them as 'towering high... surpassing all earthly things even as the earthly is surpassed by the divine', adding that 'with them esteemed Rome elevates herself to eternity – there is no sight more impressive in the entire world'. It was the Christian emperor Theodosius I who sounded their death knell. His general Stilicho removed gold plates from temple doors, and not long afterwards Goths and Vandals plundered what still remained one of the wonders of the Roman world.

In later centuries the temples crumbled. In 882 the Church of St Mary (later called Santa Maria in Ara Coeli, 'Altar of Heaven') was built where the Sibyl was said to have prophesied to Augustus Christ's coming, saying 'behold the altar of God's first born'. By the twelfth century, the pastureland for goats, the Capitol, was known as Monte Caprino, but in 1143 a popular revolt against the depredations of popes and nobles saw the Roman people meeting on its summit to re-establish a Senate (whose number the Pope subsequently managed to reduce to one). In the sixteenth century Michelangelo redesigned the piazza del Campidoglio along with surrounding palaces, the Palazzo dei Conservatori ('Magistrates' Palace', on the site of the Temple of Jupiter Optimus Maximus) and the Palazzo Senatorio (on the Asylum, above the Tabularium). The Palazzo Nuovo on the Arx, completed in 1654, was designed deliberately to mirror the Palazzo dei Conservatori. To this sublime perfection was added the late nineteenth-/early twentieth-century Altar of the Fatherland (the Victor Emanuel II Memorial). Today it is difficult to imagine the glories of the ancient Capitol, but fortunately for literature and history this was not always so. In his memoirs Edward Gibbon recalled:

> It was at Rome, on the 15th October, 1764, as I sat musing amidst the ruins of the Capitol, while the bare-footed friars were singing Vespers in the Temple of Jupiter, that the idea of writing the decline and fall of the city first started to my mind.

THE CAPITOL Some Important Dates and Remains

C14th BC	Habitation south of the Capitol; dedications near altar of Saturn.
C9th–8th BC	Iron Age village in Asylum area.
? C8th BC	Dedication of Temple of Jupiter Feretrius.
early C6th BC	Tarquinius Priscus begins Temple of Jupiter Optimus Maximus.
509 BC	Tarquin the Proud completes temple; subsequently dedicated by Horatius.
390 BC	Gauls attack Capitol.
344 BC	Temple of Juno Moneta dedicated.
133 BC	Tiberius Gracchus assassinated near Temple of Jupiter.
83 BC	Fire destroys much of Capitol.
45 BC	Caesar approaches Temple of Jupiter on his knees during triumph.
44 BC	Caesar's assassins take refuge in Temple of Jupiter.
AD 69	Fighting between supporters of Vespasian and Vitellius.
AD 80	Fire destroys much of Capitol.
AD 393	Theodosius I bans pagan religions; Stilicho removes gold from temple doors.
AD 410	Alaric sacks Rome.
AD 455	Vandals sack Rome.
AD 882	Church of St Mary (Santa Maria in Ara Coeli) on Capitol.
AD 1143	Senate declared on Capitol.
AD 1536	Michelangelo commissioned to redesign Campidoglio.
AD 1764	Edward Gibbon inspired to write *The Decline and Fall of the Roman Empire*.
AD 1911	Altar of the Fatherland inaugurated.

The easiest approach to the Capitol is by Michelangelo's Cordonata, to the right of which are grottoes where wolves and eagles, symbols of Rome, were caged in classical times. Two marble **statues of the Dioscuri** flank the top of the Cordonata, removed from the Ghetto in the sixteenth century. Here, on the balustrade are two marble sculptures, the first-century AD (so-called) Spoils of Marius, and statues of Constantine I and II. In the piazza del Campidoglio stands a replica of a gilt-bronze equestrian statue of Marcus Aurelius. Further on, in a garden north of Santa Maria in Ara Coeli, are foundations perhaps belonging to the Temple of Juno Moneta.

The jewel in the Capitol's crown are the **Capitoline Museums** housed in the Palazzo dei Conservatori and Palazzo Nuovo, linked by an underground passageway, which include remains of the **Temple of Veiovis** and part of the **Tabularium**, and afford fine **views of the Roman Forum**. Further views of Rome may be had from the terrace outside the museum's excellent café. Within the Palazzo dei Conservatori the **foundations of the Temple of Jupiter** take pride of place.

Of many objects on display, highlights include: remains of a colossal **statue of Constantine** in the museum's courtyard; the **Spinario** (a bronze statue of a boy removing a thorn from his foot); a bronze (fourth-century BC?) head of a man identified as **Lucius Junius Brutus**; a bronze statue of a **she-wolf** (whose date is controversial – anything from the fifth century BC to the fourteenth century AD) suckling a sickly sweet Romulus and Remus (added in 1471); the original of **Marcus Aurelius's equestrian statue**, whose copy stands in the piazza; the so-called **Capitoline Venus**; **centaurs** from Hadrian's Villa at Tivoli; and the impressive **Dying Gaul**, a copy of a third-century BC Pergamene bronze statue, which inspired Lord Byron.

• •

CHAPTER 11
CAMPUS MARTIUS:
FIELD OF MARS, SHRINE OF HEROES

At night in dreams I hold you fast. I follow where you run – across the Campus Martius and down, cruel lover, to the seething Tiber.

Horace, *Odes*, 4.1, 37–40

Largo di Torre Argentina is no ordinary Roman square. Yes, there are elegant buildings flanking it, façades delicately painted in palettes of pale cream and terracotta, and there is even a fine theatre, Teatro Argentina, where Rossini premiered his *Barber of Seville*. Although here, as everywhere in Rome, impatient traffic grinds aggressive gears at changing lights, and bi-tone shrieks of sirens herald frantic flows of yet more fleets of ambulances and police cars, somehow in the square itself life moves at a hushed and altogether slower pace. For down there, 6 m (20 ft) below the modern streets, is an archaeological treasure trove: remains of four temples dating from the fourth to second centuries BC, as well as baths and colonnades and part of Pompey's theatre.

It is also a cat sanctuary, whose inhabitants slink lazily across ancient pavements or stretch on worn-down temple steps, or wash luxuriantly as they recline amid tall grasses and (with half an eye) watch passing butterflies. What do they care for the umbrella pines (except that they give shade), or for the forest of tall columns (as brown and gnarled as tree trunks) that enclose the ruined shrines? For them this is a place of refuge, where injuries can be treated and food enjoyed, while in a warm, secluded room abandoned strays can sleep in safety, unaware that just a leap away (in another warm, secluded room, whose walls can still be seen) on the Ides of March in Rome's Year 710, Caesar, the most powerful man in all the world, stabbed by a cabal of rival senators, bled out his life and so became divine.

Mars and Venus

The time and place of Caesar's death were fitting: he was, after all, Rome's greatest general, and both the Campus Martius and the month of March were named from Rome's war-god, Mars. Not that he was always a war-god. In all probability Mars (whose full Sabine name was Mamers or Mavers) was originally a nature deity, a country Lar, sometimes identified as Silvanus, spirit of the fields and forests, who protected crops and flocks and boundaries, and by extension guarded cities. He was also a god of prophecy: at his oracle at Reate (modern Rieti), he told the future through a woodpecker. In Rome Mars was one of an ancient triad, in which he and Quirinus were second only to Jupiter; all were served by powerful priests, the *flamines maiores*. (Indeed, Mars and Quirinus were thought by some to be the same.)

Romans considered Mars to be their ancestor, father of Romulus and Remus by the Alban priestess, Rhea Silvia. Since Romulus was ultimately descended from Venus's son, Aeneas, too, this meant that Romans had two divine parents, whom mythology had bound since time immemorial.

On a Pompeian fresco Venus reclines in
the arms of Mars, while cupids play
with the war god's weaponry.

The tale appeared as early as Homer's *Odyssey*, and was picked up with gusto
by Roman poets such as Ovid.

Venus was married to the limping blacksmith, Vulcan, but this did not
stop her embarking on a love affair with the significantly more alluring Mars.
The two enjoyed secret night-time trysts, but they gradually became bolder,
enjoying long lazy afternoons in one another's arms. Which was how the
sun-god saw them, as he drove his chariot across the skies. He immediately
told Vulcan, who resolved to catch the lovers *in flagrante*. Unknown to Venus,
he arranged a bronze net above their marital bed, so fine that (in Ovid's
words) 'not even the most delicate threads of a spider's web hanging from
the rafters could surpass his airy web', and so sophisticated that 'it moulded

to the lightest touch and slightest movement'. Then he announced that he was going away for a few days to his favourite island, Lemnos.

Venus's reaction was predictable: she immediately invited Mars to join her. So passionate was their lovemaking that they did not notice the net descend and wrap around them until they were caught, immobile, in its coils. Now Vulcan returned, and, opening the ivory doors, summoned the other gods to see his wife's disgrace. The outcome was not entirely as he wished. Many declared they were so captivated by her beauty that they would gladly suffer such humiliation, if only they could find themselves in Mars's position. 'The gods laughed', Ovid concludes, 'and for a long time it was the best-known tale in heaven.'

Anna Perenna

The goddess Anna Perenna tricked Mars, too, in an event celebrated in an annual festival on the Ides of March held near the Largo di Torre Argentina by the Tiber's banks at the via Flaminia's first milestone. Here men and women erected huts or made crude tents from poles draped with togas before indulging in heavy drinking, praying to live for as many years as the cups of wine that they drank. In his *Fasti*, Ovid records how, as merry-making continued:

> They sing whatever show-tunes they have learnt, easily moving arms to match the lyrics, and, setting wine cups aside, they form rough chorus lines, your stylish girl-friend dancing with her hair undone.

Even Romans could not agree who Anna Perenna was. Some said she was an old woman originally from Bovillae, a Latin town about 18 km (11 miles) southeast of Rome along the Appian Way. When the plebs downed tools in 494 BC and took themselves off (some said) to the Aventine Hill, Anna helped maintain their resistance against the Senate. Every morning, 'her white hair bound in a headband, she would bake country pancakes with tremulous hands' and distribute them, still warm, among striking workers. When the dispute ended, the people expressed their gratitude to Anna by erecting a statue in her honour, while in time the gods made her immortal.

Enter Mars. He lusted after the virgin Minerva, and sought Anna's aid to seduce her. At last Anna assured Mars that Minerva was willing. With swaggering anticipation, the god decked out his love nest, and, when the veiled bride was brought in, he took her in his arms and kissed her passionately.

He soon realized he had been duped – the bride was old Anna herself. When news got out, Mars was humiliated, Venus delighted, and Anna laughed with glee – which was why, Romans said, they told ribald jokes and sang licentious songs at her festival.

Another, even more intriguing, version of Anna's biography maintains that she was none other than Queen Dido's sister. Ovid provides a sequel to the Carthaginian queen's suicide, in which the spurned Numidian King Iarbas, seizing the moment, captured her grieving city. As its population scattered, Anna commandeered a ship and sailed to Malta, whose peace-loving king, Battus, offered her asylum. Two years later, Anna's scheming brother, Pygmalion of Tyre, still smarting at Dido's trickery, launched a fleet to kidnap her and return her to Phoenicia. Poor nervous Battus could not countenance a war. So Anna again set sail, and eluding her brother's sentinels, tacked north for Sicily. A mighty storm blew up, and the ship was blown off course until at last the timbers fell apart and Anna and her crew were washed ashore in Latium.

Walking one day barefoot along the beach beside Lavinium, Aeneas met her, half-drowned. Almost unable to believe his eyes, he reassured her: he meant no harm; he would repay the hospitality that she and Dido once showed him. So he brought her home and introduced her to his wife. Lavinia appeared to welcome Anna, but she was in fact consumed by jealousy and plotted murder. As Anna slept, Dido's ghost came to her bed and warned her of impending peril. In terror the poor princess fled 'as a doe flees when she hears the howl of wolves', and next morning, apart from footprints in the mud, there was no trace of Anna – until by the banks of the River Numicus, the searchers heard her voice: 'I am a nymph of tranquil Numicus, and, concealed in the perennial river, I am known now as Anna Perenna.'

Never one to pass up an alternative, Ovid records other theories about Anna's identity: she was the moon goddess, worshipped 'because she fills the year with months'; she was Rome's equivalent of Themis, Greek goddess of law and order; she was Io, the Argive princess, transformed into a cow by Juno (jealous of Jupiter's desire), who wandered the earth until, restored to human form in Egypt, she was worshipped as Isis. Others said that she was so primeval that she had once nursed Jupiter.

Anna's populist credentials, not to mention her connection with Mars, made her the ideal candidate for a festival of merrymaking on the Campus Martius. Not only were nearby voting pens used in elections where (in theory) the people could wield power, the Field of Mars also saw the culmination of the reigns of three powerful rulers in circumstances that helped shape Rome's destiny.

Romulus's Apotheosis

Once the Campus Martius was quite literally fields, a broad area of flat land prone to flooding bounded by the Capitol to the east, the Quirinal and Pincian Hills to the north and a wide loop of the Tiber to the south and west. In Romulus's day it contained a shallow lake, the Palus Caprae ('Goat's Marsh'), where the Pantheon now stands. Here, having defeated Veii, ravaged her fields and then made peace, as Romulus addressed his triumphant troops, praising their valour and outlining Rome's future glory, darkness engulfed the sun, thunder boomed and rain lashed down, while thick fog shrouded the plain – and when it cleared Romulus had vanished.

The soldiers were first bewildered, then distraught, but gradually a remarkable realization dawned: the city's founder, fifty-eight years old and in the thirty-fourth year of his reign, had been raised to heaven and made a god. Livy records how a few days later this truth was confirmed when Proculus Julius (a member of the powerful Julii clan from Alba Longa) reported:

> At dawn this morning, Romulus, the city's father, suddenly came down from heaven and appeared before me. Trembling and confused, I stood before him reverentially, praying that it might not be impious to look him in the face. And he said: 'Go, tell it to the Romans that it is the gods' will that my Rome should be the head of all the world. So let them hone their military skills, and know, and teach their children that no force on earth can withstand Rome's might.'

Julius had good reason to report Romulus's goodwill, for there were ugly rumours that he had, in fact, been killed in the nearby Temple of Vulcan by disaffected senators, who subsequently dismembered his body, removed the pieces hidden in the folds of their togas, and buried them at home. Now, however, the deified Romulus announced that henceforth he should be worshipped as the god Quirinus (after whom Romans were occasionally called Quirites).

In fact, Quirinus was originally a Sabine god, with a sanctuary on Rome's Quirinal Hill, whose cult only later became associated with Romulus. Like Mars, Quirinus combined interests in war and agriculture. The myth of his dismemberment and burial is interpreted as representing early fertility rituals, though in the first century BC the story of Romulus's assassination at the hands of senators and subsequent deification provided neat parallels in the aftermath of Julius Caesar's death.

The Tarquins' Last Harvest

It was after the expulsion of Tarquin the Proud, Rome's last king, that the Campus Martius was dedicated to Mars. Previously, it had belonged to the royal estate, but now to mark a new era it was presented to the public. Tarquin's flight from Rome coincided with the start of harvest. On Mars's Fields rich crops of wheat stood dry beneath the sun. Although they might have fed the urban poor, it was decreed that – now that the area was sacred to Mars – it would be sacrilege for any mortal to consume them. Instead a workforce was despatched with scythes and baskets, and instructions to destroy the harvest.

Once they had cut the corn they carried groaning panniers to the river bank, and threw them into the water. The Tiber was sluggish and shallow, and the baskets got stuck on mud-banks in the middle of the stream. As time went on, more mud and debris clustered round them, and from the Tarquins' last harvest there arose Tiber Island (Isola Tibertina). 'Later I believe', writes Livy, 'work raised and strengthened it, so that it might be sufficiently high above the water and strong enough to bear the weight of temples and porticoes.'

Caesar's Apotheosis

In the first century BC bridges were constructed to link Tiber Island to the mainland, but even as the second (the western Pons Cestius) was being completed, violence on the Field of Mars transformed Rome's future in an act of such significance that, although firmly rooted in fact, it quickly accrued an aura of mythology. It happened on the day of Anna Perenna's festival, the Ides of March, and – as with Romulus's assassination – hostile senators were implicated (this time indisputably). By 44 BC the Field of Mars was relatively built up, with temples, hippodromes and other public buildings, as well as private tombs sprawling west from the ancient city. Indeed it was in the *curia* ('meeting room') of his rival Pompey's theatre complex that perhaps sixty senators, nervous that he intended to end the Republican constitution, surrounded Julius Caesar and repeatedly stabbed him to death.

Within two generations this sordid reality was remoulded to form part of the ongoing story of Rome's destiny. In *Metamorphoses*, Ovid tells how the gods needed Caesar to be deified, so that his successor (and adopted heir) Augustus might become the 'son of god'. When she learns of the conspiracy to kill him, Venus, 'Aeneas's golden mother', begs each god in turn to pity her, reminding them how she was compelled to watch 'my son Aeneas forced into endless wanderings, storm-wracked, entering the silent world

Julius Caesar, the ruthless general and canny politician, who traced his ancestry to Venus, was assassinated in the Campus Martius in 44 BC.

of shadows, doing battle against Turnus', adding: 'Do you see those lawless blades being sharpened? Don't let them strike, I beg you!' Meanwhile, the world is filled with omens, as it was in the lead-up to Romulus's apotheosis:

> They say that weapons were heard clashing amid black clouds, and terrifying trumpet calls and horns foretold the profanity from heaven. The sun's face darkened, too, and gave a lurid light across the worried earth.

Blood rains down and statues weep, the dead walk, dogs bay mournfully, while augury predicts disaster. But although she tries to save Caesar by protecting him in a veil of mist (as she once saved Aeneas at Troy), Venus is thwarted by Jupiter himself. The assassination is essential, he assures her, for it will result in the rule of Augustus under whom all earth and sea will bow to Rome, and peace will reign throughout the world. With which Jupiter instructs Venus to go down to the Campus Martius and free

Caesar's murdered soul. Ovid's description is the epitome of masterful (if hyperbolic) myth-making, drawing on past literary images such as that of Virgil's comet at Troy:

> Scarcely had Jupiter spoken than Venus, nurturing goddess, stood where the Senate was convened, though invisible to all, and took her Caesar's newly liberated soul up from his body, not letting it dissolve into the air, and bore it to the heavenly stars. As she held it, she felt it shine and catch alight, and she let it go free from her breast. The soul soared higher than the moon, and, dragging a long fiery tail, it shimmered like a star.

Becoming Gods on Mars's Field

Caesar's body was burnt in the Forum, but many of his successors were honoured with an elaborate cremation and apotheosis ceremony on the Campus Martius, site of the Mausoleum of Augustus and his family. The early third-century AD Herodian describes such an event in detail. After the emperor was buried with full honours, his wax effigy was laid on a large ivory couch draped with cloth of gold and placed in the portico of his palace on the Palatine. For seven days senators sat, dressed in black, drawn up in rows on the couch's left, while noble women dressed in white sat on the right, and doctors attended the effigy, proclaiming its worsening health. Then, when it was deemed dead, young aristocrats carried the couch along the Sacred Way into the Forum, where it was exhibited on a high platform to the accompaniment of mournful hymns.

Finally it was carried to a broad piazza in the Campus Martius, where a pyramidal pyre stood four storeys high, filled with kindling, incense and fragrant perfumes, the fruits of empire, and hung outside with sumptuous fabrics woven with gold thread, as well as gold and ivory reliefs. When all were assembled, riders circled the pyre – and chariots, too, their drivers wearing state robes and masks with the likenesses of Rome's most famous generals and emperors – before blazing torches were thrown on to the pyre from each of its four sides. As flames shot through the blazing edifice a trapdoor at the very top was opened, and an eagle set free to soar above the Field of Mars, the River Tiber and all Rome, far from the palls of black smoke that billowed into the clear air. The eagle 'is believed' (Herodian writes) 'to bear the emperor's soul from earth to heaven, and from that moment he is worshipped with the other gods'.

The Campus Martius in History and Today

The early Campus Martius was a floodplain, bounded on two sides by a loop in the Tiber and on the others by Rome's hills, with the swampy Palus Caprae at its centre. Under Rome's kings, much was royal agricultural land, but with Tarquin the Proud's expulsion in 509 BC it was reclaimed for the public, and dedicated to Mars (god of both military victory and fertility) for use as pasture and parade ground. Gradually public buildings (temporary then permanent) and tombs of prominent citizens – notably Augustus – began to encroach. In the Republic's final years, even tenement blocks sprang up. Occasionally ravaged by fire, the Campus Martius's buildings were invariably restored until Christianity put an end to temples, and floods and barbarian incursions saw baths and circuses ruined or destroyed. In the late Middle Ages and Renaissance the area became repopulated, with many streets and piazzas sharing the layout of earlier buildings.

The westernmost end of the Campus Martius, where the Tiber bends, was home to a sanctuary of Dis Pater and Proserpina, two underworld gods (worshipped at a buried altar ceremonially unearthed for use). It assumed new significance as the site of Secular Games (*Ludi Saeculares*), said to date back to Tarquin's expulsion. Legend attributed the Games' origin to divine instruction given to a Sabine man, Valesius: seeking to cure his children's sickness, he was told to give them water warmed at Tarentum; he naturally assumed the oracle meant Tarentum in South Italy, but, sailing downriver, he stopped briefly at the Campus Martius, to boil water for his ailing offspring; they were cured immediately, and in a dream he learned of both the buried altar and the gods who must be worshipped there. Under the Republic the Secular Games (whose theme was cleansing and renewal) were held roughly every century, but Augustus (following the Sibylline Books) decreed their celebration every 110 years. His Games of 17 BC saw both pomp and propaganda, including nocturnal sacrifices, theatrical productions, wild animal hunts, chariot racing and a hymn commissioned from the court poet, Horace.

The Tarentum was the starting point for another Roman institution: the annual race to identify the October Horse. On the fifteenth day of October, the month marking the end of the agricultural and campaigning season, two-horse chariots raced in honour of Mars, with the right-hand horse of the victorious pair being sacrificed to the god. At once its tail was severed and carried to the Forum, where the still-fresh blood was sprinkled at the Regia; meanwhile two teams of plebeians from Sacra Via and Subura fought to possess the head. Other games and races were held in the Circus Flaminius, an area first designated in 220 BC.

Under the Republic the Campus Martius played an increasing part in Rome's public life: armies assembled here before marching to war, victorious generals camped here before celebrating triumphs, and from 435 BC the Villa Publica (literally 'Public House', but in fact an open square containing a municipal building) was the seat of censors, whose job was to count and account for the population of both city and empire. Nearby was another enclosure associated with public life: the Ovile (literally 'sheep pen'), where voters elected annual officials, replaced by the marble Saepta Julia, begun by Julius Caesar, dedicated by Agrippa in 26 BC, and later the site (variously) of gladiatorial games and an antique market.

On the Campus Martius three other types of public buildings – baths, stone amphitheatres and permanent stone theatres – first appeared in Rome. Pompey's theatre, one of three built in the Campus Martius in the first century BC, was begun in 61 and completed less than ten years later. A magnificent complex, its auditorium was crowned with a temple to Venus Victrix (Venus of Victory), while a huge portico stretching behind the stage (with Greek statues and a garden adorned with plane trees and fountains) included the meeting room where Caesar was assassinated. In 29 BC Statilius Taurus built Rome's first stone amphitheatre on the site of the present Palazzo Cenci, while baths were built nearby by Augustus's lieutenant, Agrippa, complete with aqueduct and large artificial pool.

Agrippa was responsible, too, for the first incarnation of the Campus Martius's most stunning surviving temple, the Pantheon, and, although it was rebuilt in its present form by Hadrian, the inscription on its architrave still acknowledges Agrippa's role. Dedicated to the Olympian gods and members of the imperial family, its *pièce de résistance* is its dome. With a diameter of nearly 46 m (150 ft), it remains the widest solid-construction dome ever created, half a perfect sphere, whose base, if whole, would graze the temple floor. It owes its survival to the Pantheon's conversion into the Church of Santa Maria ad Martyres. The bronze ceiling of its porch was less fortunate. It was removed and melted down for Bernini's baldacchino above the great altar of St Peter's.

Writing late in Augustus's reign, Strabo furnishes a vivid description of the ancient Campus Martius:

> Here nature is enhanced by art. The plain is wide, easily allowing for chariot races and other equestrian activities, while the common people can exercise with balls and discuses or wrestling. The works of man with which it is adorned, the grass that grows green all year round, the crests of hills beyond the river that stretch down to the

banks: all afford such a theatrical backdrop that one is loath to tear one's gaze away. Close by is another open area with a circular portico, and sacred groves, three theatres, an amphitheatre and many splendid temples all near one another – so magnificent that the rest of Rome seems almost like an afterthought. Since they consider it so very sacred, the Romans have erected memorials here to outstanding men and women. The most noteworthy is the Mausoleum, a high mound set on a foundation of white marble

· ·

CAMPUS MARTIUS Some Important Dates and Remains

509 BC	Campus Martius claimed for the Roman people.
435 BC	Villa Publica delineated.
431 BC	Temple of Apollo built west of the Capitol.
220 BC	Circus Flaminius constructed in southeast of Campus Martius.
C3rd BC	Temples C and A in Largo di Torre Argentina.
C2nd BC	Further temples (including Temples D and B in Largo di Torre Argentina and others to Hercules and the Muses, Juno Regina and Diana).
55 BC	Theatre of Pompey inaugurated.
44 BC	Caesar assassinated and cremated.
29 BC	Rome's first stone amphitheatre. Mausoleum of Augustus begun.
27 BC	Agrippa's Pantheon begun (dedicated in 25 BC).
25–19 BC	Baths of Agrippa and Aqua Virgo aqueduct built.
23 BC	Marcellus (Augustus's heir) buried in Mausoleum of Augustus.
17 BC	Theatre of Marcellus inaugurated. Augustus celebrates Secular Games.
13 BC	Theatre of Balbus inaugurated.
9 BC	Ara Pacis Augustae dedicated.
AD 80	Domitian restores many buildings destroyed by fire; constructs stadium, odeon and several new temples.
AD 126	Hadrian's Pantheon dedicated.
AD 145	Temple of Hadrian dedicated.
? AD 180	Column of Marcus Aurelius begun.

near the river, covered to its height in evergreen trees. At its top is a bronze statue of Augustus Caesar, and inside are his remains as well as those of his family and closest friends. Behind is a vast sacred grove with beautiful walkways. In the centre of the Campus Martius is the place where Augustus was cremated surrounded by two walls, one of marble, the other of iron, and planted inside with poplar trees.

• •

AD 276   Campus Martius enclosed within Aurelian Walls.
AD 410   Mausoleum of Augustus desecrated by Alaric.
AD 609   Pantheon converted into Church of Santa Maria ad Martyres.
AD 1581   Montaigne laments haphazard building work.
AD 1938   Ara Pacis Augustae moved and reassembled.

Although the Campus Martius's roughly 243 ha (600 acres) have been built upon comprehensively since medieval times, much of its classical layout survives: for example, the piazza Navona describes the shape of Domitian's stadium dedicated in AD 86. Indeed, the area contains such a cornucopia of often hidden gems that not all can be covered here, and at least a day should be devoted to a leisurely stroll amid its treasures.

Southwest of the Capitol at the eastern limits of the Field of Mars, impressive remains of the first-century BC **Theatre of Marcellus**, planned by Julius Caesar and completed by Augustus, are built into a sixteenth-century palazzo. Nearby stand three columns of the **Temple of Apollo Medicus** dedicated in 431 BC and rebuilt four centuries later. A short distance northwest is **Largo di Torre Argentina** with its complex of four Republican temples (accessible to the public after 2021): 'Temple A' believed to be the **Temple of Juturna**; 'B', a rotunda, the **Temple of Fortuna**; and 'C' the **Temple of Feronia**, a nature goddess, who presided over the rights of the lower classes, much loved by Rome's plebeians. Abutting the temples' tufa pavement are foundations of the room attached to the **Theatre of Pompey**, in which Caesar was assassinated. To the west the curve of the piazza di Grotta Pinta preserves the shape of the theatre's auditorium. Since 1994 Largo di Torre Argentina has housed a cat sanctuary.

Due north is the breathtaking **Pantheon** (literally 'Temple of All Gods'), built by Hadrian, dedicated in AD 126, subsequently converted into the

Church of Santa Maria ad Martyres, and boasting the world's largest unreinforced concrete dome (whose central *oculus*, open to the sky, still admits rain and snow). To the northeast the converted **Temple of Hadrian** (with impressive columns) houses the Chamber of Commerce. Nearby is the piazza Colonna, whose **Column of Marcus Aurelius** carries scenes of the emperor at war.

Further north near the Tiber is the huge circular **Mausoleum of Augustus** and his family. For years this important structure (once topped with a grove of trees, and used variously throughout history as fortress, cockpit for animal-baiting and theatre-cum-concert hall) was neglected. Now being restored, it will open to the public. Housed in a glass-and-travertine cube overlooking the Mausoleum is the **Ara Pacis Augustae** ('Altar of Augustan Peace'), one of the most important structures to survive from Augustan Rome. Originally sited further south (near San Lorenzo in Lucina on the via del Corso), it was discovered piecemeal over four centuries and reconstructed in 1938. Exquisite sculptures combine mythological scenes (including of Aeneas, Romulus and Remus) with a procession of leading Romans (Augustus himself is mutilated). Supposedly the shadow of the **Montecitorio Obelisk** (now in the **piazza di Montecitorio**), the gnomon of a large sundial, was designed deliberately to fall on the Ara Pacis on Augustus's birthday (23 September). Southwest from the altar across the Tiber is the **Mausoleum of Hadrian** (subsequently converted into the Castel Sant'Angelo).

Within the Campus Martius several fine museums hold Roman or Etruscan collections, notably the **Museo Baracco** and **Palazzo Altemps**, among whose treasures are the **Ludovisi Throne** (with carved scenes of Venus's birth flanked by a chaste matron and a naked flute girl), a marble **Gaul committing suicide** (a first-century BC replica of a Greek bronze) and a fine third-century AD **sarcophagus** with battle scenes.

Further north beyond the Borghese Gardens, the **Museo Nazionale Etrusco di Villa Giulia** is a must for anyone interested in Etruscan and early Roman history or mythology. Its highlights include the sixth-century BC **Sarcofago degli Sposi** from Cerveteri with exquisitely sculpted husband and wife, the bronze **Cista Ficorini** from Praeneste (modern Palestrina), showing fine representations of the Argonaut myth, and sixth-century BC **terracotta statues of Hercules** and **Apollo** from Veii (probably the work of Etruscan master sculptor, Vulca).

• •

CHAPTER 12
THE AVENTINE HILL:
POWER TO THE PEOPLE

It is agreed that treetops trembled on the Aventine, and the
earth sank under Jupiter's great weight. The king's heart pounds;
his blood drains from his body; and his shaggy hair bristles.

Ovid, *Fasti*, 329–32

On this terrace outside the fifth-century AD Church of Santa Sabina, its wooden doors still ornate with scenes from the two Testaments, we may be forgiven for lingering to gaze on Rome in wonder. The Aventine falls steeply to the Tiber ribboning its way across the urban valley, while far off in an aureole of haze St Peter's dome trembles like a vision in a dream. Heat rises. Trees give shade. If only this were all there was to see!

Now, though, we must turn and walk through shaded residential streets, past cars abandoned randomly on pavements, with scooters squeezed improbably between, balconies that trail with flowers, and open windows from which music drifts, up to an unprepossessing square, where children's gaudy swings and chutes sit empty and unloved behind a tall iron fence. Today the only view is of the school and bright apartments that surround the square. Yet once from here the distant peaks of the blue Alban Hills were seen to stand clear on the far horizon. So it was to this place, now named in his memory, that Romulus's lesser twin once came to scour the skyline for an omen. And, if destiny had not decided otherwise, it was here that Remus might have trumped his brother to become the undisputed founder of the Roman state – here at piazza Remoria, here on the Aventine, hill of the underdog, hill of the city plebs, the people's Palatine.

Remus and Rome

From the Aventine Hill's southern summit Remus watched for the omen that would decide the site of early Rome. The Aventine was his preferred location. Near the river, easily protected, it was, he thought, ideal. Romulus, his twin, disagreed. The Palatine, he said, was better, which was why, some said, he chose to search the skies from there. Others, however, maintained that he, too, watched from the Aventine – on its northern summit, where later temples to Minerva and Diana would be built.

All agreed, though, that, from wherever they were looking, Remus saw six vultures before Romulus saw twelve – which led to further arguments. Did timing trump numbers or *vice versa*? Romulus won; he chose the Palatine; and the Aventine became thought of as its less successful neighbour. However, so associated was it with Remus, that when he was murdered shortly afterwards, he was buried on the Aventine at a site named ever after as Remoria.

Numa and the Nymph

In the valley between the Aventine and Caelian Hills was a grove sacred to the Camenae, water nymphs who breathed inspiration into men, Rome's equivalent of Greece's Muses. One was Egeria, and with her the city's second king, Numa Pompilius, enjoyed a close association.

A Sabine from nearby Cures, Numa was born the very day that Rome was founded. Now, thirty-eight years later, Rome was rudderless. The previous year, Romulus had ascended into heaven, since when powerful senators had taken it in turn to rule for five days each. The arrangement was not working. So, since Romulus was childless, they asked Numa (his colleague Titus Tatius's son-in-law) to accept the crown. Reluctantly he did.

Numa was a wise man. It was said he was a pupil of the Greek Pythagoras, who ran a school in Croton (Cortona) in southern Italy, though chronology shows this was impossible. While his relationship with Egeria was equally unlikely, it was well chronicled. Each evening he slipped off to her spring to consult and commune with her, and some even whispered that they were married. Indeed, so keen was Numa to flaunt his relationship with Egeria, that one morning he invited leading Romans to inspect his house. They found it poor and spartan. Yet when he summoned them to dine with him that evening they were amazed. According to Dionysius of Halicarnassus:

> When they arrived at the appointed hour, he showed them rich couches and tables groaning with many fine cups, and when they reclined to eat he set before them a banquet of such magnificence that it would be almost impossible for any man at that time to have prepared it so quickly. The Romans were staggered, and from then on were convinced that he was married to some goddess.

Others said that Numa invented the relationship to boost his kudos. However, most agreed that it was with Egeria's guidance that Numa taught his fellow citizens the best way to worship their gods, and how to live in peace and harmony – something that was unfamiliar to a nation founded on war. When he died, Egeria was disconsolate. She abandoned Rome in favour of Lake Nemi, where she lay down at the mountain's foot and wept so bitterly that Diana took pity on her and transformed her into an ever-flowing stream.

Numa Outwits Jupiter

Numa enjoyed an equally unconventional relationship with Jupiter – he was one of only a few mortals who tricked the god and got away with it.

Perched on a rock, the woodland deity
Faunus plays the panpipes on a fresco
from Pompeii's House of Jason.

For some time Rome had been plagued by drought, accompanied by such terrifying lightning storms that it was clear that the gods were displeased. So Numa consulted Egeria, who advised him to learn the ritual of expiation from two woodland deities: Picus and Faunus.

Neither would readily reveal the mysteries. Instead, when they came to drink deeply of a spring beneath the Aventine, and further slake their thirst with wine, Numa watched, concealed in a dark cave, until they fell asleep. Then he stole outside and shackled them. When they discovered their predicament, they demanded that Numa release them, but he refused, insisting that they first help stop the incessant salvoes of Jupiter's lightning bolts. They were not strong enough, the two gods groaned: only Jupiter had power over his weapons, but they swore that they could summon him, if Numa freed them.

As Picus and Faunus chanted dire incantations the air was torn by lightning, forests trembled and the very earth sank low as Jupiter descended from heaven to stand in awesome glory on the Aventine. 'If I have made pure offerings, and if I too am pure,' the trembling Numa begged him, 'grant an end to your thunderbolts!' To which Jupiter replied by demanding a sacrifice. 'A head!' he cried. 'Of an onion cut in my garden!' replied Numa. 'A man's!' the god added. 'I'll give you the hair!' retorted Numa. 'A life,' demanded Jupiter. And Numa agreed: 'I'll sacrifice a fish!'

Delighted by Numa's quick wit and refusal to make human sacrifice, Jupiter promised that, if the king made the necessary offerings, 'tomorrow I shall provide you with sure signs of empire'. So next morning, when frost still glistened on the ground, Numa summoned the Roman people, and, sitting on a maple throne, his head covered in a pure white shawl, he raised his hands and called on Jupiter to honour his promise. Three times thunder rolled. Then the god sent down his sign...

The Sacred Shield

As the last thunder echoed round the seven hills, the Romans saw, floating gently down from heaven, a shield shaped like a figure of eight; and as it touched the earth a disembodied voice proclaimed that, as long as it was kept safe, Rome would rule the world. It was a talisman as sacred as the Palladium that Aeneas had preserved from Troy. So cunning Numa commissioned (from Mamurius, his master-craftsman) eleven replicas, exact in every detail, which he ordered to be kept under close guard. Rome's fate lay in the shield, and now because no-one knew which one was the original, he reckoned that no-one would try to steal it. Throughout Rome's history the shields were kept safe, watched over by the Salii, twelve dancing priests of Mars.

Only on the first day of Mars's month (March) could the shields leave Mars's temple: then the Salii paraded, singing and dancing, through the streets, striking a rhythm on the shields with rods, praising gods (and, later, emperors) before returning to the temple for a lavish meal. The only deity not honoured in their hymn was Venus, goddess of peace and love.

Flora and Mars

Mars was associated with another Aventine nymph: Saturn's daughter, Flora, goddess of flowers and blossom, whose temple stood on the hill's lower slopes. Indeed, Mars owed his birth to her.

When Minerva sprang from Jupiter's head, Juno (another goddess with a temple on the Aventine) was jealous. Why, she grumbled, should her husband have a child on his own without her? And if *he* could manage it, surely she, his wife, should do the same. She was on her way to complain to all-encircling Ocean, when she stopped, already exhausted, at Flora's door. That evening, as the two conversed, Juno was expressing her determination to try every treatment possible to let her conceive, when something in Flora's reaction made her pause. Surely she knew a way! Three times Juno begged her to reveal the necessary treatment; three times Flora (fearful of Jupiter's reaction) demurred. Finally Juno swore a mighty oath never to reveal who helped her – and Flora, reassured, plucked a magic flower (so potent that one need only 'touch a heifer with it, even one that's barren, and she will conceive') and laid it on Juno's stomach – which was how, in time, in far-off Thrace, she gave birth to warlike Mars, and why (when Mars's son Romulus founded his new city) the god was determined that Flora should have her temple there.

Although an altar to Flora was said to have been set up by Romulus's co-ruler, Titus Tatius, her Aventine temple was not built until 238 BC. After years of drought and famine, priests consulted the Sibylline Books, which urged both its foundation and the establishment of games in her honour. Spanning late April and early May, these games marked a period of revelry and licence. Ovid's *Fasti* describe how 'brows are encircled with woven garlands, and fine tables heaped with roses. Drunk, the party-goer, his hair wreathed with linden bark, leaps in dance, possessed by wine's artistry, without a care. Drunk he sings at his lovely mistress's marble door, his hair dripping with flowers...' It was a time for animal hunts (but not of lions and other savage beasts – sensitive Flora found them much too frightening) and drama. Ovid gives an insight into these theatrical performances:

> Light drama's what she likes. She's not – believe me! – she is just *not* the kind of goddess who goes in for tragedies. And as for why a cast of prostitutes performs at these games, the reason's not hard to find. She's not one of the crabby kind; she's not pretentious either. She wants to open up her rites to a plebeian chorus; she wants to use the grace of youth when it is in flower.

In fact, it was not just naked prostitutes who took part in these shows. The games of AD 68 included an elephant that walked a tight-rope.

Pomona's Wooing

Pomona, too, another nature goddess, was connected with a temple on the Aventine. While Flora was the spirit of spring, Pomona's province was autumn's mellow fruitfulness. Skilled with secateurs, she pruned and shaped, grafted cuttings, irrigated trees and generally devoted her life to gardening. No other joy came close – especially not the joys of Venus. Mortals wooed her; Pans and satyrs chased her; even Silenus and Priapus pressed their suit. Pomona rejected all of them, shutting herself up in her walled orchard.

Two generations before Romulus, the Etruscan shape-shifting god of ripening fruits, Vertumnus, was so besotted that he determined to possess her. As he proclaims (in a poem by Propertius):

Now in Madrid's Museo Arqueológico Nacional,
a fecund Vertumnus carries his cornucopia
overflowing with fruit.

I can bend over my crook like a shepherd; I can cart baskets filled with roses through the dust. Why tell you of my greatest fame – that every gift the garden gives is in my hands? Dark cucumbers and swollen gourds and cabbages tied with narrow twine all mark me out. No meadow flower grows that is not placed on my brow, or languishes before me. And because my single form can con*vert* into many, in my native language I am called *Vert*umnus.

Now Vertumnus transformed himself into an old woman and, shuffling into Pomona's garden, where he enthusiastically praised her horticultural skills, he kissed her repeatedly 'in such a way' (writes Ovid) 'as no real old woman would'. Then, warning Pomona of the dangers of resisting Venus, he proceeded to extol the virtues of a young and handsome, faithful, constant gardener... Vertumnus. And further to emphasize his point, he told the tale of Anaxarete, a gorgeous Trojan princess, who was beloved by Iphis. Anaxarete was cold-hearted, and nothing he could do could sway her. At last he hanged himself. When the haughty maiden saw his body on its bier she stood transfixed, unmoving, as chill spread from her heart throughout her body and transformed her into stone. Alas for Vertumnus! Even such a cautionary tale made no impression on Pomona. So he threw off his disguise and revealed himself in all his glory as a young, potent man. Immediately Pomona fell in love with him.

By the first century BC Vertumnus was considered an ancient Roman god, whose maple-wood icon was as old as the city itself, and whose bronze statue had been crafted by none other than Numa's sculptor, Mamurius. In reality, however, he was introduced only in the third century. In 264 BC, when Etruscan Volsinii fell to Rome, the victors brought Vertumnus back to their city and built a temple in his honour on the Aventine, where they worshipped both him and his beloved Pomona.

Liber and Liberty

Where the Aventine began to rise from the swampy Murcia Valley, the site of the Circus Maximus, was a temple of even more profound significance. It was dedicated to the Aventine Triad, like Flora and Pomona rampant nature gods: Ceres, goddess of harvests, and her companions (originally her children) Liber and Libera.

For early Italians Liber was associated primarily with fructuous, sticky liquids – not least honey. In his *Fasti* Ovid tells how the god collected swarms of bees and shut them inside a hollow tree. So enthusiastic were his companions when they tasted the resulting honey, that they searched for more throughout the forest. One, Silenus, found a honeycomb inside a rotting elm tree. So that the bees might be off guard, he nonchalantly (and apparently accidentally) steered his donkey in its direction before greedily reaching up to steal the honey. All at once the bees streamed out and stung the old man all over, and as he fell his donkey kicked him hard. Soon all his sons, the satyrs, were standing round him laughing at his blustering indignation, while Liber applied healing mud to Silenus's swollen face.

Although the tale may have originated in Italy, Ovid sets it in the Thracian mountains, since, well before the early first century AD (when he was writing) Liber had become associated with the Greek Dionysus (aka Bacchus). He, too, presided over nature's fecundity, though his preferred liquid was wine. Even the gods' names seemed similar: both the Latin 'Liber' and one of Dionysus's cult titles, 'Eleuthereus', meant 'free' (or 'unfettered'). So the two fused into one, with Liber ceasing to be considered Ceres' son, and Libera becoming identified with Proserpina. At the same time, the crowds of revelling nymphs and satyrs, creatures of the countryside, who traditionally followed Bacchus in riotous processions, became associated with the urban poor, not least when they cheered their generals through Rome's streets in triumphal cavalcades.

It was no coincidence that Rome's temple to the Aventine Triad was built within a generation of her last king's expulsion, and the establishment of the Republic. It was dedicated in 493 BC by the war leader (or 'dictator') Aulus Postumius, in accordance with a vow made in time of famine, conflict and consequent disgruntlement among the urban plebs. Now, on Remus's hill, the commoners had their own holy trinity to match the patricians' triad on the Capitol, and just as that temple had its Father Jupiter, so Aventine Liber became known as 'Father', too.

Liber's Festivals

The Aventine Triad's gods were worshipped at Greek Eleusis in an initiation ceremony promising life after death, but, although some element of this belief may well have featured in Liber's spring festival in Rome, the emphasis here focused far more upon carnal joys. Presided over by an old woman wreathed in ivy, the Liberalia (held on 17 March) was a period of ribald merrymaking. A giant wreathed phallus, symbolic of fertility, was carried through the streets; bawdy songs were sung and jokes exchanged; dramas were staged on makeshift stages; and boys celebrated their transition into manhood.

Some patricians viewed Liber and his counterpart Bacchus with suspicion. Things came to a head in 186 BC when a Greek (described by Livy as 'an amateur sacrificer and prophet') introduced into Rome 'occult rites performed at night' open to both men and women and accompanied by wine and feasts. As the Bacchanalias spread, so did rumours of debauchery and murder, and the anxious establishment became convinced that the cult was a covert political movement aimed at overthrowing the state. Rewards were offered to denounce cult members; city gates were guarded to prevent escape; and, when more than 7,000 people were implicated, many committed suicide or were executed. Now the Senate would decide when Bacchanalias were held – and only five initiates might attend each one.

Whether there really was a revolutionary plot is difficult to tell, but Rome's reaction to this cult of Bacchus is oddly similar to its response to another eastern religion: Christianity. Its rites, too, they claimed, were hotbeds of debauchery, characterized by drinking wine and eating human flesh; it, too, must be suppressed; and any who did not renounce it must be executed.

A drumming bacchante, piping satyr and prancing panther accompany the young god, Liber, as he dances on this first-century AD bas relief in London's British Museum.

Bacchus and Ariadne

Despite his disruptive connotations, Bacchus (as Liber was more widely known) was popular throughout the Roman world. Mosaics and paintings showed him sometimes as a florid boy, sometimes riding a panther-drawn chariot with nymphs and satyrs in his train, sometimes accompanied by his consort, Ariadne.

When the Athenian Prince Theseus sailed to Crete to slay the Minotaur, Ariadne fell in love with him, helped guide him safely from the deadly labyrinth, and ran away with him to what she hoped would be a blissful marriage. However, Theseus abandoned her on Naxos, where heartbroken she bewailed her fate. Bacchus spied her from afar, and immediately fell in love with her, took her to heaven and made her his wife. If only it had ended thus. Ovid writes that even Bacchus almost abandoned her. After a successful evangelical campaign in India, he returned like some triumphal Roman general with a gaggle of captives, including a beautiful, nubile princess with whom he had been dallying. For poor Ariadne history

Driving a chariot drawn by four magnificent tigers, Liber rides
in triumph on a fine mosaic now in the Archaeological
Museum of Sousse, Tunisia.

seemed to be repeating itself. Again beside the seashore she poured out
her lament.

> All the while Liber was listening to her complaints. (He happened
> to have been following her.) He took her in his arms and dried her
> tears with kisses; and he said: 'Let's go to highest heaven together!
> You've been joined to me in marriage; now be joined to me in name!
> Your new name will be Libera!'

So saying, he transformed her crown into the constellation called Corona
Borealis ('Northern Crown'), providing yet another explanation for Libera's
identity. Originally his sister, now his wife, even for the Romans she was
the Aventine Triad's most shadowy member.

Secessions of Plebs

Associated with the urban poor, the Aventine Hill became the focus of one, and perhaps two, major demonstrations of their power. These were the 'Secessions of the Plebs', mass strikes against the ruling elite in which workers withdrew their labour until grievances had been addressed. The first took place shortly before the dedication of the temple to the Aventine Triad in the uneasy aftermath of the expulsion of the kings. Many felt they had simply exchanged one bad political system for another – since not only were they ground down by Sabine wars, they felt unrepresented in government while being saddled with crippling debts owed to flinty patricians.

In 494 BC they downed tools and left the city to encamp on a nearby hill – but when history came to be written, no-one could remember which. Some maintained it was the Sacred Mountain (Mons Sacra, modern Monte Sacro) near the River Anio (modern Aniene) about 5 km (3 miles) north of ancient Rome. Others were convinced it was the Aventine, because of its association with the working class. As the strike dragged on with seemingly no hope of resolution, and both sides became increasingly tetchy, the Senate despatched a negotiator, Agrippa Menenius Lanatus. Addressing the plebs in (what Livy calls) 'the rough and ready style of the age', he recounted a parable:

> In the days when the human body's parts did not pull together as they do now, but each member did and said exactly what it liked, the other members were indignant that everything that had been won by their care, hard work and diligence ended up in the stomach, while the stomach sat there quietly at the centre and enjoyed the fruits of their labour. So they entered into a pact: the hands must not bring food to the mouth; the mouth must accept nothing it was given; the teeth must not chew it. But while in their anger they were determined to force their will on the stomach by starving it, each of the other members and the entire body were reduced to extreme exhaustion. At last it became clear that the stomach, too, had an important role to play, and that it gave as much nourishment as it received by returning blood (which keeps us healthy and alive) to all parts of the body, maturing it through the digestion of food, and distributing it equally throughout the veins.

'By making this comparison', claims Livy, 'and by demonstrating how internal sedition between parts of the body was like the plebeians' anger with the Senate, he changed the people's minds.' In fact, it was not quite so simple. The Senate was forced to create a new political office, the powerful Tribunes of the Plebs, and many outstanding debts were cancelled. Even then, however, all was not resolved. Because crops had not been sown during the secession, Rome faced famine (as Menenius so vividly predicted), and in the troubled months that followed Coriolanus, sickened by powers granted to the poor, abandoned Rome to become its bitter enemy.

By 449 BC feelings again ran high. Members of a Board of Ten, appointed to revise the laws, were acting high-handedly. They assassinated one of their critics, a former Tribune of the Plebs, but the episode that sparked secession involved (like many other key elements in Roman myth and history) a woman. One of the Board abducted a beautiful plebeian schoolgirl, Verginia, claiming that she was his slave. When her father, a general, and her fiancé, a former Tribune of the Plebs, intervened, he was forced to convene a court of law. As arguments became more heated, the girl's father demanded that he be allowed to question her privately. When she was summoned, he took her aside 'to the stalls near the Temple of Venus Cloacina', snatched a butcher's knife and stabbed her through the heart, exclaiming: 'This is the only way I can assert your freedom!' The crowds erupted; riots ensued; and eventually the working class took themselves off first to the Aventine, then to the Sacred Mount, and finally back to the Aventine. Only when they had wrung new concessions from the Senate, strengthening their power, was the crisis averted.

This was not the last time that the Aventine witnessed violence against the people's representatives. In 121 BC the charismatic Tribune, Gaius Gracchus, an outstanding champion of the poor, whose policies inflamed the Senate and provoked urban violence, took refuge in the sixth-century Temple of Diana. Here, disillusioned, he bitterly cursed his city, before fleeing across the Tiber. Realizing that his cause was lost, he committed suicide in a sacred grove. Three thousand of his followers were put to death, their bodies dumped into the river.

Diana and the Cow of Destiny

Diana's temple had once witnessed a somewhat more propitious episode in Roman history – or perhaps mythology. Built on the Aventine under Servius Tullius (r. 579–535 BC) to rival the fabled Temple of Diana at Ephesus, it acquired an enviable status. Indeed, when a hefty, fine-proportioned heifer was born on a wealthy Sabine farm, augurs proclaimed that the city of whoever sacrificed the creature to Diana would rule the world. Sensing the hand of destiny upon his shoulder, the Sabine farmer took his cow to Rome, onto the Aventine and to Diana's Temple.

As he prepared to make the sacrifice, Diana's priest (who had heard the prophecy) rebuked him. The Sabine had not purified himself. He was unclean! He must wash in the Tiber immediately. Determined that everything be done according to divine prescription, the Sabine scuttled off into the valley, where the river was in flood – while the Roman priest devoutly sacrificed the heifer to the goddess, 'a cause' (writes Livy) 'of the greatest satisfaction to both king and people'.

The Aventine Hill in History and Today

With its summit just under 46 m (150 feet) above sea level, the Aventine is Rome's most southerly hill, separated from the Palatine by the Murcia Valley, originally part of the Tiber's flood plain. Indeed, the Aventine may once have been named 'Mons Murcus', while the local goddess, Murcia, may have become identified with Venus Verticordia (Changer of Hearts), in which guise she (surprisingly) ensured that the lustful remained chaste.

Traditionally Remus watched for auguries, and was buried, on the Aventine – as was the Sabine Titus Tatius, who ruled with Romulus. During early Rome's existence the Aventine remained wooded pastureland dotted with shrines. Tradition suggests (probably rightly) that it was first settled in the seventh century BC, when Rome's fourth king, Ancus Marcius, defeated and destroyed the Latin town of Politorium (near Lavinium), removing its people and re-housing them here, a policy he repeated with three other Latin settlements: Ficana, Tellenae and Medullia. Thanks to their presence, and its proximity to the Tiber, the Aventine became one of Rome's most thriving commercial centres, as the evidence of Monte Testaccio ('Potsherd Mountain') attests. Nearly 1 km (half a mile) in circumference and 35 m (115 feet) high, this ancient rubbish dump, formed between the first century BC and the third century AD, is estimated to contain remains of more than 53 million amphorae imported from throughout the Roman world. Even before its formation, however, the Aventine was already home to many successful plebeian families, as well as to a multiplicity of shrines and temples.

Throughout the Republic – and especially after 456 BC, when it was declared public land, and building plots were distributed to the poor – the Aventine was associated with the urban plebs and their struggles to achieve political representation. In 449 BC the Second Secession of the Plebs began and ended here, and it may also have been the site of the earlier secession in 494. In the third century BC, trade guilds seeking a headquarters building chose the Temple of Minerva on the northern summit, next to the sixth-century Temple of Diana – where in 121 BC Gaius Gracchus, Tribune of the

Plebs, found temporary asylum before committing suicide. By now the Murcia Valley was home to one of Rome's major entertainment hubs, the Circus Maximus. A venue for events ranging from dramas to animal hunts to elaborate military parades, over time it became best known as the crucible of chariot racing (where four teams, each dressed in distinguishing colours, thundered round the track to the roar of 150,000 spectators) – a place where the patricians of the Palatine quite literally faced the Aventine's plebeians.

Under the Empire, thanks to its proximity to the Forum, Palatine and Capitol, the Aventine became colonized by aspirant aristocrats, while poorer

- -

THE AVENTINE HILL Some Important Dates and Remains

753 BC	Remus's augury and death; foundation of Rome.
late C7th BC	Defeated Latins resettled on Aventine by Ancus Marcius.
C6th BC	Temple of Diana built.
494 BC	First Secession of Plebs (perhaps) to Aventine.
493 BC	Aulus Postumius dedicates temple to Aventine Triad.
456 BC	Aventine declared public land and parcelled out to city poor.
449 BC	Second Secession of Plebs.
392 BC	Temple of Juno built.
264 BC	Temple of Vertumnus and Pomona built.
238 BC	Temple of Flora built.
C2nd BC	Temple of Minerva built.
186 BC	Bacchanalian 'conspiracy'.
121 BC	Gaius Gracchus takes refuge in temples of Diana and Minerva.
AD 49	Claudius includes Aventine within *pomerium*.
AD 410	Alaric sacks Aventine.
AD 422	Church of Santa Sabina built.

Most of the temples and other buildings that once covered the ancient Aventine have been built over. Even the topography is difficult to read. The best place to appreciate the site's potential is the **Church of Santa Sabina**, Rome's oldest basilica, complete with original wooden doors showing scenes from the lives of Moses and Christ, including one of the earliest representations of the crucifixion. Inside, the church is elegant in its simplicity (most of its original mosaics are lost), while views across Rome from the adjacent Giardini degli Aranci (Orange Garden) are stunning.

- -

residents migrated across the river. In AD 49 Claudius included it within the *pomerium* (Rome's religious boundary), and when Alaric occupied the city in AD 410 the now rich Aventine, home to wealthy Christian matrons, bore much of the brunt of his depredations. Trade suffered desperately. As wharves and warehouses fell into disuse, the Aventine was gradually abandoned. The Middle Ages saw a resurgence in fortunes. Fine mansions sprang up amid exquisite churches, and even today on the Aventine it is still possible to find oases of calm.

· ·

Nearby to the east stood temples of Diana and Minerva. Further east and south, beneath the fifth-century Church of Santa Prisca, are remains of a **Mithraeum**, deliberately destroyed around AD 400. A nearby house (built in AD 95 and extended in 110) may once have been home to the emperor Trajan.

More can be seen around the Aventine. To the northeast, much of the **Circus Maximus** is now an unloved public park, but part of its southern structure, renovated, with good signage and open to the public, is well worth a visit. Many will be tempted to strike north from here along the via di San Gregorio, beneath arches of the **Aqua Claudia aqueduct**, and past the fourth-century AD **Arch of Constantine** to visit the **Colosseum**, the first-century AD showcase for the worst excesses of man's inhumanity built by the emperor Vespasian. The structure is impressive, its purpose not. A slaughterhouse where countless men and women, not to mention animals, died to entertain the mob, like other amphitheatres it should (in the present author's opinion) be treated with the same respect accorded sites of more modern mass killings, not as the theme park it has become. Escaping the excited crowds, travellers are encouraged instead to book a tour of **Nero's Golden House** beneath the Caelian Hill, whose frescoes and augmented reality displays are breathtaking.

To the south of the Aventine, outside a fine stretch of the late third century AD **Aurelian Walls**, the **Pyramid of Cestius** (base *c.* 30 m or 98 ft; height *c.* 38 m or 125 ft), dating from between 18 and 12 BC, is evidence of the mania for all things Egyptian that gripped Rome following Augustus's victory over Cleopatra in 30 BC. To the west is the remarkable **Monte Testaccio**, the ancient rubbish dump of broken amphorae, about 35 m (115 ft) high.

Bacchanalia and initiation into Liber's cult may be shown on remarkable wall-paintings in Pompeii's suburban **Villa of the Mysteries** (outside the Porta di Ercolano).

· ·

CHAPTER 13
THE SUBLICIAN BRIDGE
AND TRASTEVERE: PROTECTING ROME

'I pray you, holy Tiber', Cocles said, 'to receive this soldier and his arms into your kindly river!' Then in full armour he leapt into the Tiber, and, though many missiles fell around him, he swam safely to his friends (an act of daring more famous in popular culture than it is strictly believable).

Livy, *History*, 2.10.11

There is a sense of constant movement: movement from impatient traffic purring unrelentingly across the high-arched Ponte Palatino, horns rasping, sirens blaring; movement from the water, too, as, divided, the river slides on urgently past the cool abutments of Isola Tibertina, whose clustered buildings – red-bricked, terracotta-tiled – glow in the early sun.

Yet there are still some pockets of tranquillity. A little downstream, high above the outlet of the Cloaca Maxima, a man sits hunched over a fishing rod, while birds perch by the river's reedy edge, or skim the surface on huge lazy wings. Like light caught in a prism, time seems to coalesce here: the freneticism of modernity coinciding with a slower pace of bygone centuries, all built on the solidity of the city's ancient past – quite liter-ally here on Isola Tibertina, for in the late Republic its banks were faced with slabs of travertine, their curving lines cut to describe the shape of a huge ship, a towering obelisk erected at its centre to suggest a mast. A god once slipped ashore here – Asclepius the Healer slithered as a snake towards the site where his healing sanctuary would stand.

Close by other wonders, too, took place. For downstream stood an ancient bridge that linked the low-lying area beneath the Aventine and Palatine with the Tiber's farther shore, modern Trastevere, outside the boundaries of early Rome, the limit of Etruscan lands, in times of war a place of danger. And, while the Tiber kept Rome safe, the ancient bridge, the Pons Sublicius, near where the traffic pours so blithely now across the Ponte Palatino, could pose a threat if it were not well-guarded. So this bridge between two cultures was the site of many an encounter that formed the basis of some of the most vivid of all legends that extolled the bravery and virtue of early Rome.

Wooden Bridge, Straw Men

A few hundred metres downriver from Tiber Island (said to have formed from corn dumped from the fields of Rome's reviled last king) early Republicans performed deeds of such heroism that they became enshrined forever in their city's myth. Many were connected with Rome's oldest bridge, the Pons Sublicius, a structure made entirely out of wood, that stood for well over a millennium, linking Rome with Etruscan lands to the west and north.

Here, near the later Pons Aemilius (whose broken arches are today called 'Ponte Rotto'), with the Tiber at its shallowest and laziest, people had forded the river since time immemorial, many driving cattle to the market later called the Forum Boarium. So it made sense to locate the first bridge here, a structure (claimed historians) begun under Numa (r. 715–673) and completed under Rome's fourth king, Ancus Marcius (r. 642–617 BC). Its purpose was not just economic (to facilitate traffic across the Tiber) but also military (to annex the Janiculum Hill, encircle it with walls and prevent its occupation by enemy troops).

Some claimed that the bridge was infinitely older, the work not of a mere mortal but of a hero: Hercules. Returning from Spain with the stolen cattle of triple-bodied Geryon (they said), he built the Sublician Bridge for a specific purpose: to let him stand midstream and throw twenty-seven human effigies of straw into the river, surrogates for the bodies of companions lost on his journeying, whom he had been unable to bury properly. The Tiber would take them to the sea, where currents would convey them back to Greece, their homeland.

Ovid did not entirely agree. Yes, the straw men represented Hercules' companions, and, yes, the intention was that the river would help repatriate them. According to him, however, when Hercules passed through Rome, many of his Greek followers were so taken with the place that they decided to settle there. All the same, they loved their native land so much that they left wills instructing their children to drop their bodies from the bridge, so that the Tiber could carry them home for burial. When the time came, their sons found this request repugnant. So they buried them in Latium, and, to atone for their disobedience, consigned surrogate straw men to the river.

Each year on 15 May priests and Vestal Virgins processed round Rome, visiting twenty-seven shrines ('Argei'), receiving a straw effigy from each, and ending on the Sublician Bridge, where they consigned the entire collection to the waters. No-one quite remembered what 'Argei' meant, but it sounded sufficiently similar to 'Argivi' ('Argives', inhabitants of Greek Argos, from where Hercules embarked on his labours) that it became associated with his followers, and the repatriation myth sprang up. There were darker explanations, too: the straw men were avatars for early Roman human sacrifices of either men aged over sixty (a combination of culling and euthanasia) or victims demanded by Jupiter (a rite that civilizing Hercules ended, tricking the god as Numa later tricked him on the Aventine).

Whatever its origin, the Sublician Bridge was an engineering marvel. Containing no iron, it was held together entirely by wooden dowels, a design that tradition ascribed to an oracle. The bridge was considered so sacred that priests were responsible for its upkeep and repair, any damage it sustained was considered a bad omen, while to destroy it would have been sacrilegious.

Plucky Cocles

Once, however, the destruction of the bridge was a desperate necessity. In the months after Tarquin the Proud's expulsion, Rome's nascent virtues had already been displayed. Not only had one consul, Collatinus, gone into voluntary exile, lest he pollute Rome with his Tarquinian name, the other, Brutus, finding his sons plotting with the enemy, presided over their execution before falling in battle, killing and killed by the exiled king's son, while a disembodied voice (perhaps the god Silvanus) proclaimed victory for Rome. His colleague, Valerius Poplicola, was more fortunate. Returning home, he celebrated a triumph, riding through the city in his four-horse chariot, thus setting a precedent for all subsequent triumphs throughout Roman history.

Meanwhile, Tarquin had been busy enlisting allies to restore him to the throne, first Etruscans from Veii and Tarquinia, then the great Etruscan king, Lars Porsenna, from Clusium. As their army approached the city, country-dwellers left their farms and flocked into the city. Called to arms, Rome's citizens swarmed across the bridge, but they were no match for the Etruscans. Soon Porsenna's men were occupying the Janiculum, as Roman troops ran for the river, jostling and elbowing their way across the bridge back to safety. Only one stood firm: Horatius Cocles. He knew that, if Romans could cross the bridge, so could Etruscans. To prevent Rome's capture, the bridge must be demolished. So he stood unflinching, as his comrades surged around him. Livy takes up the tale:

A second-century AD medallion shows Horatius Cocles swimming the Tiber as his comrades destroy the wooden bridge.

He shouted orders: use iron or fire, whatever means they could! Destroy the bridge! He would hold up the enemy attack, inasmuch as one man could. Then he advanced to the far end of the bridge. Conspicuous among those running with their backs turned to the enemy, he stood there ready for close combat, shield raised, sword drawn, one man against a hostile army, and his inhuman courage shocked the enemy.

Then two comrades joined him, and together they confronted the massed force of Etruscans, while behind them Romans worked like demons to dismantle the wooden bridge. Soon it was nearly done, and Cocles ordered his friends to leave while they could. Again he faced the enemy alone, stabbing, parrying, until at last he heard the roar of falling timber and the cheering of his men. The bridge was down. As the Etruscans pressed forward, determined to kill Cocles, he prayed to Father Tiber before leaping fully armoured into the river. Then, with missiles raining all around him, though wounded in the buttocks, he swam to the farther shore. Grateful Rome rewarded Cocles with a fine estate, and his statue was erected in the Forum; and while Livy consigned his story to mythology, the heroism of this one man, risking his life to save his people, became a glittering example of the selfless virtues that (for moralists at least) made Rome so great.

Defiant 'Lefty'

Faced with the Tiber's barrier, the Etruscans encamped on the Janiculum, and began collecting boats to launch a riverine assault. Meanwhile, as country-dwelling Romans withdrew cattle and belongings to the city, and prepared for siege, one man, Gaius Mucius, slipped unseen across the Tiber, a dagger hidden in his clothing.

On the Janiculum no-one suspected he was Roman. Indeed, since it was payday, all the Etruscan army was gathered round a dais, where Lars Porsenna sat, his secretary beside him, doling out wages. Both men looked similar. In fact, since he controlled the cash, the secretary seemed more important. Since Mucius had never seen Porsenna, he made a fundamental error: grasping his dagger, he leapt onto the platform and stabbed the secretary. As he struggled through the crowds to flee, guards seized him and dragged him before the king – which was when, according to Livy, Mucius made a bold, defiant speech:

I am Gaius Mucius, a citizen of Rome. I am your enemy and you are mine. It was my wish to kill you, but I am no more frightened to face death than I was to dole death out. To act and suffer bravely is the Roman way.

Romans, he said, were queuing up to do as he had done – there was no shortage of courageous men. It was not pitched battle Porsenna must fear but a lone assassin. From now on, he must look over his shoulder every minute of the day: his bodyguards could not protect him.

Furious, Porsenna ordered that Mucius be burnt alive, but – before he could be obeyed – the Roman countered: 'See in what low regard men hold their bodies when their eyes are set on higher glory!' Then he plunged his right hand into the fire already blazing on a nearby altar, and held it there unflinching, his gaze locked on Porsenna's. Impressed, the king let Mucius go, but still the Roman fired one parting shot. There were 300 more like him at home, who would not rest until their mission was accomplished.

Not unsurprisingly, Etruscan envoys soon turned up in Rome for peace talks and, while the Senate refused to restore Tarquin to the throne, it did return Veientine territories captured in war and gave hostages in exchange for the suspension of hostilities. Mucius was feted as a hero and rewarded with a fine estate on the Tiber's west bank. Moreover, he earned what in the circumstances was a prestigious nickname: Scaevola, 'Left-Handed', since his right hand was now useless.

Courageous Cloelia

Good myths come in three parts, and the third element in this tale of Roman virtue involves Cloelia, a noble girl, one of the hostages given to Porsenna as part of the peace treaty. While the Etruscans were preparing in no great hurry to withdraw from the Janiculum, Cloelia and some girlfriends went to bathe in the river near the destroyed Sublician Bridge. Thanks to the truce, security was slack and they were unguarded. As they gazed over to the farther bank, to Rome, they were seized with such longing that they defied the currents and swam across the river, though one – Cloelia – rode on horseback, protecting and encouraging the others.

Back home, their parents were displeased and Poplicola, Rome's leading citizen, was furious at this flagrant breach of the peace treaty. Even though they included his own daughter, Valeria, the hostages must return. So he sent them and their servants back. As they neared the Etruscan camp, however, Tarquin (wanting to make trouble) ambushed them. Only Valeria escaped, but, as Tarquin's men were rounding up their captives, Porsenna's son, Arruns, intervened and brought them to his father. Instead of punishing the girls the king was merciful. Admiring their pluck, he asked who was behind their brave escape. When Cloelia stepped forward, Porsenna smiled and presented her with a handsome horse, richly caparisoned with exquisite trappings, which was why (writes Plutarch) her statue, mounted on a horse, stood on the Sacred Way below the Palatine, though others (he admits) claimed that its subject was Valeria.

Livy used the story to praise Roman values. He writes how Cloelia and her comrades made their deliberate bid for freedom, diving into the surging Tiber and swimming to Rome as missiles pelted down around them. At once Porsenna sent representatives to demand Cloelia's return – the other girls did not concern him. 'But then,' Livy continues, 'his feelings turned to admiration. He said that her actions surpassed those of Cocles and Mucius, adding that while he would consider the treaty broken if she were not surrendered; if she *were* returned he would restore her to her family untouched and unviolated.'

So gallant Cloelia returned to the Etruscan camp, where Porsenna showered her with praise and promised her a gift – her choice of hostages, whom he would free and send back to Rome with her. She chose prepubescent boys, partly to show her modesty, partly because these were 'most liable to be mistreated because of their age'. A fearless heroine, who wins even the enemy's admiration, who is concerned above all for the safety of Rome's next generation: standing alongside Cocles and Scaevola, Cloelia completes the triad of inspiring examples of old civic virtues to which every Roman, male or female, should aspire.

Asclepius's Arrival

Mid-river, near the Sublician Bridge, the most famous temple on Tiber Island belonged to the healing god Asclepius. In 293 BC plague struck Rome. As was traditional under such dire circumstances, priests consulted the Sibylline Books, which revealed that they should send delegates to Asclepius's healing sanctuary at Greek Epidaurus, from where they must bring the god to Rome. However, when they arrived the following year, the envoys were met with hostility. Why would the priests of Epidaurus willingly allow their god to leave? That night as the delegation's leader slept, Asclepius appeared in a dream. The Roman must not worry. The god was willing.

Next morning, while all prayed for a sign outside his temple, a great crested snake coiled and slithered hissing from the inner sanctum. It was

Asclepius incarnate. As onlookers froze in terror, the serpent bowed his head towards them, flickering his tongue, before, with a last look at the sanctuary that had for so long been his home, he glided down the temple steps through city streets towards the harbour while citizens strewed petals in his path. Then he boarded the Roman ship, which soon was scudding west for Italy. When they learned of its imminent arrival, Rome's ailing citizens crowded Tiber's edge. In his *Metamorphoses* Ovid describes how:

> Incense crackled from altars along both riverbanks and smoke perfumed the air, while sacrificial knives ran hot with victims' blood. And now he had entered Rome, the capital of all the world. The serpent arched high, and leaning his neck against the mast-top, looked around to see where he would like to settle. There is a piece of land, which the river (divided into two parts) flows around. It is called The Island. The Tiber stretches both arms round it and embraces it.

A sacred snake coils beside the healing god Asclepius on this Roman copy of an original Greek statue now in the museum at Epidaurus.

As the ship approached, the serpent flopped into the churning river, and, swimming against the current reached the island's shore, where the god sloughed off his snakeskin and resumed his divine appearance. Within days the plague abated, and on 1 January 291 BC Asclepius's new temple was consecrated. Indeed, the entire island was dedicated to Asclepius, and in the first century BC its enclosing walls may have been reshaped to resemble a huge ship in recognition of his arrival, with an obelisk erected at its heart to represent the mast, and stone bridges built to link the island to the Campus Martius in the east and the Janiculum Hill in the west.

Crowned by an Eagle

The Janiculum is not included among Rome's seven hills, although it is higher than any of them (85 m, or 280 ft above sea level). Nonetheless, being a good place to watch the skies for auguries, it had important religious associations. Here, an influential player in Rome's history received a sign from heaven that confirmed his destiny.

Lucumo was the son of Demaratus, a nobleman of Corinth, who, forced to flee his home, came as a refugee to Italy and settled in Tarquinia. Here, because of his foreign parentage and despite his wealth, Lucumo found it impossible to gain political office, so he and his wife, the aristocratic and prophetic Tanaquil, decided to move to Rome. As they breasted the Janiculum Hill, they reined in their carriage, and looked for the first time across the Tiber and the bridge towards the city. As they did so, an eagle hurtled from the sky, snatched Lucumo's cap and soared high, clutching it in his beak. Then it swooped back down and replaced it on Lucumo's head. Tanaquil, delighted, embraced her husband and explained the omen: the eagle was Jupiter's messenger; by taking Lucumo's cap and then replacing it, it was giving him the crown, a sure sign that Lucumo would be king.

So it turned out. In Rome Lucumo changed his name to Lucius Tarquinius, and when old King Ancus Marcius died, the citizens (keen that Ancus's sons should not succeed him) elected Tarquinius (r. 616–579 BC) to the throne. It was a wise choice. During his rule Rome's dominance increased thanks to victories he celebrated in a military triumph. Both here and elsewhere Tarquinius Priscus (Tarquinius the Elder) introduced Etruscan elements to Roman life, including the purple-bordered *toga praetexta* worn by boys and magistrates and the military cloak (the *paludamentum*). He enhanced the city, draining low-lying swamps, constructing the Circus Maximus in Murcia Valley, and laying foundations for Jupiter's Temple on the Capitol. Under him the Senate was enlarged, ennobling members of a hundred lesser families – including the Octavii (whose number would include Gaius Octavius Thurinus, later the emperor Augustus). Tarquinius's heirs left much to be desired, however: his grandson, Tarquin the Proud, brought kingship into disrepute, and his expulsion heralded the new Republic.

Janus's Hill

The Janiculum, where the eagle crowned Lucumo, took its name from Janus, the two-faced god, who looks both back and forward; he is the god of doors, who heralds the new year and gives his name to January. For late Roman philosophers and theologians, Janus (who could see both past and future) was the omniscient guardian of the universe, a cosmic deity presiding over time, the doorkeeper to heaven. In popular belief he was far more earthy.

Found at Etruscan Vulci, this fine second-century BC bust of two-faced Janus now resides in Rome's Museo Nazionale Etrusco di Villa Giulia.

In *Fasti*, Ovid recounts Janus's love for the nymph Cranae, a virgin huntress, who was also something of a tease. Whenever an admirer pressed his suit, she would coyly tell him that she could not sleep with him in meadows, but if he led her to a secluded cave, she would willingly follow. Then, as he strode off, Cranae would hide in a thicket where no amount of searching ever found her.

> Janus caught sight of her, and – overwhelmed by desire – employed soft words against the hardened nymph. She gave her usual command: to find some rather remote cave. Like some escort she follows where he leads but then abandons him. Foolish girl! Janus can see what goes on behind his back! You won't get your way – he's looking back to where you're hiding! You won't get your way! Look! What did I tell you? You're hiding under a rock, but he seizes you in his embrace and, once he's taken what he wants, he says: 'In return for having sex with me, you can be goddess of hinges. Take this in payment for your virginity.' And with these words he gave her a white thorn, with which to drive suffering from doorposts.

In fact, known too as the goddess Carna, she also looked after children, flesh and human organs. Although Janus was famous for philandering with a bevy of local nymphs, including Juturna and Camasene (who bore Tiberinus, from whom the Tiber took its name), he was mostly worshipped for more noble qualities. He was Latium's first ruler; he welcomed Saturn when that god was driven from Greece by Jupiter; and his temple in the Forum spoke of peace and war: only when the world was free from conflict could its doors be closed. Before Augustus's reign they were shut only twice, but during it three times, while later emperors imbued the ceremony of fastening the doors with pomp and ceremony, a visual reminder of the benefits of Roman Peace.

The Sublician Bridge and Trastevere in History and Today

Some classical writers believed that the Janiculum Hill across the Tiber (Latin 'Transtiberim', Italian 'Trastevere') was Rome's oldest inhabited sector, site of the ancient kingdom of Janus. Here the two-faced god welcomed his successor, Saturn, who established his own citadel on the Capitol. Others told how Aeneas's son, Rhomus, built a settlement on the Janiculum, which he named from his father 'Aineia'. Later, when Romulus defeated Veii, Trastevere's floodplain was said to have been annexed by smallholders and farmers, and even in the late Republic it was characterized by wide open spaces (villas' leafy gardens), while the Janiculum boasted sacred groves and forests, not least one on its summit sacred to Juno, home to her sacred cattle.

Tradition maintains that work on the Sublician Bridge was begun by Numa, Rome's second king, who was buried on the Janiculum. In 181 BC heavy rain dislodged two sarcophagi in his tomb, and their lids came off. One (originally containing Numa's remains) was empty; the other housed fourteen (or twenty-four) books: half were Roman laws, half Greek philosophy – Numa was said, anachronistically, to have been a pupil of Pythagoras. They were immediately impounded, read by the authorities and deemed so potentially incendiary that they were burnt in the Forum.

In 508 BC the Janiculum was seized by invading Etruscans under Lars Porsenna, intent on restoring Tarquin the Proud to Rome's throne, and the stories of Horatius Cocles, Gaius Mucius and Cloelia may have been deliberately invented to conceal Rome's actual defeat. Traditionally a red flag was hoisted atop the Janiculum to warn of enemy approach. It fluttered next in 477 BC, when (after massacring 300 members of Rome's Fabii family) Veientes swooped on Rome, occupying Trastevere for a year before being driven off.

Close to Mucius's estates in Trastevere was the farm of another noble Roman, Cincinnatus. In 458 BC, having withdrawn from politics after a scandal involving his son, Cincinnatus was tilling his fields, clad in a workaday tunic, when a senatorial delegation arrived. They requested that he change into his toga and then explained their mission: the army was cut off in the Alban Hills, the city needed a 'dictator' (a technical term meaning someone holding supreme power for a year) and Cincinnatus was Rome's chosen candidate. Within two weeks, he had received the enemy's surrender – causing each man to pass beneath a 'yoke' constructed from three spears, a symbol of their subjugation – and resigned his post. Nineteen years later, Cincinnatus was again appointed dictator, this time to quell a popular uprising. Again he resigned immediately his job was done (it took three weeks this time), and in later years this son of the soil, who refused to cling on to power, became yet another example of old Roman virtues.

While the last 'Secession of the Plebs' in 287 BC saw Rome's poor encamped on the Janiculum, successfully demanding that plebiscites be accorded the force of law, for centuries Trastevere, which in Roman times included Tiber Island, as well as the Janiculum and Vatican Hills, was mostly peaceful. The island, home to Greece's healing god Asclepius since 292 BC, was notable for containing only shrines and temples. Meanwhile, the land beyond the river blossomed with gardens and increasingly chic villas. Egypt's Queen Cleopatra was ensconced in Julius Caesar's estate here when he was assassinated in 44 BC. His will left his gardens to the people, and in 2 BC Augustus flooded part of them to stage a *naumachia*, a sea battle with more than thirty ships, many thousand oarsmen and 3,000 soldiers.

Under the empire Trastevere's character changed as workshops, wharves and tenements sprang up, with barracks for fire-fighters and sailors from Ravenna, whose job was to rig awnings in the Colosseum. Further north, the emperor Caligula began building a circus, where in AD 64, following Rome's Great Fire, Nero executed many Christian scapegoats. In 68 it may have seen St Peter crucified upside down, where later the first basilica to bear his name was built by the emperor Constantine. Trastevere saw martyrs, too: in 222 St Calixtus was scourged before being thrown from a window (with unerring aim) into a well, while in 303 St Cecilia (now patron of music) and her husband St Valerius (probably a member of the ancient Valerii family) were killed in their home, after being liberally roasted in a nearby bath house.

In 410 Trastevere suffered at the hands of Alaric, and by the middle of the next century, like the rest of Rome, it was largely abandoned. In the Middle Ages Trastevere contained lush estates and vineyards, though by now palaces and villas shared the landscape with monasteries and churches – not least the burgeoning Vatican, whose power continued to increase. In 1849, fighting French papal allies on the Janiculum, Garibaldi tried to seize the city. In 1870 the so-called Risorgimento at last triumphed, and the next year, as Italy was united, the Pope withdrew to the Vatican. For Trastevere, political triumph spelled disaster: gardens were grubbed up, archaeological sites smashed and housing blocks built with no regard for history. Not for nothing has this episode been called 'Rome's destruction'.

THE SUBLICIAN BRIDGE AND TRASTEVERE
Some Important Dates and Remains

late C7th BC	Lucumo receives portent on Janiculum.
642 BC	Ancus Marcius completes Sublician Bridge.
509 BC	Tiber Island traditionally created from Tarquin the Proud's grain.
508 BC	Lars Porsenna occupies Janiculum. Cocles, Scaevola and Cloelia.
477 BC	Veientes occupy Janiculum Hill.
458 BC	Cincinnatus called from his estates in Trastevere to be dictator.
292 BC	Asclepius arrives in Rome.
287 BC	Third Secession of Plebs.
181 BC	Numa's tomb discovered on Janiculum.
142 BC	Pons Aemilius (Ponte Rotto) completed as first stone bridge across Tiber.
62 BC	Pons Fabricius built linking Tiber Island and Field of Mars.
44 BC	Pons Cestius built linking Tiber Island and Trastevere; Caesar entertains Cleopatra in his villa.
2 BC	Augustus holds *naumachia* in Caesar's gardens, during dedication of Mars Ultor temple.
C1st AD	Tenements begun in Trastevere.
c. AD 40	Caligula's circus begun in his mother, Agrippina the Elder's, gardens.
? AD 68	St Peter martyred in Caligula's circus.
AD 69	Sublician Bridge destroyed by flood and subsequently repaired.
AD 222	St Calixtus martyred.
AD 303	St Cecilia and husband Valerius martyred during Diocletian's persecutions.
AD 319	Constantine begins first Basilica of St Peter.
AD 410	Trastevere devastated by Alaric, then abandoned.
AD 537	Goths occupy Trastevere.
AD 552	Narses reclaims Rome, which is now virtually deserted.
AD 1849	Garibaldi fights French on Janiculum.
AD 1871	Reunification of Italy; 'Rome's destruction'.

Thanks to late nineteenth-century builders, little of ancient Trastevere survives, though many streets follow the course of classical predecessors. A Roman **latrine** may be visited on via Garibaldi, while foundations of a **Syrian Sanctuary** lie in the grounds of Villa Sciarra, now a public park. Of greater interest are **firemen's barracks** (Augustus VII Coorte dei Vigili), open by arrangement. The area is charming, and a leisurely stroll easily takes in the Churches of **Santa Maria in Trastevere** (reputedly Rome's oldest) – from a window nearby St Calixtus was thrown to his death – and **Santa Cecilia in Trastevere**, near which the eponymous martyr and her husband were tortured. Pipes feeding the sweat room where they were roasted can be seen, while a vase (now a fountain) in the enclosed garden may once have graced the villa of the Valerii. Travellers should also visit the delightful **Tempietto del Bramante** situated in cloisters beside the **Church of San Pietro in Montorio**, once believed to be the site of St Peter's crucifixion.

Behind St Peter's Basilica the **Vatican Museums**, a treasure trove of classical artefacts, attract such crowds as to make visits a frustrating ordeal. It is worthwhile booking the (expensive) 'breakfast tour' before doors open to the public. Exhibits include **sculptures from Hadrian's Serapeum at Tivoli**, **gilt-bronze peacocks** from Hadrian's Mausoleum, the **Apollo Belvedere**, a first-century BC marble showing **Laocoön and his Sons**, a massive **porphyry basin** from Nero's Golden House, the Etruscan bronze **Mars of Todi** and the **Primaporta Augustus**, his right arm outstretched, his breastplate showing scenes redolent of Roman Peace. Tickets include access to the **Sistine Chapel**, where Michelangelo's paintings include fine depictions of Sibyls.

Nothing survives of the Sublician Bridge – or of **Tiber Island**'s Temple of Asclepius, probably located beneath the piazza (the Church of San Bartolemeo is said to lie over its sacred well, while the Hospital of the Fatebenefratelli attests to the island's continuing association with health care). Good views are afforded of the ruined **Ponte Rotto**, the second-century BC Pons Aemilius. A walk around the travertine pavement surrounding the island brings us beneath the first-century **Ponte Fabricio** (now a pedestrian bridge) and to the carving of a ship's prow complete with Asclepius's coiled serpent, commemorating the god's arrival in Rome.

* *

CHAPTER 14

THE ROMAN FORUM:
SENATE AND PEOPLE

When he entered Rome, the focus of all power and virtue, and
visited the Forum and the Rostra (famous for its power in days
gone by), he was overwhelmed, and, as his eyes took in the scene,
he was transfixed by its sheer multiplicity of marvels.

Ammianus Marcellinus, *Res Gestae*, 16.10

The sound of street performers carries with great clarity – a jazz trio, its guitarist plucking out a tireless loop of well-loved songs: 'O Sole Mio'; 'I Just Called to Say I Love You'; the theme from 'The Godfather'. Predictable, they form a curiously soothing counterpoint to hawkers importuning tourists with their cheap tat on the busy via dei Fori Imperiali or the polyglot cacophony of tour guides here in the Roman Forum, their rolled umbrellas raised, scarves tied like banners round slim metal poles, leading tired, footsore cohorts across modern walkways and well-trodden ancient stones past honeyed columns and the ruined afterglow of power.

Down from the Arch of Titus on the Sacred Way they pour, skirting the temples of Vesta and the Divine Julius Caesar, out into the Forum proper. It seems such a modern phenomenon, this gathering of peoples from across the world, snaking endlessly towards the Capitol, some led by wonder, others by a sense of duty, the belief that there are things that must be seen, that what they saw will form the basis of rich conversations with the folks back home, all paying homage to Rome's glorious history.

In some respects these crowds, like the guitarist's music, are on a loop. Following flags, feet like theirs will trudge these stones tomorrow, just as they did yesterday, last week, last year – and two millennia ago, when, trumpets blaring, hobnails crashing on the cobbles, hooves sparking, horses snorting, soldiers singing ribald songs, polyglot spectators crowded marble steps, to store up memories (which in turn would fade or blossom) of triumphs won over distant enemies, of the Roman Empire's ongoing, tireless quest to unite the peoples of the world under one unquestioning belief, one universal certainty, one everlasting truth: that here, in this square mile of commerce, government and law, beat the undying heart of the greatest civilization that mankind could ever know.

Between Life and Death

The Forum was not always central to Rome's urban life. In early history it was a verdant valley, the site of springs, whose waters flowed to the Velabrum, a low-lying area near the Tiber between the Capitoline and Palatine Hills. For part of the year, when the river broke its banks, it was a flooded swamp where, thanks to its shifting, liminal nature, shrines to gods of the underworld sprang up on its Palatine shores.

Even in later years the Forum was thought to house a portal to the dead. This was the Lacus Curtius ('Curtian Lake'), said by some to be where the Sabine cavalryman Mettius Curtius was forced to abandon his horse to the cloying marsh during his people's battle with Romulus's Romans.

Marcus Curtius and his horse
plunge into the abyss on this
first-century BC relief.

For others the place had darker, yet more glorious, connotations. They told how in 362 BC an earthquake caused a fissure to open in the Forum. Attempts to fill it with earth proved fruitless. Soothsayers were consulted, and they gave the same response: Rome must sacrifice her greatest asset to the abyss. But what *was* Rome's greatest asset? Wise heads could not agree, but (as Livy vividly records):

> Tradition tells how Marcus Curtius, a young man with a distinguished war record, rebuked them for doubting that any asset was more Roman than weapons and bravery. As silence fell he turned towards the temples of the deathless gods that tower over the Forum and to the Capitol as well, before, stretching out his hands now to the skies, now to the yawning chasm and the gods below, he dedicated himself to death. Then, riding a horse decked out as splendidly as he could manage, he plunged fully armoured into the void. Crowds of men and women threw offerings and fruits in after him.

This did the trick. By the late Republic the Lacus Curtius was paved and dry, a place where citizens would throw coins to ensure the emperor Augustus's health and long life. Even this, though, harked back to more primitive times: the coins were little more than offerings to spirits of the underworld who still haunted this most numinous of sites.

Black Stone

Not far from the Lacus Curtius another shrine was thought to mark life's passage into death. The Lapis Niger ('Black Stone') was named either from the black block bearing an archaic inscription buried in a shrine with dedicatory objects in the fourth century BC, or from the black marble paving laid above it in the first. It was a site of immense spiritual power, but by Augustus's day no-one knew why. Some called it an 'ill-omened place', speculating that, intended as the grave of Romulus (who was, of course, translated bodily to heaven), it later entombed his foster-father, Faustulus, who fell in battle here. According to the second-century AD grammarian, Festus, others claimed it was the grave of Tullus Hostilius, another Roman king – or of his grandfather Hostus.

Another tradition maintained that it was here (not in the Campus Martius) that Romulus was murdered by disgruntled senators. Perhaps people were misled by its position next to the Curia (Senate House), or maybe because it was near where Julius Caesar's body was cremated on an improvised pyre after Mark Antony whipped up high emotions in the crowd with his famous funeral speech delivered from the adjacent Speaker's Platform.

Between Two Fires

Two sanctuaries of fire gods flanked the Roman Forum. Near the Black Stone beneath the Capitol stood the Volcanal, the open-air shrine of Vulcan, the blacksmith husband of Rome's ancestral goddess, Venus. Here, on the spot where Romulus and Tatius were said to have made peace between their Latin and Sabine peoples, Vulcan was worshipped as protector of the hearth, the male equivalent of Vesta. In the Volcanal priests tended an eternal flame and an annual fire festival, complete with games and sacrifice, was celebrated in the god's honour on 23 August. Both Cacus (the fearsome ogre killed in his cave by Hercules) and the populist king, Servius Tullius, were said to be his sons – as were Caeculus, founder of Praeneste (modern Palestrina), and (some said) Rome's own founder, Romulus.

Facing the Volcanal across the Forum stood the elegant round Temple of Vesta, a goddess believed to have been brought by Aeneas from Troy to Lavinium, from where she came first to Alba Longa and then (in the reign of either Romulus or Numa) to Rome. Served by six high-born priestesses, the Vestal Virgins (who swore an oath of chastity for thirty years, and, if found to have broken it, faced death by being buried alive), Vesta was renowned for her virginity. But (according to Ovid's *Fasti*) she very nearly lost it.

One day Cybele, the eastern mother goddess, invited all the gods to picnic on Mount Ida. There was singing and dancing and general merry-making, but as Vesta lay down on a grassy knoll, tumescent Priapus, 'red guardian of gardens' caught sight of her 'as he stalked nymphs and goddesses, wandering this way and that':

> I don't know if he believed she was a nymph or knew her to be Vesta – he claims *he* didn't know – but salacious hope took hold of him. He tried to creep up unseen on tiptoes, his heart thumping. But luckily old Silenus had taken the donkey (upon which he'd ridden there) to drink at the banks of the soft flowing river. And as Priapus, god of the elongated Hellespont, was on his way to getting started, the donkey began braying – just at the wrong moment! The raucous noise terrified the goddess. She leapt up. The others rushed to see – and Priapus slipped through their aggressive hands.

At Vesta's Festival on 9 June, Roman donkeys normally employed in turning grindstones in mills and bake-houses were adorned with festive garlands from which special loaves of bread were hung. On the Hellespont, however, donkeys were not so lucky. In retribution for their role in frustrating Priapus, citizens of Lampsacus sacrificed them to the rampant god.

Despite her chastity, Vesta was not unfamiliar with the phallus. Phantom phalluses had a habit of appearing near her hearth. Plutarch reports how one sprang up in Alba Longa: an oracle demanded that the king's daughter have sex with it, but, repulsed by the idea, she palmed the duty off onto a serving girl. On discovering this, the king was about to kill the pregnant slave when Vesta, appearing in a dream, forbade him. Left to die by the Tiber, the resultant twins were suckled by a she-wolf, before returning as adults to Alba and slaying the king. Despite the names being different (the king is called Tarchetius) parallels with the myth of Romulus and Remus are obvious.

Another divine phallus sprouted near the Roman Forum at the hearth of King Tarquinius Priscus (whose palace was near Vesta's temple). A beautiful young captive, Ocrisia, discovered it and told her mistress, the prophetic

Queen Tanaquil, who realized that it presaged great things to come. So she ordered Ocrisia to dress as a bride and give herself willingly to the phallus, as a result of which she conceived Rome's sixth king, Servius Tullius – though her lover's identity (whether one of the royal Lares or Vulcan himself) remained a mystery.

Rome's Kings Before Servius Tullius

King Servius Tullius's life was inextricably linked to the Forum, but it is worth noting that many of his predecessors left their mark here, too. The wise, god-fearing Numa (*r.* 715–673 BC) first established his palace in the plain below the Palatine, introducing (if not Romulus) the Vestal Virgins to Rome from Alba Longa and establishing Janus's temple in the Argiletum northeast of the Forum. Numa was succeeded by the warlike Tullus Hostilius (*r.* 673–642 BC), who built the Senate House (the Curia Hostilia) in Rome's Forum, but met a legendary death. When he destroyed Alba Longa, he spared its temples, but abandoned their rites. This provoked Jupiter to hurl boulders onto Mount Albanus, once site of Jupiter's pan-Latin shrine, the earliest and most revered in Italy. Shortly afterwards an otherworldly voice boomed from a sacred forest near the mountain peak, issuing rebukes for abandoning ancestral gods and commanding the rites' re-establishment. It was clear what must be done, but even instituting a nine-day festival could not save Hostilius. Succumbing to plague, he tried to win Jupiter's good grace by performing private rituals. He bungled them, upsetting Jupiter so much that he incinerated both Hostilius and his palace with a lightning bolt.

Next came Ancus Marcius (*r.* 642–617 BC), who combined expansionism with piety, but failed to pass the crown to his ambitious sons. Instead, in the Roman Forum the popular assembly proclaimed Tarquinius Priscus (*r.* 616–579 BC), an incomer from Etruscan Tarquinia. A fine general, who repulsed attacks by Sabines and Etruscans, and increased the scope of Roman rule, he enhanced Rome, not least by his construction of the Great Sewer (Cloaca Maxima), channelling the Forum's streams into one large drain that debouched into the Tiber. Later the sewer was covered over and a barrel-vaulted tunnel built to accommodate the needs of the expanding city.

The Miracles of Attus Navius

Although Tarquinius Priscus's reign was foretold by gods, this did not stop him coming into conflict with his leading augur, Attus Navius. When the king proposed increasing the number of knights (*equites*) and naming their new colleges after himself, Navius opposed him. Correct procedures must be followed; favourable omens must be found.

> This angered the king, who scorned the augur and (it is said) declared: 'Come on, then, holy man! Divine through your augury if what I'm now thinking can be done!' When Attus consulted the omens he said that it could. 'Well,' said the king, 'what I was thinking was that you could cut this whetstone with this razor. Here, take them! Do what your birds declared that you could do.' Then, without any hesitation, Attus sliced right through it.

Livy, the author of this passage, describes a statue of Navius, his head covered, in the Forum not far from the Lacus Curtius and Black Stone, to the left of the Senate House 'where the incident occurred', while Dionysius records that it was erected by Tarquinius Priscus himself and placed 'near the sacred fig tree'.

The position of this fig tree involved another of Navius's miracles, for it was said to be the very tree under which the she-wolf once suckled Romulus and Remus. Originally it grew by the Tiber's banks beyond the Palatine, but it possessed such sanctity that Navius believed it should stand in the Forum near the Senate House. So miraculously he made it move to a place that had once been struck by lightning, and so was already endowed with an aura of the divine. Here it was tended carefully by priests, fearful that its withering might portend Rome's weakening power.

Crowning Servius Tullius

Although many of Tarquinius Priscus's deeds are rooted in history, tales of his death and the accession of his heir, Servius Tullius (*r.* 579–535 BC), belong to legend. At this period the palace was home to Tarquinius, Queen Tanaquil, their daughter, Gegania, and Servius, now their son-in-law. It was clear to all that Servius was being groomed as Tarquinius's heir – thanks both to his natural gifts and signs sent from the gods. Not only had his conception been unusual, but as a young man, a fiery halo was seen playing around his head – which Tanaquil interpreted as evidence of divine backing.

Even thirty-seven years after his accession the two sons of the previous king, Ancus Marcius, resented Tarquinius, accusing him of usurping the throne, and they were determined to prevent Servius from doing the same. So they sent two thuggish shepherds to the palace. As soon as they were granted audience they began a vociferous argument, demanding that the king deliver judgment on their (fictitious) quarrel. Then, as Tarquinius sat listening intently to the arguments of one, the other took an axe and smashed it into the king's head.

While bodyguards seized the fleeing assassins, onlookers rushed to the king's aid – but Tanaquil sent them all away. Then she bolted the doors and summoned Servius, demanding that he take the throne and avenge his father-in-law's death. All that was left to do was manage expectations. From an upper window Tanaquil called for silence. The king (she lied) was only stunned; he had regained consciousness; all would be well – but meanwhile Servius Tullius would rule in his place. For days, they maintained the subterfuge, with Servius presiding over lawsuits, sometimes passing judgment, sometimes deferring verdicts 'until he consulted Tarquinius', while tightening his grip on power. When Tarquinius's death was finally proclaimed, Servius ascended the throne safe in the knowledge that he would be unopposed. Ancus Marcius's sons had already slunk off in exile to the seaside near Lavinium.

Servius Tullius, the Etruscan Macstarna?

In his lost work on the Etruscans, the emperor Claudius is said to have equated Servius Tullius with the Etruscan hero, Macstarna. This Macstarna was an ally of two brothers, Aulus and Caelius Vibenna, who, some maintained, helped Romulus in his war against the Sabines (in the eighth century BC), while others claimed that they supported Tarquin the Proud (in the sixth century BC). According to Claudius, after much fighting Macstarna came to Rome with the rump of Caelius Vibenna's army, whom he settled on a hill, called thereafter the Caelian.

In fact, the story of Macstarna appears to have belonged to swash-buckling folktale. In Vulci, a fourth-century BC wall painting in the François Tomb shows a scene from it. If interpretations are correct, a group of enemy soldiers, including Cneve Tarchunies Rumach (perhaps Gnaeus Tarquinius of Rome), have captured Macstarna, the Vibenna brothers and their friends. Larth Ulthes, the Etruscan king, has managed to creep in, free some of them and give them weapons. As the prisoners enthusiastically slaughter their captors, Macstarna gently unties Caelius Vibenna's hands. Sadly there is no record of a Roman Gnaeus Tarquinius, and 'Macstarna' may simply be an Etruscan version of the Latin *magister* ('magistrate'). We may never know what significance Macstarna and his companions held to whoever commissioned the François Tomb, but the memory of Claudius's histories reminds us of a wealth of Roman and Etruscan mythology now largely forgotten.

Servius Tullius and Fortuna

Romans believed in the power of Fortuna, Lady Luck, so it is no surprise that Servius, for whom everything had gone so swimmingly, attributed much of his success to her. She it was who caused fire to play about his head when he was young; because of her Queen Tanaquil made him swear never to abdicate; so, as Plutarch piously observes, 'Servius's rule belongs entirely to Fortuna, since he received it unexpectedly and kept it against his will.' Indeed, he made Fortuna his patron goddess, establishing a temple for Fortuna Primigenia ('First Born') on the Capitol, and claiming that (just as the nymph Egeria consorted with King Numa) she regularly visited his palace, slipping in by night through an open window, called in Plutarch's day the Porta Fenestella ('The Gate of the Little Window').

Around 120 BC a magnificent sanctuary to Fortuna Primigenia was dedicated in Praeneste (modern Palestrina), whose sprawling remains still dominate the town. In the next century, however, civil wars and constant shifts in fortune reminded Romans just how capricious the goddess could be. Two authors had cause to lament her fickleness.

Fickle Fortuna, Lady Luck, holds a cornucopia in her left hand in this marble statue now in the Vatican Museum.

Ovid, who mysteriously fell from grace in AD 8, before eking out a miserable exile on the Black Sea, imagined her on a quivering orb (the 'wheel of fortune'), which 'shows she's unreliable: she forever stands atop it with unsteady feet. She's less firm than a leaf or breeze.... All human concerns hang by the thinnest thread; what once was strong is dashed by sudden chance.' A little later, Seneca (who would be murdered by his erstwhile pupil, Nero), observed that Fortuna 'grants the prize of monarchy with mocking hand.... She raises you up, only so that she can bring you low.' Six centuries earlier, Servius might have agreed – for the Roman king was to die at the hands of his own family.

Servius Tullius's Murder

Once more (as in Greek tragedies, writes Livy) family jealousy and ambition led to murder. Servius had arranged for his two daughters (both called Tullia, the feminine form of their family name) to marry the two sons (or grandsons) of his predecessor, Tarquinius Priscus: strong-willed Tarquin the Proud married gentle Tullia the Elder, while his meek brother Arruns married Tullia the Younger, a total termagant. But each of the dominant partners found the other irresistible, for (as Livy darkly comments): 'evil possesses its own magnetism; like attracts like; and so it was with Tarquin and the younger Tullia'. The two conspired in secret. Like some Roman Lady Macbeth, Tullia egged Tarquin on to villainy, and soon two deaths were followed by a marriage. The plotters were united.

Then Tullia turned her gaze to the main prize: setting Tarquin on the throne, so that, as queen, she might wield power. But although Servius was now old, he showed no signs of infirmity. He must be overthrown, and 'twere well it were done quickly. Determinedly, Tarquin shored up support. Then, when he judged the time was right, he made his move.

Striding into the Forum, surrounded by armed guards, he took his seat in the king's place before the Senate House, and as crowds gaped aghast he ordered the town crier to summon the senators to appear before *King* Tarquin. His subsequent oration echoed through the Forum: Servius should never have been king; his reign was illegal; he had stolen from the rich to aid the undeserving poor. It was not long before reports reached the palace, and Servius was bustling to the Senate House, demanding to know what was going on. 'A king's son,' replied Tarquin, 'deserves a throne far more than any slave does! We have let you insult your masters long enough!'

The House erupted in confusion; the public poured in, seeking to support one side or the other; and Tarquin bodily manhandled Servius outside before throwing him down the steps onto the pavement. As the old man staggered towards Vesta's temple and the palace, Tarquin's bodyguard caught up with him and killed him. This was not the only outrage. Almost at once, Tullia drove into the Forum, triumphantly addressing Tarquin as king. Then, as she turned to leave, her driver suddenly reined in his horses. Servius's mutilated body lay directly in their path. Livy continues:

> Crazed and urged on by the avenging Furies of her sister and her former husband, Tullia is said to have driven her carriage over her father's corpse, before, befouled and contaminated, she transferred some of her murdered father's blood, sticking to the bloody vehicle, to her own household gods and her husband's. It was these gods' anger that ensured that the violent start to Tarquin's reign was followed not long after by a violent end.

Tarquin's first edict was to prevent Servius's burial. Romulus's body was not buried, he sneered: why should the slave-king's be? It was a sign of things to come. Proud and overbearing, Tarquin ruled with an increasingly iron fist until, incensed by his son's rape of Lucretia at Collatia, a coterie of senators instigated an uprising that drove him from the throne and so inaugurated the Republic.

The Dioscuri

Tarquin did not take his banishment lying down. With Octavius Mamilius's troops from Tusculum, a city in the rolling hills, he prepared to march on Rome. The Roman army met them by Lake Regillus (now a waterless crater near Frascati). At first the battle's outcome hung in the balance. Mamilius was killed, but so were many leading Romans. Then, fearing that they would be overcome, the Roman general ordered his patrician cavalry to dismount and fight on foot. When they saw the upper classes sharing their danger, he maintained, the plebeian infantry would fight with greater spirit. The tactic worked. Tarquin was beaten back, and the Republic saved. In the final phase of fighting, so survivors said, they saw two young men, glorious in strength and beauty, dismounting from their snorting steeds and plunging with such bravery into the thick of battle that the enemy could not withstand them. Dionysius takes up the story:

> Hostilities ended in the late afternoon, at which time two youths appeared in the Roman Forum, dressed in armour, tall, handsome

and identical in age, looking like they had just been combatants in battle, leading horses slathered in sweat. As they watered their horses and washed them at the fountain [Juturna's Spring] that rises near the Temple of Vesta and forms a small, deep pool, many gathered round and asked if they had news from the camp. And they told them all about the battle and how the Romans had won. But when they left the Forum (it is said) they were never seen again, despite the city prefect conducting a diligent search. Next day the council received a report on the battle, including the appearance of the two divine youths. When they learned this they concluded (as we might, too) that the same gods had appeared in both places, and they understood that the apparitions were the Dioscuri.

Some said that the Romans marked this miracle by building a temple to the Dioscuri near where they appeared. Not Livy. According to him the Roman general at Regillus vowed a temple to the horseman, Castor, if he helped defeat the enemy – Pollux (traditionally more of a boxer) crept in by default. Livy should have known better. For this was not the only time the Dioscuri were associated with victory. In 168 BC, Publius Vatinius, was on his way from Reate (modern Rieti) to Rome when he met two dashing young horsemen, who announced that the Romans had just defeated Perseus of Macedon. Vatinius immediately rushed to the Senate House to share the news, but the senators were unconvinced, and threw him into jail for spreading rumours. Later, however, news came confirming Vatinius's report, and, when he was freed, he discovered that others had seen the same young men, too, watering their horses by Juturna's Spring, and the doors to the Dioscuri's temple had mysteriously swung open.

In Greek mythology the Dioscuri (Castor and Pollux) were twin brothers of Helen (whose abduction caused the Trojan War) and her sister Clytemnestra (who killed her husband Agamemnon at its conclusion) – quadruplets born from a single egg after their Spartan mother Leda was impregnated first by Jupiter in the guise of a swan, then by her human husband, Tyndareus. As a result, two of the children (Helen and Castor) were immortal, while the other two were not – so when Pollux was killed in a cattle raid, Castor, condemned to live without him, was disconsolate. He prayed that he, too, might die, and, although Jupiter refused his wish, he suggested a compromise. Neither fully dead nor fully alive, each should spend alternate days on earth and in the underworld.

The twins' mutual devotion inspired the Romans. Their ancestors worshipped them (perhaps as their Penates) at Lavinium, so they readily

Castor and his horse form part of a larger second-century AD
mosaic now in the Museo Histórico Municipal de Écija in
Seville, Spain.

accepted not just that the Dioscuri were the constellation Gemini, but that
they protected sailors, sometimes appearing in the phenomenon now called
St Elmo's Fire. They were considered so benign that Cicero, observing how
'man's practice and tradition have ensured that, in thanks and gratitude,
we confer the status of gods on famous benefactors', listed as examples of
such gods Hercules, Asclepius and the Dioscuri. 'All these', he concluded,
'were considered gods, because they were outstandingly good and immortal,
since their souls lived on enjoying everlasting life.' He might have added that
all were blue-blooded patricians – when the Dioscuri's Temple (one of the
fledgling Republic's first) was erected in the Forum, not a few plebeians must
have grumbled that in life they were high-status princes. Perhaps some also
complained that they were Greeks.

Greeks in the Forum

Other Greeks, too, graced the Forum. Around 300 BC, the Delphic oracle advised Roman emissaries to erect bronze statues of the bravest and wisest Greeks at either side of the Comitium, the flat area in front of the Senate House where the popular assembly met. Given his connection with King Numa, their choice of Pythagoras as the wisest was uncontroversial, but the Athenian renegade Alcibiades (who died a century earlier) was an odder choice. The decision to erect a statue of another Greek figure, Marsyas, nearby was equally surprising.

Marsyas was a satyr, half-man, half-goat, who lived by the banks of the reedy River Meander (in modern Turkey). When Minerva threw away her *aulos* (an oboe-like instrument), complaining that it caused her cheeks to bulge unprettily, Marsyas picked it up and discovered that he was a virtuoso. So vainglorious did he become that he challenged Apollo, god of music, to a competition, enlisting the Muses as judges. At first it was impossible to choose the better player but, when Apollo suggested each accompany himself on his chosen instrument while singing, poor Marsyas could no longer compete. To punish the rustic upstart, Apollo hung him from a tree and flayed him alive.

While Romans referred to their statue as Marsyas, surviving depictions suggest that it may originally have represented another satyr, Silenus. They show him naked, his left hand grasping a bloated wine skin, his right hand raised, proclaiming the freedom of the state: the companion of Bacchus in his guise as Liber, god of liberty. A notorious pick-up point for ladies of loose morals (Augustus's daughter, Julia, was said to have prostituted herself here), the statue of Marsyas became a symbol of the triumph of the common man, erected at a time when power was shifting (albeit slightly) towards the city's plebs.

The Roman Forum in History and Today

From around the tenth century BC, the upper edges of the marshy valley later occupied by the Roman Forum were used for burial. By the seventh century, huts were built nearby, now associated with the 'Regia', Numa Pompilius's palace, where Rome's sacred shields and spears were housed. Legend suggests that the palace was subsequently dedicated to the Pontifex Maximus (Rome's chief priest), whose duties included supervising the Vestal Virgins in their adjoining temple and residence. Later that century, work (traditionally associated with Tarquinius Priscus and Servius Tullius) was carried out to drain the swamp, fill it with earth and create a flattened area, divided into two zones for political and commercial purposes: the Comitium and Forum.

Around the time of Tarquin the Proud's expulsion in 509 BC, the Regia was burnt (whether the events were linked is unclear). Meanwhile, political focus shifted to two locations bordering the Comitium: the Senate House (Curia Hostilia), traditionally built by Tullus Hostilius on the site of a temple marking Romulus's reconciliation with the Sabines, already sited on a raised platform to protect it from flooding; and the Speaker's Platform, from which orators addressed crowds in the Comitium. Around 498 BC two temples were dedicated on either side of the Forum: to Saturn and the Dioscuri (or just Castor).

Evidence for much of the fifth century is scanty, but in 390 BC Gauls under Brennus sacked the Forum. Many older Romans refused to leave, sitting motionless and silent, an eerie sight to greet their enemy. Nothing could elicit a reaction until, mesmerized, one Gaul stroked a senator's beard. The Roman struck him with his stick, the spell was broken, and the Gauls massacred everyone they found. In 338 BC, the Comitium was rebuilt, and the old Speaker's Platform, now adorned with prows of vessels sunk by Rome's fleet at the Battle of Antium, became known as the 'Rostra' (*rostrum* means 'prow'). Nearby two temples were raised to Concordia ('Political Stability') in 367 and 305 respectively, while in the mid-third century BC a *macellum* ('food hall') was constructed to the north.

In the second century four basilicas were built, containing law courts with commercial and office spaces, evidence of growing economic confidence that reached its zenith with the sack of Carthage and Corinth in 146 BC. In the first century BC, bombastic egos, responsible for the miseries of civil war, transformed the Forum into a truly monumental space. Not content with encroaching onto the Comitium with his massive Basilica Iulia, Julius Caesar created a Forum annex to the north, dominated by a Temple of Venus Genetrix (Mother Venus), proclaiming both his and Rome's direct descent from the goddess. His heir, Augustus, constructed a further Forum focused on his Temple of Mars Ultor (Mars the Avenger), vowed in the wake of Caesar's assassination. Augustus's Forum included two porticoes: in the niches of one stood statues of Aeneas with Ascanius, Anchises and other famous Julii, including Alba Longa's kings, while the other displayed Romulus and great Republicans. A statue of Augustus riding in a triumphal chariot stood in the centre of the square.

Augustus (who boasted of finding Rome clad in brick, but leaving it dressed in marble) further monumentalized the old Forum, building a temple to Julius Caesar (where that would-be king had been cremated) and raising a triumphal arch to celebrate his own victory at Actium. His successors took the process further, turning the Forum into a breathtakingly impressive stage set to showcase ceremonies honouring both city and emperors, as imperial triumphs passed through the Forum along the Sacred Way before climbing onto the Capitol. When more space was needed, emperors went to extraordinary lengths to find it. For his Forum (inaugurated in AD 112), Trajan removed much of the ridge connecting the Capitoline and Quirinal Hills: when his column (part of a great library complex), complete with a helical frieze commemorating victory over Dacia, was erected the next year, its top – soaring 38 m or 126 ft into the air, and once crowned with a 5-m-tall (16-ft) statue of the emperor himself – marked the original ground level.

The Forum suffered badly under Theodosius, whose edict of AD 393 banning non-Christian religions marked the end of pagan temples, and later, too, at the hands of plundering Goths and Vandals. Still Rome struggled on. In AD 470 the Rostra was even enlarged, but the glory days were over. Some of the Forum's more suitable buildings were reused as churches: the Curia Julia became the Church of San Adriano, while the Temple of Antoninus and Faustina was converted into the Church of San Lorenzo in Miranda. Others housed Roman barons. Still others were quarried for building material. By the Renaissance, the Forum was a place of romantic ruins, and when Edward Gibbon visited in 1764 he noted:

> The forum of the Roman people, where they assembled to enact their laws and elect their magistrates, is now enclosed for the cultivation of pot-herbs or thrown open for the reception of swine and buffaloes.

The first systematic excavations began shortly afterwards. Today the artfully restored Roman Forum is one of Europe's most popular tourist destinations. In 2016, it attracted 6.4 million visitors (more than six times the size of the classical city's population at its height).

C10th BC   Burials in archaic necropolis.

c. 600 BC   Forum paved.

509 BC   Tarquin the Proud expelled; Regia burned.

c. 498 BC   Temples of Saturn and of the Dioscuri dedicated.

390 BC   Gauls sack Forum.

367 BC   Temple of Concordia built.

338 BC   Rostra adorned with ships' prows.

305 BC   Second Temple of Concordia built.

c. 250 BC   Macellum built.

184 BC   Basilica Porcia built.

179 BC   Basilica Aemilia built.

169 BC   Basilica Sempronia built.

121 BC   Basilica Opimia built.

54 BC   Julius Caesar begins new Forum.

46 BC   Basilica Julia (completed by Augustus in AD 14).

44 BC   Julius Caesar rebuilds Senate House as Curia Julia.

2 BC   Augustus consecrates Temple of Mars Ultor.

AD 82   Arch of Titus built.

AD 112   Trajan's Forum inaugurated.

AD 113   Trajan's Column raised.

AD 141   Temple of Faustina dedicated by Antoninus Pius
(who shared it on his death in 161).

AD 203   Arch of Septimius Severus built.

AD 283   Diocletian rebuilds Curia Julia in its present form after fire.

AD 312   Basilica of Maxentius built.

AD 393   Theodosius's edict closes pagan temples.

AD 410   Goths sack Rome.

AD 630   Curia Julia converted into Church of San Adriano.

Containing arguably Italy's greatest density of important archaeological
remains, the Roman Forum is a palimpsest of different eras, which can be
hard to decipher. Travellers should note that, because of restoration works,
certain areas may be inaccessible.

A path from the entrance on via dei Fori Imperiali passes the (originally
second-century BC) **Basilica Aemilia** (right) and second-century AD
Temple of Antoninus and Faustina (converted by the twelfth century
into the Church of San Lorenzo in Miranda) to covered foundations of
the **Temple of Julius Caesar**, probably built over the site of his funeral
pyre of 44 BC. Immediately west lies the old Forum, with sacred sites,

including the (fenced off) **Lacus Curtius**, with a modern 'Navius's fig tree', close to which Marsyas's statue stood. Beyond, dominated by the third-century AD **Arch of Septimius Severus** and the **Column of Phocas** is the Comitium, with the **Lapis Niger**, **Volcanal** and (considerably more spectacular) **Rostra** and **Curia** (Senate House). Continuing beyond the arch, the path climbs past the second-century BC **Umbilicus Urbis** (marking the centre of the city and the world), turning almost 180 degrees to lead up the **Clivus Capitolinus** past scanty remains of the **Temple of Concord** (originally built in the second century BC, and reconstructed by Tiberius), the first-century AD **Temple of Vespasian** and the fourth-century AD **Portico of the Dii Consentes** (the Forum's last pagan monument) (right). Towering on the left are columns of the **Temple of Saturn**, inaugurated in the fifth century BC. Returning to the Arch of Septimius Severus, the **Vicus Jugarius** runs off beneath the Temple of Saturn, with the huge first-century BC **Basilica Iulia** on the left (and fine views over the Forum).

Back along the **via Sacra** (Sacred Way) at the Temple of Julius Caesar, one path leads (right) past an entrance to the **Cloaca Maxima** to the **Temple of the Dioscuri** (originally fifth century BC, but dedicated in its present form in AD 6) and **Lacus Juturnae** (Juturna's Spring). Another leads to the **Temple of Vesta** (home to Rome's sacred flame, as well as the Palladium and Penates), and the **House of the Vestal Virgins** complete with ponds and rose garden. Between the Temple of Vesta and the Temple of Antoninus and Faustina is the site of the **Regia**. Continuing, the via Sacra passes (on the left) an **archaic necropolis**, the **Temple of Romulus** (not Rome's founder but the son of Maxentius, r. AD 306–312) with original bronze doors, and the vast **Basilica of Maxentius**. Atop the hill (the Velia) the first-century AD **Arch of Titus** bears sculptures showing the emperor's triumph following the sack of Jerusalem. Nearby is thought to be the site of the Tarquinii's palace. From here paths lead to the Palatine Hill and (past Hadrian's **Temple of Venus and Rome** rising to the left) the Colosseum.

Visitors should not ignore Rome's other Fora, which, although vandalized by Mussolini's via dei Fori Imperiali, are now beginning to enjoy the attention they deserve. On the same side of the via dei Fori Imperiali as the Roman Forum is **Caesar's Forum** with the **Temple of Venus Genetrix**. On the other side are (from southwest to northeast): **Vespasian's Forum of Peace** (dedicated AD 75); **Augustus's Forum** with remains of the **Temple of Mars Ultor** dedicated in 2 BC; and **Trajan's Forum** (now accessible) from which the sheer scale of **Trajan's Column** can be best appreciated. The **Hemicycle** (part of Trajan's Market) and Museum (**Museo dei Fori Imperiali**) are also well worth visiting.

* *

CHAPTER 15
TARQUINIA:
TOMBS, KINGS AND REFUGEES

Chosen by lot, this group [of Lydians] left their country and made their way to Smyrna, where they built a fleet, into which they loaded everything that could be carried on a ship. Then they put to sea in search of a new land and new living, until at last – after sailing past lands of many different peoples – they arrived at the land of the Ombrici, where they founded cities and remained ever since. They no longer call themselves Lydians, but Tyrrhenians [Etruscans] after the prince, who brought them there.

Herodotus, *Histories*, 1.94

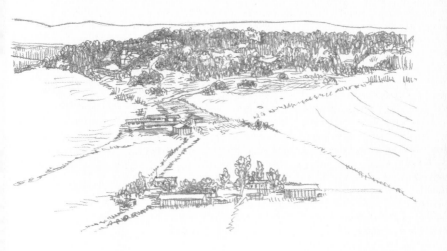

Straggling flocks of shaggy cumulus drift white across an azure sky. Their shadows animate the tawny soil below, cresting undulating hills and sliding into shallow valleys, where rich ploughed fields are bordered by lush hedgerows, and ranks of tall umbrella pines stand sentinel beside straight sandy tracks. And, pale against the blue horizon, silhouettes of mountains shimmer in the autumn sun. Sea salt mingles with the scent of warm dry soil. Breeze carries birdsong. Life animates the very air.

Here on this lush, gentle ridge, where a grey cat lounges in the sun and insects thrum from grasses, echoes of ancient lives continue to pulse underground, deep in chill chambers hewn from frozen stone. Descend damp iron steps and you can see them still through finger-marked glass doors: a fisherman letting down his net from a blue-prowed ochre boat as dolphins arc beside him, and a huntsman trying to down a flock of soaring birds – blue, red and white; men and women dancing lustily to music from a lyre-player and flautist beside a huge jar garlanded with turquoise flowers; nude long-haired youths replenishing broad wine cups for banqueters reclining on low couches decked with yellow-, red- and blue-checked blankets in tents with chequered roofs. Here, too, are olive trees heavy with black fruit, fine-feathered cockerels, leopards, lions with claret bodies and blue manes, flexing shoulders as they gaze down on the scene below, where dancers writhe by trees festooned with ribbons. Elsewhere, other lions are mauling spotted deer; a dog sinks teeth into a hooded man as blood spurts from his arms and shins and thigh; a blue-skinned demon dances, clutching bearded speckled snakes. These fading images of such vitality and vibrance, showing lives tinged with mystery and terror, speak of beliefs far distant from our own, and offer tantalizing hints of an alien society: the world of the Etruscans.

Etruscans' Arrival in Italy

Legend tells that Etruscans, like Romans, were originally migrant refugees from Asia Minor. According to Herodotus, during the reign of their second king, Atys, an eighteen-year famine beset the Lydians. Being a resourceful nation, they alleviated their misery by inventing dice, knucklebones (a game not unlike dice), ball games 'and every other kind of sport except for draughts', alternating days of obsessive play (when they forgot their appetite) with days of eating. At last, however, with no end in sight, Atys divided his people into two groups, deciding by lot who should stay and who should emigrate. While he remained, his son, Tyrrhenus, ruler of the refugees, led his people on a voyage west, until (like Aeneas and his Trojans) they arrived in Italy. Here in the land of the Ombrici (who almost certainly gave their name to Umbria, but whose territory Herodotus describes as stretching to the Alps) they made their home and built their cities, changing their name from Lydians to Tyrrhenians in honour of their leader. 'Tyrrhenians' was Greek for 'Etruscans'.

Inevitably there were other explanations. Writing under Augustus, Strabo linked the Etruscans to Pelasgians (warlike Arcadians, who spread throughout Greece from Crete to Thessaly, colonizing Argos and Athens on the way), adding that, first settling the islands of Lemnos and Imbros, 'some migrated to Italy with Tyrrhenus, son of Atys'. A further twist was added by the local fifteenth-century AD poet, Lorenzo Vitelli, who erroneously linked the name Cornetum, by which Tarquinia was then known, with Coritus, father of Dardanus, founder of Troy. While modern historians remain unconvinced by a Lydian–Etruscan link, scientific research on Etruscan DNA has failed to come up with alternative origins, and may even hint that the myth contains a shred of truth.

Tages

Tyrrhenus's son (or brother), Tarchon, founded Tarquinia, known to the Etruscans as Tarchuna. As Tarchon tilled the fertile plough land, he came across a clod of earth which metamorphosed before his very eyes into a young boy. At once the prodigy began to speak. Its name, it said, was Tages, and (according to a sceptical Cicero, quoting Etruscan annals) although it looked like a child:

> It had the wisdom of a seer. Amazed and frightened at the sight, the ploughman cried out in wonder. A crowd gathered round, and soon all Etruria had assembled there. Tages addressed this substantial audience at length, while they enthusiastically took in and wrote down all he had to say. His entire speech was a discourse on the science of soothsaying.

Even as the child spoke, his audience saw him ageing. By the time he finished he was a weak old man, who died, disintegrating into dust. His knowledge remained, however, and 'in later years, new discoveries were learned, tested in accordance to Tages' principles, and added to the original collection'.

This was the art of haruspicy, whereby experienced soothsayers examined fresh entrails of sacrificial victims to foretell the future, a science that both Etruscans and Romans considered vital. Books on haruspicy were written, and a model of a sheep's liver (the Liver of Piacenza) survives, showing the organ divided into zones, according to the health of which forecasts were made. Each bears the abbreviated name of an Etruscan god, while the perimeter is marked into sixteen areas, possibly corresponding to the Etruscan zodiac.

Tarchon the Younger and Aeneas

Virgil, accepting that Etruscans were Lydian immigrants, writes that in the following generation, Tarchon's son, Tarchon the Younger, leader of the Etruscan Confederation, was an important ally of Aeneas. Eager to defeat Ardea's Turnus and the disgraced Etruscan King Mezentius of Caere (modern Cerveteri), Tarchon offered command of his army – and his throne – to Rome's Evander. Evander rejected it, however, citing a prophecy that only a foreigner could be victorious. So Aeneas rode to Caere, where Venus presented him with a new suit of armour forged by Vulcan, including a shield bearing images of Rome's future greatness. At Caere, Aeneas met Tarchon, and cemented an alliance.

For much of the *Aeneid*, Tarchon is shadowy, coming into his own only in a late battle scene, when Jupiter galvanizes him and he dashes across the plain outside Lavinium, tearing an enemy rider from his horse, and clinging to his struggling foe he tries to stab him with a broken spear point. Many Romans would have been surprised by his bravery – their usual view of Etruscans is summed up in Tarchon's speech to his followers, who shrink from doing battle with the warrior queen Camilla:

Etruscans, never ready to face pain, always slacking! What fear, what cowardice has gripped your spirits? Has a woman frightened you, made you turn tail? Why do we carry weapons if we can't use them? You're quick enough to join the nightly tussle of lovemaking, or join the dance when Bacchus's curved flute invites you. Well, keep your powder dry 'till dinner time, when tables groan with wine cups, if that's your pleasure, if that's all that you care for! Wait till the haruspex proclaims good omens, and summons you to banquet in deep sacred groves.

Etruscan Luxury

While Etruscans were considered pious because of their knowledge and conduct of religious observances, they also enjoyed a reputation as the most decadent of people. They were stereotyped as fat and flabby, and at least two fourth-century BC historians took great glee in imagining their excesses. While Timaeus of Tauromenium (present-day Taormina) wrote of banqueters served by naked slave girls, Theopompus of Chios took things further, recounting:

A fresco from Tarquinia's fifth-century BC
Tomb of the Leopards shows a banquet in progress.

It is quite normal for Etruscans to share their womenfolk. These women take great care of their bodies, and often even exercise with men, and sometimes with each other (it is no disgrace for women to be seen naked). Moreover, they banquet, not with their own husbands, but with whatever man is present, making toasts to whomever they wish. They greatly enjoy their drink and are stunningly beautiful. Etruscans rear any baby that is born, without ever knowing who the father is.... When they meet socially or for family gatherings...the servants may usher in female prostitutes, handsome boys, or even wives; and when banqueters have had their fill of them, the servants next bring strapping young men, who proceed to lie with them, sometimes in full view of all, though usually couches are screened off. It is true that they consort enthusiastically with women, but they enjoy boys and adolescents even more.

A Greek Refugee

Given the Etruscans' reputation, it is not surprising that Tarquinia attracted at least one refugee from that most louche of Greek cities, Corinth. Dionysius records that Demaratus, a wealthy businessman, gave up all other trading partners to focus exclusively on the Etruscan market. When Cypselus, a member of a rival dynasty, became Corinth's tyrant (in 657 BC), Demaratus, fearing for his life, stowed his wealth on board a ship and sailed to Italy.

> Because of his constant trade with the Etruscans, he had many firm friends there, and especially at Tarquinia, which was then a large and prosperous city. So he built a house there, married a high-born woman and had two sons by her, whom he called by Etruscan names: one, Arruns; the other, Lucumo. He schooled them in both Greek and Etruscan learning, and, when they were of age, arranged marriages for them with noble women.

While Demaratus may be a historical figure, many legends surrounding him are now treated with suspicion. Tradition tells that he brought three craftsmen from Corinth, Eucheir, Diopus and Eugrammus; but since their names mean 'Good with his Hands', 'Clear Sighted' and 'Good Draughtsman' many think that they are merely personifications of archaic arts and crafts (unless, of course, they were nicknames). Furthermore, Demaratus is credited with introducing writing to Etruria, but while art and culture did certainly flourish in Tarquinia at this time, Demaratus's arrival was not the only reason. Like other Etruscan cities, Tarquinia already enjoyed close links with Greece, the Near East and Egypt, all of which contributed to its burgeoning cultural life. Of even greater importance to our story are Demaratus's sons, Arruns and Lucumo, for the entangled fate of their families had a profound impact on Rome's mythology and history.

Demaratus's Sons

When Demaratus was an old man, Arruns, his eldest son, died suddenly without an heir. So Demaratus left his wealth in its entirety to his second son, Lucumo. Now wealthy and ambitious, Lucumo tried to enter politics, but, being the son of an incomer and possessing no citizen rights, he was rejected at all turns. Frustrated, he learned that in a nearby city foreigners were not just granted citizenship but could also succeed on merit. So Lucumo, his wife Tanaquil and all his household made the 80-km (50-mile) journey to Rome, where, changing his name to Lucius Tarquinius (Lucius from Tarquinia) he was appointed her fifth king. All the same, he did not forget Tarquinia. Strabo writes:

> Like his father before him, he enriched Etruscan land – Demaratus through artisans he brought from Corinth, Tarquinius through Rome's resources. They say that the regalia used in triumphs and by consuls and other rulers was transferred to Rome from Tarquinia, along with fasces, axes, trumpets, sacrificial rites, arts of divination, and all kinds of public music used in Rome.

However, unbeknownst to anyone, when Arruns died, his wife was newly pregnant with a son, who (since Demaratus changed his will) was now disinherited. As a result the child bore the name Egerius ('Needy'). Nothing is known of his childhood, but he, too, went to Rome, where he served in the army of his uncle (by now King Tarquinius Priscus), and when Tarquinius forced Sabine Collatia to surrender, he appointed Egerius its garrison commander. Nonetheless, Egerius's family was destined to destroy his uncle's, for his son, Lucius Tarquinius Collatinus, married Lucretia, whose rape by Rome's prince Sextus Tarquinius prompted the overthrow of Rome's kings and the dawn of the Republic. Thus, while one branch of Demaratus's family was vilified for overbearing pride, the other was praised as liberators.

Even so, the fortunes of the two branches were similar. Although they elected Tarquinius Collatinus one of Rome's first consuls, the people hated his name – because, Livy writes, 'it was ill-omened, an anathema to freedom'. His position became untenable; even his colleague, Brutus, and his father-in-law, Lucretius, urged him to leave Rome. So in the end, the last of Demaratus's dynasty, he resigned the consulship to live with his family as exiles in Lavinium.

Painted Tombs

No Etruscan literature survives, and, while the emperor Claudius composed a twenty-volume *History of the Etruscans* (in Greek), Romans (apparently deliberately) erased many traces of their culture. Much of our knowledge is therefore based on studies of surviving art and artefacts – the greatest concentration of which is at Tarquinia. There are 6,100 tombs spanning 400 years (from around 600 BC), many originally covered with round burial mounds, and roughly 200 of them are painted.

Most depict exuberant life: dancers, banqueters and athletes, fishermen and hunters set in a fecundity of flowers, trees and teeming oceans, with leaping dolphins, birds and prowling animals. Whether these represented the real world (reminders to the dead of what they had left behind) or the afterlife remains unclear. It is suggested that they are evidence of the resurrecting power of Fufluns, a vegetation god, whom Etruscans linked to Dionysus/ Bacchus, even elaborating legends in which, the son of Semla (Greek Semele), he first abandoned and then married Princess Areatha (Ariadne).

Some scenes are baffling. Why, for example, in the Tomb of the Bulls (above a painting of Achilles ambushing Troilus at Troy) is a rampant bull charging at a copulating couple? What is the meaning of the Augurs' Tomb, where a hooded, club-wielding man is savaged by a black dog, through whose collar a nail has been driven to enrage him, while a second man (labelled 'Phersu') uses ropes to goad – or hamper – dog and victim? Is 'Phersu' connected to the Latin *persona* (mask), suggesting that he is an actor? The victim's blood and suffering seem real. So, does this represent the type of orchestrated violent death that would become popular in Roman amphi-theatres? Or does 'Phersu' represent a mythological character – perhaps Charun? Certainly attendants masked as Charun worked in amphitheatres, despatching victims with heavy mallets, before dragging their corpses offstage. Other tombs show Charun in the company of snake-wielding Tuchulcha, or Vanth, the goddess who conveyed souls to the underworld. Unlike his Greek equivalent, this Etruscan Charun is not a ferryman. Rather, he guards the entrance to the underworld, sometimes depicted as a painted door within the tomb beyond which living viewers cannot pass.

In Tarquinia's sixth-century BC Augurs'
Tomb a hooded man is savaged by a dog,
whose lead is held by the bearded 'Phersu'.

Over the centuries, the paintings' character shifts. While at first they possess a Near Eastern or Greek vitality, by the third century, when processions of dour, toga-wearing neo-Roman magistrates crowd the walls, they become more static and less obviously well executed. By 200 BC the age of painted tombs was over, but not their tumultuous history. In the Middle Ages many were robbed of their grave goods – in 1489 Pope Innocent VIII sanctioned an expedition to find gold treasures, while in 1546 locals were made to submit 2,000 kg (4,400 pounds) of Etruscan metalwork to be melted down and used in Rome's Basilica of St John Lateran. Over the next centuries painted tombs were discovered and drawn, but as one eighteenth-century visitor lamented:

The paintings appear beautiful and new when grottoes are first opened, but with the free passage of air everything is lost within a few years, and the plaster on which they are painted becomes damp and crumbly.

Opening a tomb in 1822 a local official, Carlo Avvolta, saw:

a warrior lying on the couch before me. In only a few minutes I watched him decompose. As more air entered the tomb, his armour oxidized the more, disintegrating into the most minute of particles 'till scarcely anything that I had seen was left behind.

This story of a crumbling corpse was doubly intriguing. First because it recalled Tages, the infant prodigy discovered in a furrow, who aged throughout the day, only to die and dissolve into soil by evening. And also, as news spread, it set a precedent for other romanticizing archaeologists. When Heinrich Schliemann discovered a gold face mask at Mycenae in 1876, he claimed that the face beneath, intact for over three millennia, had quickly decayed to dust, and declared: 'I have gazed on the face of Agamemnon'.

As their fame spread, treasure-hunters, sponsored by museums and collectors, pillaged the tombs, removing sections of paintings and dynamiting what remained to hide the evidence. By the 1840s nineteen painted tombs were protected by a custodian, and a local museum opened in 1875 (transferring to its present site in 1916). Between 1949 and 1960, paintings from seven tombs were removed and reconstructed in temperature- and humidity-controlled environments, including four in the museum. However, illicit digging continues. Writing in 1986, one robber, Luigi Perticarari, even boasted of his skill in extracting frescoes with a power saw.

Tarquinia in History and Today

While tombs on Monterozzi Ridge date to 3000 BC, villages sprang up on hilltops around Tarquinia only around 1200 BC (when Tarchon was said to have arrived from Lydia). In the Iron Age (or Villanovan Period) hut settlements became prevalent, but during the eighth century the main habitation moved to Civita, while Monterozzi was devoted to the dead. Now Tarquinia, 6 km (about 4 miles) from the sea, enjoyed close cultural and trading links with cities of the mainland Etruscan League as well as (through its port, Gravisca) with the Near East. Temples were dedicated to Uni (Juno) and Turan (Venus), their architecture showing increasing sophistication – by 650 (by which time Demaratus had arrived from Corinth), public buildings boasted terracotta roof tiles (only thirty years after they appeared in Greece).

Tarquinia flowered in the sixth century BC, when city walls were built, and the Ara della Regina enclosed the site of Tarchon's encounter with Tages. Monterozzi's first painted tombs appeared around 600 BC, their wealth, paintings and grave goods revealing close contact with Greece. Tarquinia's population numbered between 14,500 and 25,000, and according to Livy its people 'considered it a fine thing that a man of their blood ruled' Rome. Irked by Tarquin the Proud's expulsion in 509 BC, they allied with Veii against the Romans at the Battle of the Arsian Woods, until a mysterious voice from Silvanus's wood proclaimed their defeat. In 474 an Etruscan fleet, probably including Tarquinian ships, was defeated by Syracusans at Cumae, disrupting trade routes.

Following Rome's capture of Veii in 396 BC and a Gallic invasion in 390, while Etruscan coastal cities were harried by Syracusans, Tarquinia's relations with Rome again soured. In 358 BC Tarquinia's men defeated a Roman army, slaughtering 307 captives in ritual sacrifice, inflicting a further defeat the next year. Livy describes legionaries panicking at the sight of 'Etruscan priests brandishing serpents and blazing torches, and advancing like Furies'. In 353 BC the tables were turned, and Romans led 358 Tarquinian prisoners back to the Forum, where they flogged and beheaded them.

With Etruscan Caere (Cerveteri) forging alliances with Rome, Tarquinia was the region's leading independent player, and it was now that the Ara della Regina was enhanced with terracotta sculptures, including magnificent winged horses. However, Tarquinia was unable to resist the growth of

The delicate fourth-century BC terracotta 'Winged Horses of Tarquinia' once adorned the pediment of the Ara della Regina.

Rome just 80 km (50 miles) away. Escaping the depredations of the Second Punic War, by 205 BC her womenfolk were busy making sailcloth for Scipio prior to his victory over Hannibal at Zama (202 BC). By now the last of the painted tombs had been closed up.

Under Roman rule, Tarquinia was a nondescript provincial town, but some distinguished citizens served as senators. Meanwhile, her haruspices continued to wield influence – Spurinna, who warned Caesar to 'beware the Ides of March', may have been from Tarquinia – and their significance was still felt in AD 408, when they were consulted for the last time when Alaric threatened Rome. Tarquinia's subsequent history is unclear. Gravisca was abandoned by 549, and in 1307 Civita fell to its new neighbour, Corneto, built at the eastern edge of Monterozzi Ridge. When Domenico Bandini of Arezzo (1335–1418) visited soon afterwards, he described Corneto as:

> an exceptional town with towers, encircled by a double wall, looking across from a high hill to the sea in the far distance. Tarquinia was in its territory, a city once, now nothing but an empty name and ruins, though from it came the Tarquins who ruled Rome.

Interest in newly discovered tombs began to draw both visitors and looters, and, with Corneto renamed Tarquinia in 1922, a fine new museum was established, but despite laws to preserve surviving archaeology, *tombaroli* (tomb raiders) still ply their pernicious trade.

c. 3000 BC	First rock tombs on Monterozzi.
c. 1200 BC	Etruscan migration from Lydia? Hilltop settlements around Tarquinia.
C8th BC	Civita becomes main centre of habitation. Cultural links with Near East and Magna Graecia.
c. 700 BC	First chamber tombs. Imports of Athenian/Corinthian pottery.
657 BC	Demaratus arrives at Tarquinia.
600 BC	First painted tombs.
C6th BC	City walls, temple and harbour built. Monterozzi now becomes principal burial ground.
359–353 BC	War with Rome.
308 BC	Truce with Rome.
281 (or 268) BC	Becomes part of Roman federation.
205 BC	Women make sails for Scipio.
c. 200 BC	Last painted tombs.
181 BC	Gravisca becomes a Roman colony.
90 BC	Tarquinia becomes a fully Roman town with Roman administration.
AD 161	Baths built.
AD 1006	Corneto becomes a fortified town.
AD 1307	Corneto defeats Civita.
AD 1489	First modern 'dig' at Monterozzi tombs.

On Civita Ridge are foundations of the **Ara della Regina** and a stretch of **walls** complete with gateway. More impressive are the painted tombs on Monterozzi Ridge near modern Tarquinia. To preserve them from light, air and visitors, many open on rotation. Housed beneath small huts, they are approached down occasionally slippery metal stairs, which end at glass doors, insulating the chambers and forbidding access. Time-switches operate electric lights, for such brief periods that much effort is spent operating them – a willing companion is a useful asset. Do not be put off, however. The tombs repay the effort.

They include – closest to the ticket office and (good) café – the **Tomb of the Jugglers** (where a woman balances a vase on her head); the **Tomb of Hunting and Fishing**; the **Tomb of the Hunter** (painted to resemble a tent with a frieze of animals and horsemen); the **Tomb of the Lionesses** (musicians and dancers perform beside an urn); the **Tomba della Pulcella** (the only tomb approached along its original *dromos*); the **Leopards' Tomb** (scenes of banqueting and music making); the **Tomb of the Demon Azurri** (images of the underworld); and the **Tomb of the Charons** (guarding the doorway to death). Above ground are Iron Age tombs and markers.

Tarquinia's stunning **Museo Nazionale Tarquiniense** is housed in the fifteenth-century Palazzo Vitelleschi. Treasures include seventh- and sixth-century BC **stone relief carvings** from tomb façades, showing mythological creatures and scenes from Greek mythology; **sarcophagi**, sculpted or painted with battles (including the Amazonomachy and Centauromachy), one topped by Cerberus; Greek vases with paintings of **Dionysus, the Dioscuri, Jupiter and Europa**, and sundry **erotic scenes**; and the fabulous terracotta **winged horses**, once part of the Ara della Regina's pediment, now beautifully stabled in a dedicated room. Reconstructed from Monterozzi are the **Tomb of the Triclinium** (where dancers perform ecstatically and a cat chases partridges beneath couches); the **Tomb of the Biga** (with a chariot race complete with crash); and the **Ship Tomb** (with detailed depictions of an Etruscan merchantman).

Another local Etruscan city is Caere (**Cerveteri**), some of the tombs of whose **Necropolis of Banditaccia** resemble Iron Age huts, while others front onto wide, grid-patterned streets. Many interior chambers contain fine carving, and, while few paintings survive, the late fourth-century BC **Tomb of the Reliefs** is named from its vividly painted reliefs of objects from everyday life, giving a good idea of an Etruscan home's interior. Cerveteri's **Museo Nazionale**, with fine interactive displays, contains a good collection of Greek pottery. Highlights include the **Euphronios Krater** showing the dead Trojan hero Sarpedon being lifted from the battlefield by Death and Sleep, and a **kylix** by the same potter showing the Sack of Troy.

CHAPTER 16
CLUSIUM:
CITY OF LARS PORSENNA

So mighty was Clusium, so great the power of Lars Porsenna.

Livy, *Ab Urbe Condita*, 2.9

Light floods the valleys, picking out dark clumps of cypress and tall umbrella pines, before diffusing in the morning mist that causes climbing fields and rolling hills and tree-fringed mountains to appear to hover in the clear blue air, turning villages and bell towers into distant ghosts. Here in Chiusi, light bathes ancient stones and gateways, flooding through dark-shadowed streets, and washing terracotta walls, to sparkle on fat scarlet heads of window-box geraniums. There are bright colours everywhere: across from the museum, a flash of orange overalls as a man sweeps the cathedral portico; in the narrow square, crates, red and yellow, burgeon with salad leaves of luscious green and fruit – bananas, apples, lemons – beneath striped blue and green and pink and yellow awnings.

In the shade, men of a certain age, most grey and balding, all dressed in a uniform of blue jeans and blue zipper-jackets, lean against crumbling balustrades and watch the world – and ladies of a younger age – go by, while others stop to read white posters tacked high on a burnt-umber notice board: black-bordered death announcements: Alfredo Cupelli (72); Gennaro Necci (81); Carmela Leone (95). Yet these are not the only posters to adorn the walls. On another, a blue rabbit – an Italian Bugs Bunny – a green snail grinning on his right hind paw, points down the road with uncontained excitement, and a sign proclaims, '*Tutti i martedi*, every Tuesday, just fifty metres distant: Porsenna's Market!' How proud the old Etruscan would have been.

Osinius

There is much that is shadowy about the mythology of Clusium (modern Chiusi). So, fittingly, the first king we hear of was connected to a phantom. Virgil tells how, when Aeneas learns of his young friend Pallas's death, he rampages savagely across the battlefield, seeking his enemy, Turnus. Juno knows that, if they meet, Turnus (her favourite) will be killed, so she creates a diversion: she sends a phantom Aeneas to lure Turnus onto a ship moored nearby – the ship, writes Virgil, in which King Osinius sailed with his troops from Clusium, part of Aeneas's Etruscan alliance. No sooner does Turnus board it, than it slips its moorings and drifts out to sea, a ghost ship gliding through the waves away from danger until it touches shore at Ardea.

It is the only surviving mention of Osinius. Perhaps Virgil invented him, but more probably this reference is the only echo of a once-thriving mythology, in which Clusium played a major part. It would not be the only time that Clusium's role in history or legend was suppressed or skewed. The most controversial involved another king, Lars Porsenna, and his siege of Rome.

Lars Porsenna

Clusium was keen to curb Rome's growing power, and, in the wake of Collatia's fall in 585 BC, she joined a confederation of north Etruscan cities – Arretium (Arezzo), Volaterra (Volterra), Rusellae and Vetulonia – sending troops to help Rome's Latin and Sabine enemies. The following years saw heavy fighting and severe casualties until at Eretum, 30 km (almost 19 miles) northeast of Rome, Tarquinius Priscus inflicted a crushing defeat on the Etruscans in what Dionysius calls 'the greatest battle yet between the two nations', massacring many, increasing Rome's influence and earning himself a triumph.

However, when Tarquin the Proud was expelled from Rome in 509 BC, Clusium's then leader, Lars Porsenna ('Lars' perhaps meant 'ruler'; 'Purthne', 'supreme magistrate'), seized the opportunity to turn the tables. One tantalizing fragment of Etruscan mythology hints that Porsenna was once considered to be superhuman: when a monster, Olta (a terrifying wolf-man), devastated the territory of Volsinii (perhaps modern Orvieto), and even attacked the city itself, Porsenna conjured up a thunderstorm and destroyed him with a lightning flash.

More prosaically, however, when exiled King Tarquin turned to Clusium for help, Porsenna issued an ultimatum: Rome must either restore Tarquin to the throne or face all-out war. When his demands were rejected, Porsenna led his Etruscans south, where they were joined by disgruntled Latins from Tusculum and the surrounding districts. As they converged on Rome to encamp on the Janiculum, panicked country-dwellers, fleeing inside the walls, prepared for siege.

This was the setting for the triptych of heroic Roman tales that helped define the essence of patriotic bravery: Horatius Cocles guarding the Sublician Bridge; Scaevola plunging his right hand into the flames; Cloelia leading prisoners to safety across the raging Tiber. Some claimed that her bravery (and the cowardly response of Tarquin's son) led to a rapprochement between Rome and Porsenna. Dionysius maintains that Porsenna was so impressed by Cloelia's pluck that he returned his remaining prisoners, made a treaty with Rome and withdrew to Clusium, while Rome's Senate sent Porsenna a sceptre, gold crown and ivory throne, along with a triumphal robe, the panoply of kingship.

It all sounds very cosy, but a throwaway remark from Tacitus suggests the truth was different. Writing about civil strife in AD 69, when the Capitoline Temple of Jupiter Optimus Maximus was destroyed by fire, he observes 'that neither Porsenna, *when Rome surrendered* [my italics], nor the Gauls, when Rome was taken, had managed to profane' this temple. Pliny the Elder backs up this observation, recalling part of a treaty from the time stating that henceforth 'Romans should use iron only for agricultural equipment'. They should beat swords into ploughshares: they should be disarmed. As with Virgil's glancing reference to Osinius, so here in Tacitus and Pliny, we stumble on a hidden truth: that Lars Porsenna of Clusium defeated Rome, and occupied the city. Although he did not restore Tarquin to the throne (which suggests he simply used the deposed king as an excuse for war), he did impose terms that, for a while at least, immeasurably enhanced his kudos.

Defeat at Aricia

Toeing the official line, Livy recounts that 'abandoning his war with Rome, and reluctant to seem to have mobilized his army in vain, Porsenna sent his son Arruns with some troops to attack Aricia' (modern Ariccia) in the Alban Hills. However, the mission ended in defeat, when Latins with Greek

Etruscan warriors march to battle on this relief now housed in Chiusi's Archaeological Museum.

allies from Cumae rallied to Aricia's aid. At first luck seemed on Arruns's side, but then he found himself caught in a pincer movement. He and most of his men were slaughtered. The rest fled – not to Clusium but to Rome, where they were kindly received and housed until their wounds were healed. Indeed, while some subsequently returned home, praising their benefactors' kindness, others settled in Rome itself, in a ghetto known thereafter as the Etruscan Quarter.

Now, if Porsenna had been defeated (as Livy claims), Rome's altruistic behaviour towards her recent enemy is inexplicable. Again, a greater truth appears to lurk below the surface. Was Arruns's expedition part of a wider strategy once Porsenna had taken Rome? Was it this defeat that stopped Porsenna from exploiting his hold on Rome? And did powerful Rome later try to erase all memory of her defeat by Clusium, so that only the faintest echo has come down to us? Certainly Augustus's historians worked hard to vilify both Clusium and another Arruns, blaming them for initiating events that would threaten Rome's existence.

Enticing Gauls

There was once, writes Dionysius, a old prince of Clusium named Lucumo (his name in Etruscan meant simply 'prince' or 'nobleman'). Before he died he entrusted his young son's guardianship to Arruns, his closest friend, who nurtured the boy, caring for him as if he were his own, and ensuring he received his whole estate intact when he reached adulthood. His ward, however, soon abused his kindness.

Arruns had a beautiful young wife, to whom he was devoted, while she in turn had eyes only for him. But Arruns's ward desired her, too, and over time seduced her, 'corrupting her mentally as well as physically, and seeking her out to talk with her in public as well as private'. Arruns was devastated, but because his ward was rich and powerful there was little he could do – at least not on his own. So he hatched a plan.

He persuaded his ward to finance him on a business trip of many months to Gaul (during which, the young man reckoned, he might himself make hay in Clusium), and soon Arruns was heading north, with wagons full of delicate delights such as wine, olive oil and figs. As Dionysius explains, at this time:

> Gauls had no experience of wine made from grapes, or oil from our olive trees, but instead of wine used a foul-smelling drink made from barley left to putrefy in water, and rancid pig fat, hideous to smell and taste, instead of oil.

To these beer-swilling, lard-guzzling 'barbarians', Arruns's wares seemed miraculous, and they clamoured to know where they could get more. It was exactly what Arruns had hoped for.

> He told them that the land where these fruits grew was vast and fertile, inhabited by only a few men – and these no braver than women when it came to fighting. And he recommended that, instead of buying such delicacies from others, they should expel the current inhabitants and enjoy the fruits as their own. Persuaded by these words, the Gauls descended into Italy and the city called by the Etruscans Clusium, from where the man came who incited them to war.

While Livy describes Arruns guiding the Gaulish hordes across the Alps in the early fourth century BC, he injects a note of caution: 'Far be it from me to suggest that Arruns (or another of that town's citizens) did *not* lead the Gauls to Clusium, but it is widely agreed that other Gauls had crossed the Alps before them.' Nonetheless, the folksy tale of an 'obese Etruscan' unleashing Gaulish terror on both Italy and Rome simply to punish his wife's corruptor made for splendid propaganda – especially since only Roman courage would defeat the invaders. First, though, they must face butchery and violence – not least at Clusium.

Fabian Treachery

Livy imagines the reaction of the town's besieged inhabitants:

> The people of Clusium were terrified at this unexpected invasion. Facing them was a countless throng, their strange appearance and their weapons unlike anything that they had seen before. Often rumours came to them: how Etruscan armies had been beaten both across the Po and on the nearer side.

Envoys galloped from Clusium to Rome requesting aid. Although Rome had just conquered Veii, the city was nervous, for not only had her victorious general, Camillus (exiled on trumped-up charges of embezzlement), prayed that the gods might prove his innocence by 'making his thankless country bitterly regret his absence', but also one of her citizens had heard the Voice:

A plebeian, Marcus Caedicius, reported to the tribunes that in the silence of the night on New Street, where a shrine now stands above Vesta's temple, he had heard a voice, more resounding than any human voice, commanding him to tell the magistrates that the Gauls were coming…. It was a warning from the gods, but they ignored it. Fate was drawing closer.

Nonetheless the Senate refused Clusium's requests, though they did despatch three young men, sons of Marcus Fabius Ambustus, to remonstrate with the invaders and try to reach a settlement. 'However, they behaved more like savage Gauls than true Romans.' Incensed at the Gauls' high-handedness, or simply itching to see action, the brothers became involved in fighting. Ambushed, the eldest slew the Gaulish leader – at which the Gauls forgot their feud with Clusium and turned their sights on Rome. Even now they acted with restraint. They sent envoys of their own, demanding reparation, but Rome scornfully refused. And so it was that Brennus, the new Gaulish commander, marched south through fertile valleys, slaughtering Rome's legions at the River Allia, before pouring down into the city to pillage and to burn.

Porsenna's Tomb

At the beginning of the third century BC, Clusium became part of Rome's growing empire, but legends of her lost wealth continued to intrigue – not least the story of Porsenna's tomb. Pliny the Elder considered it a fable, but his description (quoting the earlier Varro) is enticing:

He is buried beneath [or perhaps 'near'] Clusium, at a place where there is a square monument made of squared stones. Each side is 300 feet long and 50 high. Inside this squared base is a labyrinth so tortuous that whoever enters without a ball of thread will never find their way back out. On top of the squared plinth stand five pyramids, four at the corners and one in the middle. The base of each is 75 feet wide and their height is 150 feet. They taper in such a way that a bronze orb rests on top of the whole group, and there is a conical superstructure from which bells hang by chains. When the wind sets them in motion their chimes carry for a great distance…. On top of the orb are four more pyramids, each 100 feet tall. And on top of these five more stand on a single platform.

Varro was ashamed to add the height of these last pyramids, but Etruscan legend recounts that it was equal to the height of the whole of the rest of the building. What sheer madness to seek glory by such extravagance that no-one could profit from, and moreover exhaust the kingdom's resources, when everyone praised the architect more than the man paying for it!

Fantastical though this description seems, some still believe it, and labyrinthine tunnels snaking deep beneath modern Chiusi merely add to their conviction. The tomb's location, however, remains unknown, and chances of locating it are slim: Sulla reportedly destroyed it in 89 BC. In 2012, however, archaeologists discovered five subterranean pyramids with fifth-century BC passages (contemporary with Porsenna's death) in nearby Orvieto. Excavations continue...

(Meanwhile a second search continues further south near Cosenza, where another tomb, perhaps containing looted gold, is said to lurk beneath the River Busento. This is the resting place of Alaric, in AD 410 the first foreigner to overrun Rome since the fourth-century BC Brennus. Despite concerted efforts its location, too, eludes discovery.)

Clusium in History and Today

Known in Etruscan as Clevsin, Clusium was inhabited in the eighth century BC, a cluster of small villages on a hilltop near a lake and the navigable River Clanis (present-day Chiana), amid marshy countryside. Already there are signs of Greek influence, and, like other Etruscan cities, Clusium traded widely with the eastern Mediterranean. By the sixth century, enclosed by city walls, Clusium thrived, establishing a colony of its own (Padania) and enjoying high-quality foreign imports.

The city enters written history with the enigmatic ruler Lars Porsenna, who may have captured Rome in 508 BC, curbing her military capabilities and restoring occupied territories to nearby Veii. However, defeat at Aricia put paid to his ambitions, and in 507 he returned to Clusium. The following century saw Rome expand into Etruria, but in 390 BC aggressive Gaulish tribes (possibly invited by Arruns of Clusium) besieged Clusium, then besieged and sacked Rome before being driven out of Italy.

In 295 BC war waged by Clusium and other Etruscan cities against ever-expanding Rome ended in defeat. Thereafter, Clusium was a loyal Roman ally, providing wood and grain for Rome's fleet in the Second Punic War (205 BC), but suffering during the civil wars – in 89 BC Sulla razed it to the ground, along with Porsenna's tomb, before allocating the site to war veterans. Thereafter, life was relatively peaceful. From AD 540 until the end of the tenth century Goths occupied Clusium (building the cathedral in 560). It then passed to the Lombards. However, surrounding marshes made habitation increasingly difficult, and Clusium was largely abandoned until fifteenth-century drainage projects allowed it to regain prosperity.

In the fifth-century BC Tomb of the Monkey, the eponymous creature crouches in a corner watching scenes of wrestling and horsemanship.

C8th BC	Scattered villages.
C6th BC	City walls; tunnelling begins.
508 BC	Lars Porsenna besieges (and captures?) Rome; Arruns defeated at Aricia.
507 BC	Treaty with Rome; Porsenna returns to Clusium.
390 (or 387) BC	Gauls besiege Clusium, defeat Romans at the River Allia and sack Rome.
295 BC	Defeated by Rome in Third Samnite War.
264 BC	Becomes ally of Rome.
C2nd/1st BC	Cistern constructed within tunnel system.
89 BC	Sulla destroys Clusium (and Porsenna's tomb?).
AD 540	Goths occupy Clusium.
AD 560	Cathedral of San Secondiano built on site of earlier basilica.

Modern Chiusi conceals most of Romano–Etruscan Clusium, although traces of walls survive. Beneath the town, however, is an **Etruscan tunnel system**. From the cathedral garden a narrow (sometimes low) tunnel with side passageways burrows deep beneath the cathedral and adjoining piazza to a double-vaulted cistern supported by a central pilaster. It is wrongly called the Labarinto di Porsenna; the tunnels were probably for drainage and collecting rain water.

The **Museo Nazionale Etrusco** is a trove of Etruscan, Greek and Roman artefacts. Highlights include seventh- to sixth-century BC **canopic vases**, fifth-century BC **Attic vases**, a (restored) fifth-century BC terracotta of a **woman holding pomegranates**, numerous sixth- to fifth-century BC **cinerary urns** with reliefs showing scenes from Etruscan life, and later **painted cinerary urns**, many showing Eteocles and Polyneices' fratricide (part of the Greek myth of the Seven Against Thebes). Especially impressive is the reconstructed **Tassinaie Tomb** (170–150 BC), the only surviving painted Hellenistic tomb, as well as banqueting scenes from the **Tomb of the Hill**.

Outside the walls, three Etruscan tombs may be visited, two by appointment – the **Tomba della Pellegrina** and **Tomba del Leone** – and one with restricted hours. This is the only painted tomb, the **Tomba della Scimmia** (Tomb of the Monkey), decorated in blues and terracotta, and named from the creature crouching in a corner as he watches Etruscans wrestling, boxing and riding horses.

CHAPTER 17
VEII AND THE TRIUMPH OF ROME

Veii was the Etruscans' front line, in no way inferior to Rome either in the size of its army or the quantity of its armaments. Indeed, she exalted in her wealth, sumptuous lifestyle, luxury and extravagance to such an extent that she waged many noble conflicts with the Romans for the sake of power and glory.

Plutarch, *Life of Camillus*, 2

Down the dirt road out of town, down past the cemetery, an old mill, its peeling terracotta walls bleached by the years, nestles in the warmth of the morning sun. Water gushes white across an arcing dam to linger lazily on flat blanched rocks before plunging into the vertiginous abyss beyond. Across the stream, the Mola, rise low tufa cliffs, heavy with trees and dappled light, and loud with birdsong. A steep path climbs between them to a broad plateau, earth ploughed rich orange, scattered indiscriminately with clumps of paving stones and broken walls, while on the far horizon rugged mountains stand out dark against the pale blue sky.

For now, though, we'll take another path – below the cliffs, the shaded gully to our right resounding with the plash of muffled water, dark leaf shadows dancing in the warming breeze. Here on a narrow strip of flatland is a haunting, surreal sight: a skeletal temple rising from vibrant grasses speckled with white flowers. Only foundations survive, but above in delicate steel tracery rise outlines of the columns that once soared high to roof and pediment. And what a structure it once was! Even today in Rome you can see part of its ornate terracotta architrave, with intricate paintwork and rows of antefixes (heads of goddesses and grinning satyrs), and the stunning sculptures that once stood proud upon the pediment: almond-eyed Latona; lion-skin-girded Hercules; Apollo with an enigmatic smile playing round his lips, as hair in tight braids tumbles round his shoulders.

This was Apollo's temple. The nearby stream fed his prophetic pool. But for all that he was worshipped here, he did not warn his priests of a destiny that he himself would hasten, or that Juno would turn her back on Veii to embrace a future in Rome.

Veii and Mythology

In Veii, mythology and history merge more closely than at any site we have visited so far. Most stories that survive tell of wars, which (with a few exceptions) end in Roman victories. Yet, since many take place in prehistoric times, even rationalizing Augustan historians tend to mythologize, or use heroic tropes to ennoble Roman history and stress the inevitability of Rome's success.

Strikingly, almost none of Veii's own legends survive, yet this teeming city, once one of Rome's most powerful rivals, may have possessed a rich mythology. In defeat, Veii's legendary past was eradicated. So, as we visit this deserted site today, its tranquillity far removed from the bustle of its urban neighbour, Rome, we cannot but ask: if Veii had won those ancient wars and suppressed Rome's myths, who now would know of Romulus and Remus?

Early Hostilities with Rome

While Rome fought her Sabine neighbours over women, Veii was the first city that she fought for territory. Situated by the River Cremera, one of the Tiber's tributaries, Etruscan Veii's early growth matched that of Rome, just 16 km (10 miles) to the southeast, and for more than three centuries economic rivalry sparked military tension and led at last to existential war.

Legend tells how, fearing for her future, Veii launched a scrappy raid on Roman lands when Romulus was king. Rome's response was well coordinated. As Romulus led well-drilled troops across the Tiber, Veii's men poured out to meet them – but in ragged order. The battle ended in a rout, and, when triumphant Romulus laid waste to the surrounding territory, Veii sent diplomats to cede part of their own land and negotiate a century-long truce.

The late sixth-century BC life-sized painted terracotta Apollo of Veii once adorned a temple at the sanctuary of Portonaccio.

After the hundred years had passed, Veii allied with nearby Fidenae, which, once an Etruscan town, was situated almost halfway between Rome and Veii, and was now a reluctant Roman colony. It was part of a concerted plan. Lately Alba Longa had made uneasy peace with Rome, but now her general, Mettius Fufetius, promised to join Veii and Fidenae to crush the Romans. They planned to provoke a battle, before which Fufetius would declare his support for Rome's king, Tullus Hostilius – but during which he would switch sides.

So, where the Tiber meets the Anio, the armies clashed; but Fufetius failed to honour his commitment. Instead of attacking the Romans, he withdrew to a nearby hill. Abandoned, Rome's Tullus was unfazed. He ordered his cavalry to raise their spears vertically to form a fence blocking the Veientes' and Fidenates' sightlines, then in a booming voice declared that on his orders Fufetius was outflanking his enemies' rear.

The Fidenates fled in panic, leaving the Veientes facing the full force of Rome. Then they, too, turned and ran, some leaping terrified into the Tiber, others caught and slaughtered on the banks. Fufetius was executed in the grisliest of ways, tied to two chariots and torn apart, while once-proud Alba Longa was obliterated from the map. Not Veii, however. Although defeated, the city thrived, though the gods themselves gave notice that her fortune would not last forever.

Veii's Magic Chariot

Veii's craftsmen were renowned as the most skilled in Italy. So, when Tarquin the Proud began his Temple of Jupiter Optimus Maximus on Rome's Capitol, he commissioned from them a terracotta statue group to stand atop it showing Jupiter riding a chariot. When the sculptors placed their exquisite work in the kiln for firing, however, instead of contracting, as terracotta does when moisture in the clay burns away, it expanded to such a size that the kiln had to be dismantled to remove it. Veii's haruspices decreed it was a sign foretelling power and fortune to the statue's owners. Who did own it, though? Tarquin, who commissioned it, had just been expelled from Rome, but surely Tarquin's enemies had no claim on it; instead, it must stay in Veii to ensure her future greatness. Then, a few days later, during equestrian games, the gods intervened. Plutarch reports how:

> There were the usual thrills and spectacles, but when, garlanded, the winning charioteer was driving his chariot sedately from the hippodrome, his horses took fright for no apparent reason – it was

A charioteer drives his team of two horses
on a sixth-century BC vase painting.

either divine intervention or pure chance – and bolted towards
Rome, taking their charioteer with them. He could do nothing,
neither rein them in, nor calm them with his voice, but he was
carried helplessly until they reached the Capitol, where he was
thrown out of his chariot.... The Veientes were amazed and terrified.
So they bade the craftsmen deliver their chariot to Rome.

A Voice from the Woods

Despite these divine warnings, Veii offered Tarquin her support. After all, he
was Etruscan, and Rome was an ancient enemy. So, with Tarquinian allies,
they met Rome's army in the Arsian Woods, where their territories abutted.
As battle raged, Tarquin's son, Arruns, caught sight of Rome's consul, Brutus,
the man he blamed most for overthrowing the monarchy, and he galloped to
attack. So ferocious was their hatred that neither gave thought to his own

safety, motivated only by a lust to kill. And each did kill, driving his spear deep into his foe's body, dying by each other's side.

Elsewhere, too, casualties were matched equally. Tarquinia's troops defeated the Romans; Romans overran Veientes (accustomed as they were, sneers Livy, to defeat). At dusk, as fighting ended:

> In the silence of the night from the Arsian Woods a mighty voice was heard resounding. They thought it was Silvanus's voice, and this is what it said: the Etruscans had lost one more man than the Romans in the fighting. So the result was clear: Rome was victorious.

Despair engulfed both Tarquin and his allies, and they melted into the darkness. Rome was victorious, but still she had much suffering in store.

The Fabii

In 483 BC, war broke out again when Veii made ever-deeper incursions into Roman territory, threatening to besiege the city itself. Part of Rome's problem was internal strife: the plebeian army, suspicious of its patrician generals, was not motivated to fight. The Etruscans scented victory, and by 480 Rome's generals, Marcus Fabius and Gnaeus Manlius, could not trust their men to follow orders. On campaign in Veientine territory, they skulked behind palisades, allowing the Etruscans to ride close and jeer, until at last the Roman rank and file demanded action. In the fight that followed, although the Veientes came close to victory, killing both Manlius and Fabius's brother, Rome prevailed. She had won a battle, but the war was far from over.

Next year, as Veii launched raids on Roman territory, the consul Caeso Fabius made an unorthodox proposal: entrust the war with Veii to his family, the Fabii, and let Rome concentrate on other matters. The Senate agreed, and, with the Roman people's cheers resounding in their ears, every male member of the Fabii – 306 men in all – marched into Veientine lands to dig in by the banks of the Cremera and enter Rome's mythology.

As Fabius suspected, his fort attracted Veii's ire, and soon an Etruscan army was massing to attack it. But before they had assumed formation, a squadron of Roman cavalry thundered into view, routing the Etruscans, who fled to Saxa Rubra ('Red Rocks') and sued for peace. By pretending to be easy prey, the Fabii had caught the Veientes off guard. However, their success was only temporary; Veii thirsted for revenge.

Despite the treaty, the Fabii remained ensconced by the Cremera, raiding the local countryside, and fighting detachments of Veientes; and with each success their confidence grew. Straying ever further from their fort, they met little resistance: Veii's farmers fled, abandoning their cattle, while her soldiers could not be seen for dust. So, when the Fabii spied a herd of cattle far away on the horizon, they did not hesitate. They swaggered out across the plain, blind to the armed men lying in ambush; only when they heard the Veientine war cry did they realize they were surrounded; and then the javelins came and there was no escape. Valiantly they fought their way to a low hill. As Livy records:

> It gave them opportunity to draw breath, to recover from their sudden shock. They beat back their attackers. Thanks to the terrain the little force was winning – but suddenly some Veientes, sent around the hill, appeared behind them on the summit. Their advantage was lost. The Fabii were all killed, and their fort overrun. 306 men perished to a man. Because of his youth only one of the Fabii remained alive to preserve the family line and be of greatest help to Rome in times of war and turmoil.

While details of the battle can be dismissed as legend – they are almost identical to the (nearly contemporary) story of the 300 Spartans at Thermopylae – Veii's success is undeniable. Within months, her army had poured south to Rome, and occupied the Janiculum. Rome rallied, however, and after many hard-fought battles the Veientes were forced home. Once more they had squandered their chances. They did not have many left.

Lars Tolumnius's Dice Game

Less than forty years later, Fidenae rebelled again, cementing an alliance with Veii's king, Lars Tolumnius. Alarmed, Rome sent four ambassadors to Veii to protest. Ushered into Lars Tolumnius's reception rooms, they found the king playing a game of dice. Before they could speak, a delegation from Fidenae burst in, demanding that Rome's envoys be summarily executed. As the Fidenates finished, Lars Tolumnius made such a splendid throw, that he shouted out in triumph: 'Excellent!' – at which, thinking that he was giving his approval to the execution, armed men leapt up and cut the Roman envoys' throats, an act so brutal that it made war inescapable.

In Rome the news was met with outrage. Statues of the victims were erected in the Forum, and legions mustered. Some said it was just a ghastly misunderstanding, but Livy thought otherwise:

It is unbelievable that he would not have stopped playing dice when his allies from Fidenae arrived to consult him on an execution that would break international law – and that he did not thereafter view his error with disgust. More likely he wanted to make the Fidenates complicit in his crime, so that they would entertain no hope of a rapprochement with Rome.

Again the two sides met near the confluence of the Tiber and the Anio near Fidenae, and again Rome won – but not before Lars Tolumnius covered himself in glory. Even Livy gives him grudging praise: 'None of the Etruscan cavalry fought as bravely as King Tolumnius,' he writes. 'He prolonged the battle, continually attacking Rome's horsemen as they scattered to pursue fugitives.' At last he met his match. Cossus, a Roman officer, recognized him 'harassing the frightened Romans, swooping through their battle lines dressed in royal attire', and charged him. Tolumnius was unhorsed. He struggled to stand, but Cossus smashed him repeatedly with his shield, stabbing him until the king was dead, intoning: 'If gods wish any sanctity on earth, I offer this slaughtered victim to the murdered envoys' ghosts.' Rome and her piety had prevailed. Veii was just years from destruction.

A Second Troy

As Rome and Veii grew in power, they 'faced each other with such savage hatred that there was no doubt that whichever was defeated would be wiped out'. Rome's chance came when Veii appointed a king whom other members of the pious Etruscan Confederation despised, since he flaunted his wealth, and withdrew from a religious festival when they refused to appoint him joint priest. Now, knowing that Veii had no allies, the Romans began a siege. When they realized the siege would last not only for the fighting season but over winter, too, some of Rome's soldiers grumbled. Their arguments were met by Appius Claudius, a doughty senator who (like Livy, who reports the speech) knew his Greek mythology:

> A city was once besieged for ten years by all Greece for one woman's sake! And so far from their homes! So many miles! So many seas! We will besiege a city for perhaps a year, just twenty miles from home – almost within sight of Rome! Who are we to complain?

He convinced the reluctant Roman soldiery, but the siege was badly handled. As in the Greek camp at Troy, so at Veii generals worried more about their egos than bringing matters to a swift conclusion. When one was attacked, and another refused to help him, entire battalions were forced to stream back to Rome's walls for protection. Years dragged on; indiscipline set in; and while some troops engaged in unsanctioned skirmishes, others traded insults across no man's land – which was how the gods revealed Rome's destiny.

The summer had been scorching; the earth was cracked; streams and rivers had dried up. Yet unaccountably the Alban Lake was rising. Bewildered, Rome sent a delegation to the Delphic oracle, but even before it returned, at Veii the gods intervened. As the warring sides traded familiar insults, an old Veientine man shouted out that Rome would never take his city until she drained the water from the Alban Lake. The Romans mocked him – until, learning that he was a haruspex, they realized his words might be prophetic.

A Roman guard arranged a private consultation with the old Etruscan, but when he arrived the Romans kidnapped him and sent him to be interrogated by the Senate. The haruspex claimed to have no memory of prophesying, since the god had spoken through him, but he did know that Etruscan books of knowledge said that, when the lake rose and Romans drained it, Veii's gods would desert her and the city would fall. The Delphic oracle confirmed his words, adding that, once the lake was drained: 'you, Roman, shall boldly attack the enemy walls, remembering that victory over the city you have besieged for so long has been granted by these fates that are now revealed'.

The Romans began digging (or repairing) tunnels through the Alban Hills and cutting irrigation channels through the Latin plain below, and in the jingoistic words of Livy:

> No sooner was the water drained into the fields than the Fates stretched out their hands for Veii. Marcus Furius Camillus, the man destined to destroy it, was appointed Dictator.... With the change in leadership everything suddenly changed, and Rome experienced new hope, new courage, even a new fortune.

Veii's Fall

Camillus reinvigorated the stale siege, now in its tenth year, tightening discipline, building new stockades and beginning a tunnel through the tufa to emerge underneath the Temple of Juno on the citadel. The sappers worked tirelessly until at last they neared their goal. Then, praying to Juno and Apollo, Camillus launched his attack.

The Veientes were bewildered. This sudden onslaught on their well-protected walls seemed reckless. As soldiers ran to their posts, Veii's king sacrificed a heifer at Juno's altar, declaring that 'victory would come to whoever teased apart the entrails'. Only feet away below the ground Roman soldiers, lurking at their tunnel mouth, heard his prophetic words. Then, tumult! The earth erupted and armed men poured out. While some seized the entrails and rushed them to Camillus so that he might separate them, others unleashed carnage. As Veii's women and children rained roof tiles from burning buildings, and her menfolk ran to save them, Rome's legionaries clattered through bloody streets or breached abandoned gates, slashing, stabbing, slaughtering.

When it was over and Veii was burnt and plundered, even Camillus could not believe the wealth of booty. Piously he prayed that, if any god or man believed Rome's luck to be excessive, he, Camillus, might bear the brunt of any retribution, which he asked might be as light as possible for both himself and Rome. Then, as he turned, he stumbled. What did this stumble mean? No-one knew for now, but when the Gauls invaded Rome just six years later, and Camillus beat them back, there were those who remembered his prayer and its aftermath, and saw in Brennus Veii's failed avenger.

Livy's epitaph for the lost city draws parallels between the epic siege of Veii, the last of Rome's neighbours to stand between her and conquest, and the siege of Troy:

> So Veii fell, the richest of all Etruscan cities. Even in defeat she showed her greatness. She was besieged for ten years, winter and summer without any let-up, and inflicted many more casualties than she sustained. And in the end, as Fate brought things to their conclusion, she fell by cunning, not by force.

Juno Embraces Rome

Juno's enmity towards the surviving Trojans, Rome's founders, permeates Virgil's *Aeneid*. Yet, following Veii's fall, the goddess was persuaded to look favourably on Rome. Livy's description is worth quoting in full.

> With all secular assets stripped from Veii, they started to remove the temple offerings, and the gods themselves – but as worshippers, not looters. Young men, hand-picked from the army, were assigned to convey Queen Juno to Rome. So, having purified their bodies and dressed in white vestments, they entered her temple in a state

of pious veneration, laying hands on her at first with profound reverence, since according to Etruscan custom only one priest from one specific family was permitted to touch her.

But when one of them, touched by divine inspiration or making a puerile joke, asked, 'Juno, do you want to go to Rome?', the rest shouted out unanimously that the goddess had nodded her head. Another story tells that they heard a voice, too, saying that she was willing. Certainly we hear that after she was raised from her plinth by lightweight lifting gear, she was almost weightless and easy to carry, as if she went of her free will. She was carried unharmed to the Aventine, her everlasting seat, where Camillus's vows had summoned her, and he later dedicated her temple.

With Juno safely on the people's hill, Rome's civic pantheon was nearing its completion, while, with Veii, her adjacent Troy, defeated, the city looked forward to a glorious future. Even her defeat by Brennus and his Gauls a few years later could be seen as part of a divine plan, for from it, thanks to Camillus (a 'second Romulus' in Livy's words), Rome emerged stronger and more determined, her character sharpened on a forge of steel, her spirit moulded by her legends, her people ready to take on the world.

Now in the Altes Museum, Berlin, and dating to around 500 BC, this magnificent terracotta antefix showing the horned head of Juno once adorned an Etruscan temple.

Veii lay 16 km (10 miles) northwest of Rome on a tufa plateau protected on two sides by cliffs and streams near the River Cremera, a tributary of the Tiber. The area was inhabited in the Bronze Age, but in the ninth century BC the community was joined by settlers from Tarquinia. Over the next four centuries Veii's power grew, until by 500 BC it controlled all lands north of the Tiber from Capena and Falerii to the sea, and northwest to Lake Bracciano. Although showing little sign of centralized town planning, Veii was now a teeming city intersected by a wide main street.

As its growth matched Rome's, it was inevitable that the two should clash. Livy records at least seven wars, using relations with Veii both to heroize Rome's past and to draw parallels with Greek history and mythology. His account of the Fabii's self-sacrifice in 477 BC is too suspiciously close to narratives of the Battle of Thermopylae to be coincidental, and he similarly finds links between the sieges of Veii and Troy.

Archaeology confirms Veii's defensive capabilities – including late fifth-century BC ramparts and tufa walls built around the entire plateau, and an elaborate system of cisterns and drainage tunnels – while the city's wealth is seen not least at the Sanctuary at Portonaccio, where the Temple of Apollo was lavishly decorated. Although painted tombs are rare, rich burials include the seventh-century BC Chigi Tomb on Monte Aguzzo, from which a delicately painted vase showed scenes of war and Greek mythology.

Destroyed by Camillus and with her lands annexed by Rome, Veii's independence ended in 396 BC. The site was soon resettled as a bustling agricultural town, but its glory days were over. A new road, the via Cassia, bypassing Veii in the second century BC, confirmed its status as a backwater. By the fourth century AD Veii was largely abandoned. Clustering in the plateau's northwest quadrant, Roman Veii was a fraction of the size of its predecessor, and although inscriptions describe a theatre, baths, a Temple of Mars and a Porticus Augusta, no traces have been found. Excavations have been scanty. In the early nineteenth century the Forum was discovered, together with colossal heads of Augustus and Tiberius. More recently a sanctuary has been excavated at the edge of the plateau, and arrowheads from Camillus's siege discovered at the northwest gate.

Wealthy Roman villas studded the neighbouring hills. Augustus's wife Livia's 'Villa of the Hens' was at nearby Prima Porta.

C10th BC	Scattered settlements on plateau.
C9th BC	Tarquinian settlers arrive.
c. 750 BC	Romulus defeats Veii.
C7th BC	Settlements coalesce to form city. Defeated by Tullus Hostilius.
c. 510 BC	Tarquin the Proud commissions terracotta chariot.
509 BC	Defeated by Romans at Battle of the Arsian Woods.
483 BC	War with Rome.
477 BC	Fabii massacred at Battle of the River Cremera.
406 BC	Roman siege of Veii begins.
396 BC	Camillus destroys Veii.

Now a protected archaeological park, Veii (Veio in Italian) lies close to Isola Farnese. From the car park, a track fords the Mola torrent leading (right) via a paved Roman road into the **Portonaccio Sanctuary**. A partial metal superstructure outlines the height and dimensions of the **Temple of Apollo**, near which is a **pool** for ritual ablutions and a massive **altar**. To the north, the painted **Tomba Campana** is open by appointment. Above is the citadel, or piazza d'Armi. Little can be seen here – the villa and healing sanctuary are both enclosed by high fences. Elsewhere fragments of paved road and tantalizing foundations lie exposed in ploughed fields, while black tarpaulin protects exposed remnants of city gates.

Many finds from Veii are housed in Rome's Villa Giulia museum, including three colossal late sixth- or early fifth-century BC painted **terracotta statues of Apollo, Hercules and Latona**, probably the work of Vulca, and other terracotta temple fittings from the Portonaccio Sanctuary, **terracotta statues of Minerva and Hercules** from a sanctuary on Veii's citadel, a **princely burial** complete with chariot remains, the delicate **Chigi Vase** (originally made in Corinth around 640 BC) and an early fourth-century BC statuette showing **Aeneas and Anchises** fleeing Troy.

CHAPTER 18

TIVOLI:
ROME'S WORLD IN MICROCOSM

Others will praise shining Rhodes, Mytilene, Ephesus, the walls of Corinth by the double sea, Bacchus's Thebes, Apollo's Delphi, or Thessaly's famous Vale of Tempe. There are those whose one aim is to sing all day of chaste Minerva's city, pluck olive twigs to wreathe their foreheads. Others praise Juno and horse-grazing Argos, rich Mycenae. But not for me tough Sparta, or the rich plains of Larisa. No! Give me sparkling Albunea any time, as she gurgles from her source, and the cascading Anio, Tibur's groves, and orchards moist with splashing streams.

Horace, *Odes*, 1.7

A crocodile stares stonily across the still, green pool, from whose farther bank a quartet of comely caryatids gazes back, reflections rippling seductively in the warm sighing wind. Elsewhere a hero, naked save for a helmet with flowing horsehair crest, fingers his shield languidly, buttocks tightly clenched to achieve a perfect *contrapposto*, while a decapitated comrade tries without success to mirror him. Two bearded men recline nearby, both clutching cornucopias. One leans on a frightened-looking sphinx, the other on a petrified she-wolf, still suckling two baby human boys. And all the while the sun bakes down, cicadas chirp their chain-saw melody, and a sleek cat, patchwork black and white, washes in the cool shade of a column, careless of the grotesqueries around her.

Flanked by steep banks planted with tall trees, and leading to a towering half dome fronted by four tall Corinthian columns, the Canopus is just one of several pools here at Hadrian's Villa that play with the idea of space and light. For us, though, the Canopus is most relevant, because this strange mishmash of images, this cultural kaleidoscope that links Greece and Egypt and the lush landscape of Italy, bespeaks a new step in Rome's appropriation of mythology. For in the century and more since Augustus became First Citizen, Rome has achieved her destiny as ruler of the world. No longer is there any need to dwell on the inevitable path that brought her here, or her defeat of conquered nations. Rather, it is time to reconcile, to integrate, to welcome alien beliefs within the common fold. It is time to build a new mythology.

Hadrian at Tivoli

For Augustus's contemporaries it seemed entirely possible that Rome would constantly expand and one day rule the world. And as poets and historians constantly reminded, this was Rome's destiny. But by the time Hadrian became emperor in AD 117, just over a century after Augustus died, realpolitik was setting in. Defeats, reversals and pyrrhic victories, from Parthia (modern Iran) to Germania and even far-flung Britannia, caused Hadrian to adopt a controversial policy. There should be no further expansion. Rather, the limits of Roman rule must be delineated, and every effort made to ensure that existing territories were well ruled and protected.

An obsessive micromanager, Hadrian took pains to visit as many provinces as he could, and his constant travels meant that he understood the diverse nature of the lands he ruled more than any other emperor. As many alpha males still do, when he built his sprawling villa-palace at Tibur (modern Tivoli), he deliberately decorated his estate with evidence of his power. A later Roman recorded:

Hadrian rounded off his villa at Tivoli in a most remarkable way, assigning to it names of the most famous provinces and places, calling them, for example, 'Lyceum', 'Academy', 'Canopus', 'Pecile' [after the Stoa Poecile or Painted Colonnade of Athens] and 'Tempe'. And to omit nothing, there was even a 'Hades'.

While many parts of the villa contained costly statuary, on the Pecile's long wall were painted scenes from Greek and Roman mythology, encouraging contemplation of Rome's heroic past.

Hadrian was a profoundly spiritual man. His Pantheon, a temple to all the gods, in Rome's Campus Martius represented heaven and earth in microcosm, but even at Tivoli areas were dedicated to the principal religions of his day. For by now Rome was awash with foreign cults in a way that the Augustans never dreamed of – in Virgil's description of the Battle of Actium, Egypt's gods are wild and alien, enemies of Rome's civilizing deities; in Hadrian's villa they take pride of place.

Now, even as Roman mythology was being illustrated in mosaics and frescoes across the empire, a multiplicity of hitherto alien religions flooded into Rome, all with mythologies of their own. We shall end our travels by considering three, with two of which Hadrian would have been familiar, while the third he created himself.

Mithras

No Mithraeum has been found at Tivoli, yet the soldier-emperor undoubtedly knew this eastern god. Sculptures show Phrygian Mithras emerging naked from a rock, a cap on his head, a dagger in his right hand and a flaming torch in his left, in a scene that encapsulates his power. For Mithras held life-giving sway over the physical environment: once, in a desert, he shot an arrow into a rock, causing water to gush forth.

Flanked by his attendants Cautes and Cautopates, Mithras looks aside in sorrow as he sacrifices his magnificent white bull.

Although there are many interpretations of the story, most agree that Mithras crossed the world on a magnificent white bull, his pride and joy. However, when mighty Sol, the sun-god, sent a raven to command that he sacrifice the beast, Mithras could not disobey. Looking aside in sorrow, he gripped its nostrils, pulled back its head and sliced its neck with his dagger. But the creature was miraculously transformed. From its body rose the moon to take her place as the companion of Sol. While Mithras's cloak swelled to become the vault of heaven, sparkling with stars and planets, grain sprouted from the bull's tail, grapes from its blood, and from its genitals rich semen oozed into a sacred bowl, causing the earth to teem with life. Initiates believed that this was the 'Big Bang', the moment the universe was created, when, as a hymn proclaimed, Mithras 'redeemed us by shedding eternal blood'.

Many sculptures celebrate this moment, showing a serpent licking the bull's blood, as a scorpion tries to suck nourishment from its genitals. Nearby are twin attendants, Cautes and Cautopates, one raising his torch

to heaven, the other plunging his towards the earth. At the bull's death, time and seasons were created, along with day and night, whose alternating light and darkness symbolized the everlasting struggle between good and evil. In that moment, too, Sol Invictus (Unconquered Sun), who issued the command, and Mithras, who obeyed him, became united as a powerful generative force. Now they banqueted on meat, bread and wine, before Mithras mounted Sol's four-horse chariot and together they soared across the skies to the farthest bounds of heaven.

Promising souls' reunion with Sol Invictus's life-giving light, and imbued with a spirit of male camaraderie, Mithraism became popular among soldiers from the first century AD onwards. Initiations, featuring sacrifices and banquets, were conducted in subterranean temples, and members moved up the ranks from the lowest, 'The Raven', through 'Bridegroom', 'Soldier', 'Lion', 'Persian', and 'Runner of the Sun', to the highest grade of all, 'The Father'.

Isis and Osiris

Evidence for the worship of two other eastern gods, Isis and Osiris, has been found in the Serapeum at the far end of the Canopus at Hadrian's Villa. Two siblings, born from earth and heaven, they were also husband and wife, rulers who succeeded the sun-god, Ra. Under their benign rule Egypt flourished, but their evil brother, Set, could not endure such harmony. Trying to convulse the world in chaos, he murdered Osiris and dismembered him, scattering the pieces throughout Egypt, before seizing the throne. As darkness reigned, Isis and her sister Nephthys scoured the country, soaring low like falcons, swelling the Nile with tears, while Osiris's life-giving blood ebbed dark into the water. Slowly they found all the pieces, reconstructing them until his body was almost whole. Only the phallus (swallowed by fish) eluded them. So Isis made a magic prosthetic, and, with Osiris complete, she reanimated him until he was sufficiently alert for her to straddle him. As lightning flashed, Osiris's seed shot out, and in time Isis bore a son, the mighty Horus.

While Set plunged Egypt further into anarchy, Isis kept the infant Horus safe, but when he came of age, he undertook a cosmic struggle against Set and his cohorts of chaos. For eighty years the battle raged along the Nile, until Horus emerged victorious, and Osiris's spirit was set free to enter the underworld (and rule as its king). As for Set, some said he was reconciled with Horus, and, forgiven, ruled the skies; but others taught that, though dead, Set's spirit lived on, hungry for human souls, his evil counterbalanced by Horus's good, poised for a battle that would last throughout eternity.

A fresco from Herculaneum shows priests
and worshippers at the Temple of Isis.

Plutarch gives an alternative version, adding his own intriguing details:
Set had an exquisite casket made to Osiris's exact measurements, before
inviting Osiris and his friends to dinner. The banquet over, the casket was
brought in. As all admired its beauty, each guest climbed in to see if they
would fit. No sooner was Osiris inside, however, than Set hammered down
the lid and filled the cracks with molten lead. Within a heartbeat Osiris
was dead, his soul fluttering west beyond the sunset; but since his body was
unburied, it could not achieve eternal rest.

Meanwhile the Nile bore the casket out to sea, until it washed ashore
at Phoenician Byblos. As it caught in the branches of a tamarisk, the tree
blossomed with glossy leaves and flowers, its trunk enfolded the casket,
and it became so perfect that King Maneros had it cut down and used as

the central pillar in his palace. Meanwhile, in Egypt, Isis wandered the earth disconsolately, seeking news of her lost husband, until children told her of the casket floating out to sea. Tirelessly she tracked its course until she came to Byblos, where, entering the palace disguised as its prince's nurse, she discovered its last resting place. When she revealed her true identity, the awestruck king promised anything she wished. So she split open the pillar, removed the casket, and returned with it to Egypt, to hide it in the Delta's marshlands. But Set discovered it – which was when he tore the body into pieces and scattered them throughout the land.

Plutarch's version contains echoes of the myth of Ceres and Proserpina, whose mystery cults promise rebirth after death, while in Egypt the annual life-bringing cycle of Nile floods chimed well with Osiris's reconstruction, reanimation and resurrection, and the image of Isis with the divine child, Horus, provided hope and inspiration.

Antinoüs

Hadrian was fascinated by esoteric teachings, and, being politically astute, he tapped into human yearnings for life after death and massaged mythology to create a new cult intended to combine previously diverse beliefs from across the empire. Its focus was a new god: Antinoüs, once Hadrian's companion, now immortal.

This beautiful Bithynian youth was said to have been Hadrian's lover, but little is really known about him until 130, the year of his death, when he and Hadrian were touring Egypt. A contemporary Alexandrian poet describes them on a lion hunt. Identifying Antinoüs as Mercury's son, the story tells how Hadrian protected his lover as the wounded creature attacked. Then, on the day of Osiris's festival near Hermopolis ('Mercury's City'), Antinoüs drowned in the Nile. Dio Cassius gives telling details:

> Antinoüs died either because he fell into the Nile (as Hadrian writes) or by being offered up as sacrifice (which is the truth). I have mentioned previously that Hadrian was very curious and surrounded himself with divers divinations and incantations. He paid Antinoüs the greatest honours, either because of his passion for the boy, or because he had died willingly – for such a willing sacrifice was necessary for the purposes he had in mind...

These purposes soon became clear: no sooner was Antinoüs dead than Hadrian's grief – or political *nous* – went into overdrive. Claiming to have

The statue of Antinoüs in the guise of Osiris, now in the Vatican Museum, once adorned Hadrian's Villa at Tivoli.

seen a star shoot up to heaven, he identified it as Antinoüs's soul, declaring that his lover had become a god. Then he built a city, Antinopolis, near where the boy had drowned, established festivals and games in his honour, and erected temples and statues throughout the empire. Immediately recognizable, these showed a heart-stoppingly beautiful young man, his body well-toned, his face full-lipped and perfect, his expression constantly benign, sometimes with iconography linking him to Mercury, Bacchus or Osiris (all gods connected to the underworld).

Antinoüs's embalmed body was possibly brought to Tivoli, but while Hadrian may have been moved by genuine sorrow to preserve Antinoüs's memory and by religious awe to worship him, he was more likely manipulating Egyptian, Greek and Roman mythologies for his own end, combining beliefs from across the empire to achieve religious harmony that would, he hoped, encourage political cohesion. Moreover, he claimed that, discovering that the emperor was ill and one of them must die, Antinoüs willingly laid down his life, while the shooting star was evidence that, through faith and sacrifice, the young man had become a god. Once more religion promised salvation after death. If only Hadrian could convince himself! As he himself lay dying less than eight years later, he penned a five-line poem:

Dear little soul, dear little wanderer, dear,
charming little guest and comrade of this body!
Where will you go now,
bloodless, rigid, stripped of life?
You used to share so many jokes. You'll never joke with me again.

New World Order

There is no record of Hadrian embracing another 'mystery religion' already taking hold across the empire: Christianity. He must have come across it: Christians were blamed for the Great Fire of Rome in AD 64, and in 112, Pliny the Younger, governing Antinoüs's homeland of Bithynia, sent messages to Hadrian's predecessor Trajan, asking how to treat members of this new sect, which, while agreeing that man must 'render unto Caesar the things that are Caesar's', taught a greater allegiance to the one true God.

Had Hadrian but known it, Rome's future lay in Christianity. It took another two centuries for clever brains to reconcile the Christian God and Mammon, but they were so successful that in 313 the emperor Constantine decriminalized the now-pervasive religion, and in 393 Theodosius embraced it zealously, closing pagan temples and banning pagan rites. As Greece and Rome's old gods receded into history, their web of myths became increasingly irrelevant: since they could not be true, they were, at best, charming allegories.

Within a terrifyingly short time imperial myths of invincibility (already exposed as tenuous in border territories) were exploded, too, when Alaric and his disgruntled Visigoths sacked Rome in 410, desecrating not just basilicas and palaces but also the mausoleums of Hadrian and Augustus, emptying their urns of ashes, trampling on Rome's pagan soul. That Rome survived and grew again was thanks only to its now being the headquarters of the Western Church, ensconced across the Tiber from the ancient seats of power, the Forum, Capitol and Palatine, on a once lowly hill, the Vatican.

But spiritual memories are long. People are attached to myths and to their heroines and heroes. Many saints share attributes with pagan predecessors. Even the Pope's title, 'Pontifex Maximus', had belonged to the highest priest in ancient Rome. Julius Caesar and Augustus, Nero, Hadrian, Constantine: all held it as the gods' representatives on earth – and 'Papa', 'Pope', means 'father', too, a status Jupiter and Augustus bore.

All things change, and myth evolves, as Ovid, ending his *Metamorphoses*, reflects:

Thus great Atreus yields his fame to Agamemnon, Aegeus his to Theseus, and Peleus to Achilles; as indeed – a parallel more suited to those two gods [Caesar and Augustus] – Saturn yields to Jupiter. Now Jupiter rules heaven's palaces and the three-fold kingdom of the earth, while Augustus rules the world. Each is our father, each our ruler now.

I entreat you – gods, who came here with Aeneas, leading his path through sword and fire; and you, too, native gods; and Father Quirinus, our city's founder; and Mars Gradivus, Quirinus's father; and you, Vesta, worshipped as one of Caesar's own Penates; and with Vesta, Phoebus, too, who dwell beside her hearth; and Jupiter, who hold the high Tarpeian Rock; and all other gods that it is holy for a poet to entreat – may it come late, when we're already gone, that day on which Augustus quits the world he governs now, and soars to heaven to hear the prayers of those he's left behind!

And now I've reached my work's end, which neither Jupiter's wrath, nor fire, nor steel, nor all-consuming time will ever wipe away. Let the day come that has power over my body (although nothing else); let it end the uncertain season of my years. For, with my better part, I'll soar, immortal, high above the stars, and my name shall last forever. Wherever Roman power extends across the conquered earth I shall be read aloud, and, if poetic prophecy holds any truth, I'll live for ever, everlasting in my fame.

Tivoli in History and Today

Like many Italian towns, Tibur was said to have been founded by refugees, Greek Arcadians, seeking shelter after wars with Thebes. In fact, it was a fourteenth-century BC settlement, an important member of the Latin League, with its own prophetic shrine, where a Sibyl was the mouthpiece for a local water-nymph.

Independent for centuries, Tibur allied itself with invading Gauls in 360 BC, and, although beaten in fierce battle, showed such pluck that it attacked Rome (unsuccessfully) the following year. In 338 BC, however, Tibur was defeated and absorbed into the Roman fold, and in 90 BC its people were granted Roman citizenship. It soon became popular with the urban elite, including Augustus and Maecenas, and poets such as Statius and Catullus. Nestling in the Sabine hills, with cool cascades and forests, it provided the setting for plush summer villas, while surrounding farmland offered comfortable incomes to men such as Horace, wishing to act out a life of rustic innocence.

Tibur's most ambitious building project was Hadrian's Villa. Begun around AD 120, it occupied a site of more than 120 ha (300 acres), with more than thirty building complexes joined by porticoes or linked by pools, while underground service tunnels meant slaves could transport necessities unseen by their patrician masters. On Hadrian's death in AD 138, the villa was abandoned.

TIVOLI Some Important Dates and Remains

C14th BC	Signs of early occupation.
360 BC	Allies with Gothic invaders, defeated by Rome, but attacks Rome next year.
338 BC	Absorbed by Rome.
90 BC	Roman citizenship accorded.
late C1st BC	Becomes a favourite location for elite villas.
c. AD 120	Hadrian's Villa begun.
c. AD 128	Hadrian takes up (occasional) residence.
AD 273–74	Zenobia in residence.
AD 547	Fortified by Belisarius.
AD 1001	Comes under papal control.
AD 1461	Pope Pius II builds Rocca Pia.
AD 1550	Villa d'Este begun.
AD 1835	Villa Gregoriana begun.

Hadrian's Villa affords an ideal setting for a day trip from Rome. At the entrance, a visitors' centre contains a useful **model**. Nearby the **Pecile**'s walls once bore frescoes of mythological scenes. Close by is a rectangular pool. A path (left) leads to the **'Naval Theatre'**, a circular construction surrounding an island building containing living spaces and baths, Hadrian's private retreat. The palace proper is nearby, with its **library court**, **hospitalia** (residential quarters) and **pavilion**, whose windows overlook an area landscaped to suggest Greece's Vale of Tempe. A path leads (left) to the **Temple of Venus** with views of modern Tivoli. Another (right) leads

From AD 273–74, Queen Zenobia of Palmyra, defeated by Aurelian, enjoyed months of gilded captivity at Tibur. The town shared Rome's decline. A stronghold for Count Belisarius in 547, it fell to the Ostrogoth army of Totila. By the eleventh century, it was under papal control, when its setting again attracted moneyed power-brokers. In 1461, Pope Pius II built the Rocca Pia, a reminder of his power, but the most famous palace was the Villa d'Este, stunningly decorated with formal gardens, built for Cardinal Ippolito II d'Este in 1550. Pope Gregory XVI's Villa Gregoriana, whose parkland utilizes the waters of the River Anio, was added in 1835.

to the **Great Peristyle**, **Hall of the Doric Columns**, and **piazza d'Oro**, named from the many treasures discovered in what was once a colonnaded complex complete with libraries.

Heading back towards the Pecile, turn left past **bath houses** to the **Canopus**, modelled on the Nile Delta's Sanctuary of Serapis. A long rectangular pool in an artificial hollow is partially surrounded by (replica) statues (the originals are in the nearby **museum**). At the south is the **Serapeum**, a tall, semi-circular, half-domed building, which may have served as a dining room. Southeast lies the **Academy**, with a temple to Apollo and an odeon. Further still lies the area called **Hades**. Back near the Pecile is a **nymphaeum**, while outside the site near the car park an overgrown **theatre** lies behind the perimeter fence.

In Tivoli itself the Sanctuary of Hercules Victor is currently closed, but the **Temples of Vesta** and **the Sibyl** (the assignation of whose names is arbitrary) are well worth visiting and viewing from a nearby bridge, where their position atop a sheer cliff above the gushing River Anio can be best appreciated. Many treasures from Hadrian's Villa are housed in Rome's museums, including remarkable mosaics (one of **Doves at a Waterbowl**) in the Capitoline Museum, and statues from the Serapeum, including a **bust of Isis** and a Parian marble **statue of Antinoüs as Osiris** in the Vatican Museum.

If energy and enthusiasm permit, the **Villa Gregoriana** with waterfalls and grottoes can be entered near the Temple of Vesta, while the **Villa d'Este**'s gardens will bring solace to the soul of any weary traveller.

RECOMMENDED READING

There are many books on Greek myths, but their Roman and Etruscan cousins are less well served. Particularly to be recommended is:

Wiseman, T. P., *The Myths of Rome*, Exeter, 2004

Other works include:

Bonfante, L. and Swaddling, J., *Etruscan Myths*, London, 2006
Gardner, J., *Roman Myths*, London, 1993
March, J., *The Penguin Book of Classical Myths*, London, 2008
Matysak, P., *The Greek and Roman Myths*, London and New York, 2010
Maurizio, L., *Classical Mythology in Context*, Oxford, 2016

A useful sourcebook is:

Neel, J. (ed.), *Early Rome, Myth and Society*, Hoboken, NJ, 2017

Books evoking Roman life, including attitudes to myth and legend, include:

Angelo, A., *A Day in the Life of Ancient Rome*, New York, 2009
Carcopino, J., *Daily Life in Ancient Rome*, London, 1941

The Mediterranean is well served by travel guides. For the traveller in search of Classical remains the most useful are the Blue Guides, which contain brief histories of most of the sites mentioned in this book, as well as clear site plans. Those wishing to spend an extended length of time in Rome might also find the following of interest:

Claridge, A., *Rome, An Oxford Archaeological Guide*, New York, 1998
Coarelli, F., *Rome and Environs, An Archaeological Guide*, Berkeley, Los Angeles and London, 2007
Masson, G. (revised Fort, J.), *The Companion Guide to Rome*, Woodbridge, 2009

Quotations from classical texts in this book have been translated by the author; but there are many readily available English versions of most of the works quoted. They include:

Cicero, *On the Nature of the Gods*, trans. H. McGregor, London, 1978
Dionysius of Halicarnassus, *Roman Antiquities*, trans. E. Cary, London, 2015
Herodotus, *The Histories*, trans. T. Holland, London, 2014
Homer, *The Homeric Hymns*, trans. N. Richardson, London, 2003
Homer, *The Iliad*, trans. E. V. Rieu, London, revised 2003
Homer, *The Odyssey*, trans. E. V. Rieu, London, revised 2003
Horace, *The Complete Odes and Epodes*, trans. B. Radice, London, 1983
Livy, *The Early History of Rome*, trans. R. M. Ogilvie, London, revised 2002
Ovid, *Fasti*, trans. A. Wiseman and P. Wiseman, Oxford, 2013
Ovid, *Metamorphoses*, trans. E. J. Kenney and A. D. Melville, Oxford, 2008
Petronius, *Satyricon*, trans. J. P. Sullivan, London, revised 2011
Pliny the Younger, *The Letters of the Younger Pliny*, trans. B. Radice, London, revised 2003
Plutarch, *The Makers of Rome*, trans. I. Scott-Kilvert, London, 1965
Propertius, *Elegies*, trans. O. Lyne, Oxford, 2009

Suetonius, *The Twelve Caesars*, trans.
R. Graves, London, revised 2007

Virgil, *Aeneid*, trans. D. West, London, 2003

Virgil, *Eclogues*, trans. C. Day Lewis, Oxford,
2009

Other works, including those by Dio
Cassius, Diodorus Siculus, Herodian, Strabo
and Varro, are available in bilingual editions
published by the excellent Loeb Classical
Library.

Edward Gibbon's *The History of the Decline
and Fall of the Roman Empire* is published
in hardback by Everyman Library,
London, 2010.

ACKNOWLEDGMENTS

Rome may have been built in a day, but this book took slightly longer. I was invited to write it by Colin Ridler, T&H's inspirational commissioning editor, a modern-day Maecenas, and I thank both him and his dynamic successor, Ben Hayes, who have championed it through every stage of the process. It was an inspired decision to ask David Bezzina to provide the drawings for this volume, and I am delighted that his artistry accompanies and enhances my words.

Also at T&H I have been fortunate to work again with a team of praetorian excellence, especially Sarah Vernon-Hunt and my eagle-eyed editor, Carolyn Jones, who have overseen procedures with their usual grace and aplomb. My thanks go, too, to the other members of the superlative in-house team, not least the creative designer, Rowena Alsey, production supervisor, Celia Falconer, and publicity executive, Victoria Brown.

As before, my research involved travels throughout the Mediterranean, and I am particularly grateful to Vicki Tzavara at The British School at Athens and Christine Martin and Stefania Peterlini at The British School at Rome for presiding over my wanderings as Venus presided over Aeneas's; and, while I met with help and kindness everywhere I went, my thanks go particularly to Gloria Galante and Francesco Graziani, who at Lavinium went the extra mile to explain recent archaeological developments and inspire with reflections on the heröon, and to Lynda Johnson, who shared her local knowledge at Veio.

My profoundest thanks go to friends and family, who continue to endure and, indeed, encourage my eccentric interests: my mother, Kate, and especially my wife, Emily Jane, whose company, good sense, support and love I value more than anything, and who stoically tramps round sites and museums with me, invariably pointing out things that I would otherwise have missed and making connections that I would otherwise have overlooked. Finally I must gratefully pay honour to the Penates – in our case not household gods, or household dogs, but household cats – Stanley and Oliver, whose perception of how keyboards, pens and paper might be used is somewhat different from my own, a valuable reminder, when writing a book such as this, that the realities of both stories and objects can in the end be what we make of them.

INDEX

Mythological characters appear in Roman type; historical figures (including some who might be mythological) in *italics*; place names and buildings in SMALL CAPITALS; and Classical terms, events, buildings and institutions in *SMALL ITALIC CAPS*.

Page numbers in *italics* indicate illustrations.